**African Arguments**

Written by experts with an unrivalled knowledge of the continent, *African Arguments* is a series of concise, engaging books that address the key issues currently facing Africa. Topical and thought-provoking, accessible but in-depth, they provide essential reading for anyone interested in getting to the heart of both why contemporary Africa is the way it is and how it is changing.

**African Arguments Online**

African Arguments Online is a website managed by the Royal African Society, which hosts debates on the African Arguments series and other topical issues that affect Africa: http://africanarguments.org

**Titles already published**

Alex de Waal, *AIDS and Power: Why There is No Political Crisis – Yet*

Tim Allen, *Trial Justice: The Lord's Resistance Army, Sudan and the International Criminal Court*

Raymond W. Copson, *The United States in Africa: Bush Policy and Beyond*

Chris Alden, *China in Africa*

Tom Porteous, *Britain in Africa*

Julie Flint and Alex de Waal, *Darfur: A New History of a Long War*, revised and updated edition

Jonathan Glennie, *The Trouble with Aid: Why Less Could Mean More for Africa*

Peter Uvin, *Life after Violence: A People's Story of Burundi*

Bronwen Manby, *Struggles for Citizenship in Africa*

Camilla Toulmin, *Climate Change in Africa*

Orla Ryan, *Chocolate Nations: Living and Dying for Cocoa in West Africa*

Theodore Trefon, *Congo Masquerade: The Political Culture of Aid Inefficiency and Reform Failure*

Léonce Ndikumana and James Boyce, *Africa's Odious Debts: How Foreign Loans and Capital Flight Bled a Continent*

Mary Harper, *Getting Somalia Wrong? Faith, War and Hope in a Shattered State*

Gernot Klantschnig and Neil Carrier, *Africa and the War on Drugs: Narcotics in Sub-Saharan Africa*

Alcinda Honwana, *Youth and Revolution in Tunisia*

Marc Epprecht, *Sexuality and Social Justice in Africa: Rethinking Homophobia and Forging Resistance*

**Forthcoming**

Michael Deibert, *The Democratic Republic of Congo: Between Hope and Despair*

Gerard McCann, *India and Africa – Old Friends, New Game*

Adam Branch and Zachariah Mampilly, *Popular Protest in Africa*

**Published by Zed Books with the support of the following organizations:**

**International African Institute** promotes scholarly understanding of Africa, notably its changing societies, cultures and languages. Founded in 1926 and based in London, it supports a range of seminars and publications including the journal *Africa*.

www.internationalafricaninstitute.org

**Royal African Society** is Britain's prime Africa organization. Now more than a hundred years old, its in-depth, long-term knowledge of the continent and its peoples makes the Society the first stop for anyone wishing to know more about the continent. RAS fosters a better understanding of Africa in the UK and throughout the world – its history, politics, culture, problems and potential. RAS disseminates this knowledge and insight and celebrates the diversity and depth of African culture.

www.royalafricansociety.org

**World Peace Foundation**, founded in 1910, is located at the Fletcher School, Tufts University. The Foundation's mission is to promote innovative research and teaching, believing that these are critical to the challenges of making peace around the world, and should go hand in hand with advocacy and practical engagement with the toughest issues. Its central theme is 'reinventing peace' for the twenty-first century.

www.worldpeacefoundation.org

# Acknowledgements

This book builds on insights that I have gained over the years through my work at the International Institute for Environment and Development (IIED), a policy research institute based in the United Kingdom. This work includes research and policy advocacy on large-scale land acquisitions and agricultural investments in Africa. In particular, it includes the Legal Tools for Citizen Empowerment initiative, an effort to strengthen local rights vis-à-vis large-scale natural resource investments in lower-income countries. These activities involve extensive travelling, and collaboration with colleagues at IIED and with partners in Africa and elsewhere. So my first heartfelt thank-you goes to IIED and the partners around it for giving me the opportunity to learn about issues that I am passionate about.

IIED's work on the global land rush has been supported through multiple collaborations with development agencies, particularly the Food and Agriculture Organization of the United Nations, the International Fund for Agricultural Development, Oxfam and the International Development Research Centre. It has also been supported by the United Kingdom government's Department for International Development and by a consortium of European donors that has included, at different times, Danida (Danish International Development Agency), DGIS (Directorate-General for Development Cooperation, the Netherlands), Irish Aid, Norad (Norwegian Agency for Development Cooperation), SDC (Swiss Agency for Development and Cooperation) and Sida (Swedish International Development Agency). In addition, IIED's work on land tenure receives support from the Bill & Melinda Gates Foundation, particularly a grant to secure local land rights in parts of West Africa where small-scale agriculture is intensifying. I would like to thank these donors and partners for their support, though I should also make it clear that the views expressed in this book are mine and do not necessarily reflect those of the institutions involved.

I would also like to thank the many people with whom I have had stimulating conversations and exchanges over a number of years, and from whom I have gained so much invaluable insight. This includes current and former colleagues at IIED, particularly Camilla Toulmin, James Mayers, Steve Bass, Emily Polack, Bill Vorley, Abbi Buxton, Lila Buckley, Ced Hesse, Sonja Vermeulen, Duncan Macqueen, James Keeley, Isilda Nhantumbo, Jamie Skinner and Barbara Adolph. It also involves colleagues in Africa and elsewhere, including Liz Alden Wily, Ward Anseeuw, Jun Borras, David Bright, John Bugri, Perrine Burnod, Derek Byerlee, Man-Kwun Chan, the late Salmana Cissé, Muriel Côte, Nadia Cuffaro, Klaus Deininger, Adrian di Giovanni, Moussa Djiré, Jennifer Franco, Laura German, Giorgia Giovannetti, Ruth Hall, Mark Kakraba-Ampeh, Amadou Keita, Rachael Knight, Rebeca Leonard, Jon Lindsay, Pascal Liu, Harold Liversage, Anna Locke, Christian Lund, Paul Mathieu, Michel Merlet, Fison Mujenja, Paul Munro-Faure, Fred Nelson, Samuel Nguiffo, Simon Norfolk, Michael Ochieng Odhiambo, William Ole Nasha, Hubert Ouédraogo, Richard Owusu-Asare, Carlos Oya, Robin Palmer, Alda Salomão, Andrea Shemberg, Carol Sorensen, Emmanuel Sulle, Mike Taylor, Ramata Thioune, Jodie Thorpe, Kyla Tienhaara and many more. Sharing parts of my path with these researchers and practitioners has made a difference to my thinking and analysis. I have also had countless conversations with government officials, private sector operators, staff from non-governmental organizations and development agencies, investigative journalists and opinion leaders. My understanding of the land rush – and this book – have greatly benefited from these conversations.

At different stages, several people provided comments on parts of the book: Lila Buckley, Maryanne Grieg-Gran, Joseph Hanlon, Isilda Nhantumbo, Emily Polack, Jamie Skinner, Carol Sorensen, Camilla Toulmin and Bill Vorley. Robin Palmer, Christian Lund and Alex de Waal reviewed and commented on an earlier draft of the entire manuscript. All these valuable comments and suggestions were of great help in the finalization of this book. While my gratitude goes to these colleagues and reviewers, the responsibility for any remaining errors is mine.

Thank you to Ken Barlow at Zed Books and Stephanie Kitchen at the International African Institute, who supported the project from the beginning, provided helpful guidance through the drafting stage, thoroughly reviewed and commented on earlier drafts, and supported me as I finalized the manuscript. Thank you to Miles Irving for developing the map featured as Figure 3.1. And thank you to Ewan Smith and Ian Paten at the production team associated with Zed Books for taking the project from manuscript to book.

Finally, my greatest thank-you goes to the farmers and herders who have shared their experiences with me. As I worked on this book, I felt the weight of the responsibility associated with having been entrusted by them with their time and with information that touches the very foundations of their lives. While I made efforts to protect their identities, I hope to have done justice to their concerns and aspirations.

# 1 | Introduction

In the dry season, the road to the village of Massingir runs through expanses of dry woodland. In this flat district of southern Mozambique, villagers make a living by rearing cattle, trading charcoal and growing millet on small plots. Away from the tarmac road that connects the district to Chókwè, a town some 130 kilometres farther south and the main economic hub in the area, driving in Massingir district requires negotiating bumpy tracks. And only people in Massingir village, the district capital, have electricity. This place might seem an unlikely setting for a global rush to take control of Africa's land. But appearances are deceptive. In the district, land has been a growing source of tension in recent years. Rehabilitation works on the colonial-era Massingir dam have increased agricultural potential. Next to the dam now lies prime farmland. Just across the border with South Africa is the Krueger National Park, and the district has much potential for eco-tourism. These developments in agriculture and conservation have led to a squeeze on local landholdings.[1]

First came conservation. In 2001, the government established a million-hectare wildlife park, hoping that the elephants would bring tourists, and with them jobs and public revenues. But the new park involved plans to resettle some 1,200 families living inside the protected area.[2] The government found alternative land for these people close to the Elephants river, which runs from South Africa through this part of Mozambique before flowing into the Limpopo river. While formalities to secure the transfer of this land were never completed, in the eyes of villagers inside the park the land had been promised to them. The resettlement process dragged, however. When I visited the area in September 2008, villagers were still living in the park. And they were angry. The year before, the government had issued a fifty-year, renewable lease for part of the land that had been promised to them. The lease was allocated to a company listed on the London stock exchange. The deal involved plans to develop a 30,000-hectare irrigated sugar cane plantation and a processing plant to produce sugar and ethanol. Ethanol would be exported within the region, mainly to South Africa, and perhaps to Europe. The company promised investments of over $500 million, and a processing plant that could be operational as early as 2012. The new venture would create thousands of jobs. In Massingir, this prospect meant a great deal. Since the nineteenth century, men have migrated from the district to South Africa to take up work in the mines. Decades ago the Portuguese colonial masters promoted this practice, trading labour for South African gold. Today, many families are separated, with husbands and fathers being away for much of the year. So the promise of new employment opportunities closer to home appealed to many in the district.

But villagers in the park, who saw this land as having been earmarked for them, felt betrayed. At a community meeting inside the reserve, anxiety about what the future might hold was palpable. People complained that the elephants were damaging their crops and frightening their cattle. Yet they did not want to leave the park without clear assurances about what land they would now be given. Villagers outside the park also felt the squeeze. A neighbouring community had developed plans to use a vast area of land for conservation and eco-tourism. But mindful of the growing land scarcity in the district, the government agreed that only a much smaller area should be attributed to this group. As community leaders were persuaded to take up this offer, some villagers felt that their dream had been sold on the cheap. And it was not just land. The sugar cane venture obtained rights to abstract water from the nearby dam.[3] But farming downstream in the fertile Limpopo Valley, the 'breadbasket of the country', also depends on water flows regulated by this dam. Computer simulations raised concerns that, if the sugar cane project were to use all the water it was entitled to, downstream users would face shortages.[4]

When I met the manager of the company in 2008, he was upbeat about the project and the benefits it would bring to local people. As he drove me to the company's first irrigated plots, he said that, by 2011, the entire land area would be under cultivation. Sitting in her office in the district capital, the then district administrator – the highest government representative in the district – also had high hopes for the project. But within one year, the world had become a different place. A major financial crisis in the West had kicked in, sparked by dodgy financial innovation and the bursting of a bubble in sub-prime mortgages. The crisis made it more difficult for companies to secure lending. Also, oil prices were down from their peak of mid-2008, which reduced the attractiveness of alternative energy sources. More difficult lending and changed oil prices had fatal consequences for many biofuel projects in Africa. The venture in Massingir was one such casualty. In late 2009, the company announced the suspension of its investment owing to the intervening changes in the world economy. The government responded by terminating the lease. The ambitious investment proposal had come to nothing.

But the land was not returned to local people. The land squeeze did not disappear along with the company. For a few years, stalemate and uncertainty continued to affect land access for villagers within and outside the park. Then, in 2012, a consortium of South African and Mozambican companies expressed interest in relaunching the project. New promises were made, and ambitious targets set. The consortium pledged to invest over $700 million, and aims to produce commercially from 2018.[5] The sugar cane venture may still become a reality.

Over the past few years, the events that unfolded in Massingir have become an increasingly common occurrence in Africa. Competition for land has increased in many parts of the continent. Multiple sources of pressure are squeezing local landholdings, and large land deals for plantation agriculture have acquired growing prevalence. The sugar cane project in Massingir was one of the first of many land deals in Africa that have attracted much public attention. In Mozambique, several land deals for

3

plantation agriculture have been announced by companies based in the United Kingdom, southern Africa and Brazil – although announcements have not always translated into actual leases, and few large leases have been signed since 2009.[6] In Madagascar, a failed deal involving the acquisition of 1.3 million hectares of land by a South Korean company made headlines all over the world. In Ethiopia, Sudan and South Sudan, companies from India, the Middle East, Europe and North America have acquired millions of hectares in just a few years. In Mali, the government has signed many deals for agricultural investments in the irrigable lands of the Office du Niger area, though a military coup, the occupation of the north of the country by Tuareg and Islamist groups, conflict and overall political instability have now brought many agribusiness ventures to an end. Companies from Europe and North America have taken up large areas of land in Ghana and Tanzania. In so many different parts of the continent, land that was until recently of little outside interest is now being acquired on a large scale to develop commercial investments in agricultural production. Concerns about food and energy security among governments in richer countries, and private sector expectations that commercial returns from agriculture will increase, have fuelled a renewed interest in investing in African agriculture, and a global rush for Africa's land.

Dubbed 'land grabbing' in the media, this wave of land deals has kindled much public debate, in which strong positions are taken on the merits and demerits of the deals. Some commentators welcome this trend as the bearer of new livelihood opportunities. They emphasize the urgent need for investment in agriculture to feed the world's growing population. They point to the capital, know-how, infrastructure and market links that corporate players can contribute. Some believe that the millions of small-scale farmers who grow crops on ever smaller plots of land in much of Africa have no future in today's globalized economy. But others are less optimistic about the deals. For them, these projects are mainly driven by speculation, not agricultural production; plans involving very large plantations of untested crops in remote areas are likely to fail; and local people will lose their land and risk not being able to feed themselves. Critics also argue that large-scale investments can marginalize Africa's small-scale farmers, who constitute the backbone of agriculture on the continent, and that small-scale farmers can be competitive on global markets. The polarized debates about the land rush ultimately reflect competing visions about the future of world agriculture, and particularly about the roles of small- and large-scale farming. They also reflect different views on how to manage the complex relationship between promoting economic development and respecting local rights.

A few years since the public spotlight turned on the land deals, a vast and growing body of evidence has emerged that has improved our understanding of the phenomenon. It is still too early to assess the full implications of the global land rush. But we now know much more about who is acquiring land, where and why. We know about the political and economic forces that drive the land rush, and the factors that facilitate it. And we know more about what the land rush means for Africa and the global food system. There is still much uncertainty about what types of investment can benefit local people. But we have a clearer understanding of which investment models do not work.

This book is a journey through that evidence. The ambition is to offer an academically rigorous yet accessible reader on an issue that has attracted growing attention not only among professionals, but also in public opinion at large. The book discusses the historical roots, the scale, the geography, the drivers, the features and the early outcomes of the global rush for land. It focuses on land deals for agricultural investments in sub-Saharan Africa – and unless stated otherwise, Africa is used as shorthand for sub-Saharan Africa. The book reviews evidence from different parts of Africa, but the discussion of local and national issues draws insights particularly from developments in four countries: Ghana, Mali, Mozambique and Tanzania.

Africa has been an important recipient of land-based investments, both in absolute terms and relative to other regions.[7]

It vividly illustrates the challenges created by the global land rush – such as the paradox that food-insecure countries should be exporting food to richer states, or the problem of widespread insecurity affecting the rights that villagers have on their land. Ghana, Mali, Mozambique and Tanzania have all received strong investor interest.[8] While no selection of countries can do justice to the tremendous diversity of contexts in the continent, discussing developments in these four countries enables us to explore the features and implications of the land rush in East, West and southern Africa; in English-, French- and Portuguese-speaking countries; and in jurisdictions with different historical backgrounds, legal traditions and policy orientations.[9]

But while there is no doubt that much land has been acquired in Africa, the land rush is a global phenomenon that also affects other parts of the world, including Latin America and South-East Asia. In Laos and Cambodia, hundreds of thousands of hectares have been acquired since 2005, with Chinese, Vietnamese and Thai companies pouring in.[10] In Latin America, foreign investment in agriculture is making landownership more concentrated, and increasingly in foreign hands.[11] The discussion of land acquisitions in Africa contributes to understanding this wider, global phenomenon. Also, in discussing land deals for agriculture, the book places the analysis within the broader context of the multiple sources of pressure on land worldwide. Indeed, the surge in land deals for plantations signals a shift in the global food and agriculture system, but pressures on land are increasing as a result of multiple forces beyond farming. Take the case of Massingir: villagers here experience a resource squeeze because of the combined pressure from industrial agriculture and conservation for tourism. Elsewhere, extractive industries are taking up vast areas of land for the development of petroleum and mining resources. And across Africa, competition for higher-value land has been exacerbated by demographic growth, migration and land acquisitions by local and national elites. Transnational deals for plantation agriculture need to be placed within this wider context of multiple pressures on land,[12] and of profound transformations in rural societies.

The title of the book refers to 'land grabs'. This is what many readers immediately relate to, largely as a result of sustained media reporting that has used this terminology. Much contemporary debate about the land deals is framed in simplistic terms, pitching greedy global capitalists – the 'land grabbers' – against poor 'communities' in Africa. But in researching this topic, I did not assume that the deals are necessarily bad. A careful analysis of the evidence presents a more complex picture, in which structural factors, not just personal greed, are at play, and in which the fault lines between different interests are less clear cut than often assumed. Also, the need to reverse decades of policy neglect and to increase investment in African agriculture is widely recognized. The question is whether land deals are the best form of agricultural investment – and if not, what other options would make more sense. In navigating these issues, I approached the research with an open mind, and aimed to develop rigorous analysis of the available evidence. Overall, the findings reveal both positive and negative outcomes – though the balance of the evidence to date is overwhelmingly against large land deals.

Finally, a conceptual clarification is needed. In the book, 'land deal' and 'agricultural investment' are often used together or interchangeably. But the two notions are different – not all land deals are investments in a societal sense, and not all investments in agriculture involve land deals. Indeed, for the company, acquiring land may in itself be an investment, which could generate returns through increases in land values and through agricultural production. But for the host country, the land acquisition is merely a transfer of land rights. In societal terms, investment requires something more – for example, contributions of capital, infrastructure or know-how for agricultural production.[13] Only investments in this latter sense could have positive outcomes for local economies and societies. Also, large land deals are not the only possible avenue for commercial investments in agriculture. Investments can take many different forms and shapes. For example, companies may invest in processing, and source agricultural produce through contracts with local farmers. Plantations and contract farming can also coexist, where the company runs a 'nucleus' plantation and sources additional produce from outgrowers – that is, farmers producing under contract in the areas surrounding the nucleus estate. Some ventures involve shared ownership of the business between the company and local farmers or landholders. There are many possible models of agricultural investments, but the book focuses on land acquisitions for plantation agriculture.

The book develops four sets of arguments, each drawing on different fields of study. The first relates to history. The origins of today's land rush can be traced to long-standing, unequal relations that have cast Africa as a supplier of commodities to the outside world. The seemingly isolated Massingir district has been integrated in the international economy for decades. The deliberate reconfiguration of space and livelihoods that today increases pressures on land in the district is the continuation of a longer trajectory that goes back to colonial times. The Portuguese colonizers promoted migration to South Africa's mines. They also forced local farmers to cultivate cotton, so as to generate taxes for the colonial administration and supply Portugal's lucrative textile industry. Local farmers were integrated into international value chains dominated by the colonizers. And in the dying days of the colonial regime, the Portuguese initiated the construction of the Massingir dam, in order to develop irrigation in the Limpopo Valley and stem the ever stronger opposition to colonial rule.[14] The dam was completed shortly after independence, though it suffered from infiltration problems for years – until recent rehabilitation works paved the way to today's sugar cane venture. The seeds of contemporary plans for irrigated agriculture in the district were planted a long time ago.

Large land deals for plantation agriculture are themselves not new to the African continent. During colonial times, Western companies acquired millions of hectares in Africa through successive land rushes from the early 1900s to independence.[15] In Mozambique, settlers and companies established many commercial plantations, which were then nationalized at independence. After neoliberal reforms from the late 1980s onwards, these farms were privatized – and some have formed the object of today's land deals.[16] A similar picture emerges from different parts of Africa. In Liberia, the new democratic government recently renegotiated some deals dating back to the 1920s – and then went on to issue new concessions for large areas of land. In countries like Ghana, Tanzania and Zambia, state farms for mechanized agriculture were established in the 1970s and 1980s and have more recently been privatized, with international capital pouring in. And besides colonial, foreign and state-driven land acquisitions, national elites have been acquiring rural land in many parts of the continent for a very long time. When today's deals are implemented, they add a new layer to these historical developments that have increased pressures on land. It is impossible to understand the contemporary land rush without placing it in this longer time frame.[17]

So Chapter 2 charts the historical roots of the global land rush. It explores ruptures and continuities with the long history of social, economic and political relations that Africa has forged with the outside world. Historically, mechanisms used by corporate interests to bring Africa's commodities into the international economy have shifted between controlling farming through direct ownership and management of large plantations, on the one hand, and sourcing produce from contract farmers, on the other. Today's land rush represents a new movement of this historical pendulum in favour of large plantations – though the scale, geography and players of contemporary deals differ from those of earlier experiences. The chapter argues that three past waves of 'land grabbing' – by European colonizers, independent governments and local elites – influence today's legal frameworks, government actions and customary institutions, and that this historical legacy of dispossession shapes the features and outcomes of contemporary land deals. The potential for the deals to benefit local groups is constrained from the outset.

The second set of arguments developed in the book relates to the international political economy of the global land rush – that is, its scale and geography, and the political and economic forces that drive it. Chapter 3 challenges three common perceptions

9

about who is acquiring how much land, where and why. The first is about scale. There is great variation among estimates of how much land has been acquired. Some estimates are for over 200 million hectares of land – an area the size of western Europe.[18] But evidence suggests that, on the ground, the scale of the change is smaller than that indicated in public debates. This is partly because many deals have not been fully implemented. Yet these findings should not give ground for complacency. While much effort has gone into putting numbers on the total land area acquired, all the figures produced so far suffer from limitations that make them a poor measure of scale. More useful indicators would involve an assessment of how land acquisitions – whatever their land area size in absolute terms – are increasing overall pressures on land. And it is now clear that the deals, even where poorly implemented or not implemented at all, exacerbate competition for land. The failed sugar cane venture in Massingir illustrates why this is so: much investment targets the most valuable lands, in terms of irrigation potential, as in Massingir, or proximity to markets and infrastructure; the deals compound pressures on land from other sources – conservation and tourism in Massingir, but also mining and petroleum elsewhere; and where the deals fail, the land is often not returned to local groups.

Chapter 3 also challenges common perceptions about the nature of the land acquirers. Much attention has focused on the role of Gulf states, China and Western financiers as major acquirers of Africa's lands. But local nationals, not foreign governments or transnational corporations, are at the forefront of the land rush. Behind the much-publicized transnational land deals, local elites have increased their landholdings at the expense of poorer groups. In many parts of Africa, the relationship between people and land has been changing for many years, and the surge in transnational deals is only a part of that process. Where foreign investment is involved, Western companies and firms from within the African continent account for the lion's share of the deals – more than operators from China or the Gulf. And the growing involvement of players from Asia in African agriculture merely reflects the shifting balance of power in the global economy. In Massingir, the failed sugar cane venture was led not by the Chinese or the Arabs, but by a firm listed on London's stock exchange and mainly owned by Zimbabweans.[19] The new consortium that is now taking over the project involves South African and Mozambican firms.

Finally, Chapter 3 challenges some widespread perceptions about the drivers of the land rush. The need to produce food for the world's growing population, and particularly for the growing middle classes in large emerging economies, such as China and India, is often cited as a critical driver of the deals. But the land rush is not about feeding the planet. It is mainly about meeting demand for energy and consumption goods in richer countries and about speculation linked to rising land values. Fuel, wood, fibre and finance, more than food, are the engines of the renewed interest in agricultural investments in the global South. Structural transformations in the global food and agriculture system create powerful forces that concentrate power in corporate hands and favour large- over small-scale farming. So it is not surprising that the renewed interest in agricultural investment translates into land deals to establish large plantations. Some of the world's richest people are hoping to pocket handsome profits from the deals. But, ultimately, the root driver of the land rush is not 'them', the Chinese or the 'greedy capitalists', but 'us' – our collective expectation of ever rising living standards, coupled with the aspiration of the rising middle classes in emerging economies to enjoy similar levels of material consumption. A solid understanding of these fundamental drivers is necessary to identify levers and pressure points for effective policy responses.

The book's third set of arguments is about the law. 'Land grabbing' suggests unilateral appropriation of land. But land acquisitions typically involve contracts, and these contracts are, in most cases, broadly consistent with national law – not least because most investors want reassurances about the security of their assets. And contracts involve two parties. It is typically governments that sign the deals and make land available to investors. In fact, most governments are vying to attract investment. Until

11

its cancellation in 2009, the sugar cane venture in Massingir had strong backing at the highest level of government in Mozambique.[20] The company's office in Massingir was housed in the building of the district administration – a circumstance dictated by practical considerations, perhaps, but one with powerful symbolic connotations. And after the project failed, the government sought other investors that could continue the project. Villagers knew all this very well. Their anger was aimed at the government, not the company. The problem is that important aspects of the law reflect a disconnection between government policy and the aspirations of local people. Villagers in Massingir may see the land as theirs. But, legally, the land belongs to the government, and the government is legally empowered to allocate it to outside investors. It is the law that facilitates the wave of land acquisitions and undermines the likelihood that the deals will benefit local people. This situation should not surprise. For centuries, unfair laws have facilitated 'land grabbing' around the world – from pre-industrial Scotland to colonial Africa.[21]

So Chapter 4 discusses the role played by the law – that 'gentle civilizer of nations'[22] – in today's land rush. It argues that lopsided legal developments make international law more geared towards enabling secure transnational investment flows, than towards ensuring that these flows benefit people in recipient countries. While international law has gone a long way towards strengthening the protection of foreign investment, it offers little protection to rural people who may be adversely affected by investment flows. Also, with important exceptions, national laws tend to undermine the rights that rural people claim over their land. As outside interest in Africa's lands increases, these features make local groups vulnerable to dispossession. And a few publicly available contracts for land deals raise ground for concern as to the extent to which host countries and communities are negotiating a fair deal. Policy responses to the global land rush have focused on voluntary principles for responsible investment. But international guidance alone cannot reverse structural imbalances in hard law. While the limits of the law in pursuing social justice goals have been well documented, Chapter 4 argues that, without reforming the law and strengthening the power of local groups to exercise their rights, it is unlikely that the renewed interest in African agriculture will benefit local people.

The book's fourth set of arguments relates to the socio-economic outcomes of the deals. Whichever way one looks at it, the land rush, if sustained over time, will produce profound, lasting changes in Africa and in the global food system. The protagonists and supporters of the land deals promise that the gains will outweigh negative impacts. But are these promises being fulfilled? Chapter 5 discusses what the deals mean for host countries and communities, drawing on economic and socio-logical studies. Many investment projects are still at an early stage, and it is too early to fully assess outcomes. But there is mounting evidence that, to date, the deals have failed to deliver their hoped-for benefits. The failure of the sugar cane project in Massingir, at least in its first incarnation, provides a dire warning. The experience in Massingir also shows how large land deals can squeeze the land and water rights of the world's poorest people, in a continent where population is growing fast and most rural dwellers depend on natural resources for their food. It illustrates the vulnerability associated with these investments: the venture may bring the prospect of better livelihoods, but it may also be abandoned at short notice. Locals may end up with the worst of all worlds – losing first their land and then the prospect of employment. There are now many similar stories – failed projects, squeezed resources – from different parts of the continent. By contrast, there is to date little evidence of the benefits. Success stories are difficult to come by. Most commentators agree that investing in Africa's agriculture can promote local development and improve local livelihoods. But the fascination of many African governments with large land deals is misplaced. There is a need for different models of agricultural investment that support, not undermine, the aspirations of rural people.

For practical reasons, these four sets of argument are presented in different chapters. But the realities they describe are closely

13

interconnected. The history, political economy and law discussed in the first three chapters create a context that powerfully influences the socio-economic outcomes of the deals. The land rush brings into contest competing claims to land – whether based on occupation for generations, or on leases issued by government or traditional authorities. The arena in which these competing claims are wielded is an uneven playing field shaped by entrenched inequalities developed over history, by the local-to-global forces that drive large land deals and shape power imbalances, and by the distribution of legal rights and redress mechanisms. That uneven playing field is bound to have repercussions on the outcomes of the deals. This is not just a linear relationship of cause and effect. The outcomes of the deals, if sustained over time, can in turn foster important changes in historical trajectories, political economies and legal frameworks. For example, growing land concentration can have major repercussions on power relations at local, national and international levels.

Chapter 6 distils insights from the four substantive chapters of the book, and develops a more integrated analysis of the historical, political and legal context of the deals, and of their socio-economic outcomes. The central argument is that, in the unfolding land rush, historical trajectories, political economies and legal frameworks tend to remove control from the people who are most directly concerned. This lack of control makes it more unlikely that the deals will benefit local people, and respond to their aspirations. The chapter makes the case for placing people at the centre of investment processes, discusses ways to shift prevailing patterns of agricultural investment, and suggests the big-picture changes in policy and practice that are needed to make that shift become a reality.

# 2 | Historical roots of the land rush

*The first great land grab: the European scramble for Africa*

'Wishing, in a spirit of good and mutual accord, to regulate the conditions most favourable to the development of trade and civilisation in certain regions of Africa [...] and concerned [...] as to the means of furthering the moral and material well-being of the native populations [...]' These solemn and apparently well-meaning words were pronounced by the plenipotentiaries of the United Kingdom, France, Germany and a few other Western powers gathered in Berlin for an international conference on Africa. The words are enshrined in the preamble of the treaty that was adopted at the event. But despite the lofty aspirational statement, few would argue that this treaty reflected a genuine concern for the well-being of people in Africa. If anything, these words illustrate how even the most brutal of acts can be couched in noble language. The treaty is the General Act of the 1885 Berlin Conference, a landmark event in the process that led to Europe's colonization of Africa. Within a few years of the conference, most of the African continent was brought under European domination.

Colonization was the first great grab of Africa's land. As recent debates about 'land grabbing' unfolded, some saw parallels between the large land deals of modern times and the colonial project. The former director-general of the Food and Agriculture Organization of the United Nations, Jacques Diouf, told the press that land deals risked 'creating a neo-colonial pact'.[1] Despite these references to the past, much of today's debate about the global land rush is framed in ahistorical terms. Yet far from being a new phenomenon, large land deals have a long history in Africa. During colonialism, settlers and colonial companies took millions of hectares. Times are very different today. Africa is now made up of sovereign nations. The players, motivations and crops involved in today's land deals are different from those that drove the colonial plantations. But the colonial deals have left profound scars that still shape important aspects of today's land rush. Charting the historical trajectory dating back to colonial times is critical to properly understanding today's deals.

Of course, political and economic relations between Africa and the outside world date back to well before the Berlin Conference and the colonial experience. The Romans occupied the northern part of the continent, but after an ill-fated expedition they stayed clear of sub-Saharan Africa. The Arab conquest brought northern Africa under Islamic control. Islam also exerted important cultural and economic influence on the Sudano-Sahelian belt and on the East African coast. In the Middle Ages, trade between Europe and West Africa provided much of the gold needed for the monetarization of Europe.[2] Centuries later, Africa provided large numbers of slaves for the mines and plantations of the New World. After the Portuguese circumnavigated Africa in the fifteenth century, they occupied strategic parts of the African coast.

But throughout this long history of political, economic and cultural relations, outsiders did not venture to occupy substantial land in mainland Africa until the nineteenth century. Then, multiple forces triggered a radical shift in relations between Africa and the outside world. The Industrial Revolution in the United Kingdom and then in continental Europe and the United States increased productivity, changed transport and communications, expanded military capabilities and transformed national societies. These changes widened the thus far small gaps between richer and poorer countries, making it easier for richer countries to subjugate less powerful ones.[3] In Europe, the Great Depression of 1873–96 and protectionist measures adopted as a response to it pushed European countries to establish colonies as a way of acquiring new markets for their industrial surpluses. Africa's mineral wealth and its suitability to produce agricultural commodities were also attractive to the Europeans. Indeed, in Europe and North America, the emergence of mass consumption societies required sourcing growing quantities of raw materials for industrial production. And in several European countries, political rivalries and rising nationalism fuelled imperialistic ambitions and appetite for colonial adventures.

Contrary to popular belief, the General Act of the Berlin Conference did not carve out Africa among the participating powers. Most of its content deals with freedom of trade and navigation on two important river basins – the Congo and the Niger. But by setting rules for the occupation by European powers of territories in Africa, the General Act did pave the way for what came to be known as the scramble for Africa. Within a few years, much of the continent was brought under the rule of European powers. Colonial domination triggered the most rapid and comprehensive grab of Africa's lands in history. European colonizers asserted political sovereignty over the territories they conquered. But they also acquired ownership of vast areas of land. The main legal fiction used to do this was the concept of vacant lands, whereby lands without productive occupation were deemed to be empty and without owner (*terres vacantes et sans maître*, in French).[4] In colony after colony, legislation vested ownership of vacant lands with the state or an institution representing it (the Crown, in British colonies). Back then, population densities on the continent were lower than they are now, and many important forms of resource use were not recognized as constituting productive use. So the greater part of the land in Africa came to be owned by the colonial governments. With a pen stroke, local landholders became mere users of somebody else's land. In a few cases, colonial control over land was established in more indirect ways. In the Gold Coast (now Ghana), attempts by the British colonizers to enact legislation vesting vacant lands with the Crown were defeated by resistance from customary chiefs and a national bourgeoisie interested in acquiring rural land for speculation. But the colonial administration developed other means to control land and rural people, namely by strengthening the powers of customary authorities now allied with the colonizers.[5]

Colonial administrators used their control over land to open

17

up Africa's resources for settlers and companies, causing extensive dispossession among the local population. In many parts of eastern and southern Africa, substantial European settlement led to the taking of large shares of the colonies' land. In South Africa, the Natives Land Act of 1913 reserved to natives, who constituted the bulk of the population, only 13 per cent of the national land – a share that would be further reduced under apartheid. The vast majority of the land was taken up by the settlers. European settlers also came to own 49 per cent of the land in Southern Rhodesia (now Zimbabwe), 7 per cent in Kenya and 6 per cent in Bechuanaland (now Botswana).[6] In both settler colonies and elsewhere, Western companies took up vast areas of land to set up plantations for the commodities required by the industrializing economies of Europe and North America, such as cotton, palm oil and rubber. In Sudan, the British developed the Gezira irrigation scheme to grow cotton between the Blue and White Nile rivers. The scheme was later expanded to cover some 880,000 hectares of land, and remains one of the largest in the world.[7] In the Democratic Republic of the Congo, a British company established a 100,000-hectare plantation to grow palm oil for its flagship soap brand.[8] And in Liberia, an American company making car tyres established a 'million-acre' rubber plantation. In many of these large ventures, only a fraction of the land taken was actually cultivated.[9]

In other cases, the vesting of landownership with colonial authorities or subservient chiefs did not result in physical dispossession, but it did weaken local land rights in ways that are still felt to this day. In much of Africa, the scale of European settlement was much more limited than in the Americas, partly because of the more difficult terrain. Where centralized political structures existed and markets and trading routes were well established, as in much of West Africa, the colonizers preferred to source agricultural produce from local farmers.[10] Here, the extent of land dispossession was more limited. Many colonial crops – cocoa, coffee, cotton – were largely grown by local farmers, with European businesses focusing on trading and processing. Value extraction took place through collecting taxes and manipulating agricultural commodity prices, rather than through expropriating land. Colonial policies used coercion, regulation and economic incentives to ensure that sufficient labour would be provided to supply value chains dominated by the Europeans. Local people continued to access land on the basis of 'customary' systems. But the colonial regime brought profound changes to these systems. To promote peasant participation in cash crop production, access to land became conditional upon farmers paying taxes to their chiefs. What had been until then a patronage relationship between a subject and a chief, mainly based on political allegiance and supply of military services, was remoulded into an economic relationship between a landlord and a tenant.[11] Also, colonial authorities strengthened the authoritarian powers of custom-ary chiefs to control rural areas.[12] This manipulation of custom made local land rights more fragile. The colonizers also readapted customary systems to make it easier for settlers and companies to acquire land. For example, customary law was interpreted as establishing only use rights, rather than ownership, over land.[13] And where customary land rights were legally recognized, for instance under late colonial legislation passed by the French and the Portuguese,[14] emphasis was on individual rights over land used for housing or cultivation, to the exclusion of the usually larger parts of the customary land estate that were used for grazing, hunting or gathering, or of lands set aside for future generations.[15]

Through colonialism, the capitalist system that had emerged in Europe and North America spread to sub-Saharan Africa. Africa was integrated in the capitalist economy as a producer of minerals and agricultural commodities, and under unfavourable terms that facilitated the extraction of value from the colonies to the benefit of the colonial powers. The colonial experience is now long gone. But as today's rush for Africa's land unfolds, the colonial legacy still influences the features and outcomes of the deals in many important ways. The land rush confirms Africa's integra-tion into the world economy as a provider of raw materials. The weakening of local land rights brought about by colonialism has not been fundamentally reversed. Important features of colonial

19

land legislation – including the central role of the government in land relations, the framing of local land rights as mere use rights subject to proof of productive occupation, and the legal devices to make land available to outside investors – remain recurring characteristics of land law in Africa. And at the local level, the nature and powers of the customary authorities that are today expected to represent local interests in the face of growing outside pressures are still influenced by colonial-era manipulation aimed at exploiting, not protecting, local groups. The colonial past still casts a dark shadow on the present, making it more unlikely that today's renewed interest in investing in African agriculture will meet the aspirations of local groups.

### The second great land grab: state-led land acquisitions after independence

In northern Tanzania, land relations are tense. Developments in conservation and tourism have taken much land from local groups. In Loliondo, a division of Ngorongoro district, in the country's Arusha Region, a bitter conflict opposes the Maasai pastoralists to government authorities, tourism businesses, conservation interests and hunting blocks. There have been allegations of forced evictions and human rights abuses, and lawsuits have been brought before national courts.[16] The roots of this conflict go a long way back in time. The landholdings of the Maasai have been squeezed since the colonial era. In 1904 and again in 1911, the British protectorate that then ruled neighbouring Kenya signed the Anglo-Maasai Agreements with individuals purporting to be Maasai chiefs. The agreements dispossessed the Maasai of vast areas of land.[17] Lawsuits filed by the Maasai to challenge the legality of these agreements were dismissed on a technicality.[18] The German colonizers of what is today Tanzania also set about dispossessing the Maasai, and the British continued that work when they took over from Germany after the First World War.

The spoliation of the land of the Maasai did not end with the demise of colonialism. The 1980s saw a new surge in dispossession. In 1984, the Tanzanian government allocated some four thousand hectares of land in Loliondo to a parastatal company that made beer. The plan was to develop mechanized barley farming to supply the company's breweries. But the land was claimed by Maasai pastoralists, who continued to use much of it. A few years later, in 1992, the government allocated a hunting block covering another big chunk of Maasai land to a company with connections to the United Arab Emirates. From the late 1980s, tensions ran high, and the Maasai pastoralists became increasingly mobilized. Many of the Maasai intellectuals who today work in development agencies or civil society organizations in the region's capital, Arusha, were forged by those years of struggle. Today's land conflict in Loliondo follows intervening changes in these long-standing ventures. The brewery formalized its land title in 2003, and three years later it subleased the land to a safari operator.[19] The transfer was followed by reports that pastoralists were evicted from the land.[20] Tensions also erupted on land within the hunting block, because in 2009 the government evicted villagers from the area.[21] As in many other instances across the continent, the conflict in Loliondo represents just a new phase of a long history of tensions and contestation.

Indeed, back in the 1980s, the state farm in Loliondo was far from being an isolated case. The Tanzanian government created many such farms in different parts of the country, swallowing up land claimed by pastoralists. In Hanang, another district in northern Tanzania, the government allocated several 4,000-hectare plantations to a parastatal company in order to grow wheat. It is reported that, in their heyday, the farms in Hanang supplied a third of Tanzania's wheat requirements.[22] But they dispossessed the Barabaig pastoralists, who throughout the 1980s fought and lost multiple court battles to reclaim their land.[23] Nor were these big development schemes unique to Tanzania. State farms sprang up in many parts of Africa. In Ghana, a parastatal company was established in the 1970s to develop palm oil. Thousands of hectares of land were expropriated from local farmers in the Eastern Region and allocated to the company.[24] In Mozambique, after the Portuguese farmers left the fertile, irrigated lands of the

Limpopo Valley, cultivation was continued by state farms. Instead of getting land, local peasants were integrated as labourers on these farms.[25] In the 1990s, many state farms in different parts of Africa were privatized, and some privatized plantations form the object of today's land deals. Some recent privatizations and leases have been associated with flare-ups of conflict, especially where villagers who had encroached upon the state farms were now threatened with eviction.

Behind the state farms and the expropriations of the 1970s and 1980s were not colonial regimes, but independent governments. From the late 1950s, a wave of declarations of independence changed Africa's political landscape for good. A new generation of political leaders emerged from anti-colonial struggles and came to power. Hopes were riding high across the continent. But those who expected a radical reconfiguration of land relations were to be disappointed. Decolonization rarely resulted in stronger land rights for rural people. Many post-independence legislators provided for the continued application of colonial-era legislation. So, many African countries inherited legal systems that were geared towards centralizing resource control in the hands of the state and opening up resources for outside investors, rather than towards protecting the land rights of local people – although government powers were now to be used in pursuit of a development agenda, rather than for colonial exploitation. In fact, some new laws gave rural people even weaker rights than those that had been recognized by late colonial legislation. In the decades after independence, single-party regimes and military dictatorships strengthened the extensive role of the state in control over land and the national economy, further eroding the land rights claimed by rural people. The second big 'land grab' in Africa's history was perpetrated by African governments themselves.[26]

To be sure, the newly independent countries followed different paths to development, which translated into diverse land policies. Ghana experienced 'African socialism' first and then capitalism.[27] Mali went through socialism and then a military dictatorship. Tanzania experienced 'African socialism', the ideal of self-reliant farming, and a policy of voluntary first, then forced, villagization (*ujamaa*). After Mozambique became independent in the mid-1970s, it was ruled by a Marxist-Leninist regime and ravaged by a long civil war. But despite the different political orientations, extensive government control of land and the economy was a recurring feature in the decades after independence. In socialist countries, the collectivization of the means of production was justified through socialist ideology. Legislation nationalized all land, for example in Mozambique. Colonial plantations became state or collective farms, and other lands were subject to villagization and cooperative experiences. On the other hand, the African countries that adopted a capitalist model of development justified the central role of the state with then fashionable economic theories on the 'big push' – whereby large-scale, state-led investment was needed to promote economic development. Here too, much land was owned by the government – or else the government exercised control over land in more indirect ways. In Mali, a Land Code adopted in 1986 reintroduced the possibility of obtaining private ownership through land registration.[28] But the complex procedure required to establish private landownership meant that much land was – and still is – held by the state. Also, extensive powers of eminent domain, which enabled the government to expropriate land for broadly defined 'public purposes', allowed governments to acquire vast areas of land. In Ghana, where the colonial regime had left landownership in the hands of the chiefs, the State Lands Act of 1962 allowed the government to acquire land for a public purpose, which included commercial ventures. Based on this legislation, a significant share of the land was brought under direct government ownership.

Attitudes towards the land rights of rural people also varied in different places and phases – but again recurring features emerged. In some countries, the newly independent government challenged the power of customary authorities compromised with the former colonial masters. So legislation in Mali and Mozambique abolished customary land rights, repealing late colonial legislation that had provided these rights with some degree of legal protection.[29]

In southern and central Ghana, on the other hand, the chiefs kept the land and national law continued to recognize customary rights. However, the Stool Lands Act required revenues from land rentals and sales to be paid to the government, which would then distribute these revenues according to a specified formula. But the chiefs' continued control over much land eventually led to a rapprochement between the Ghanaian government and customary authorities, which opened up the country's land to large-scale agriculture through deals with the chiefs.[30]

Yet, irrespective of the place of customary rights and authorities under national law, land legislation in most African countries recognized only weak rights for people in rural areas. Consistently with the approach that had been taken by colonial policy, these rights were usually framed as usufruct rather than ownership, and legal protection was often subject to evidence of productive use, for instance in Mali and Tanzania. The newly independent governments maintained the legal fictions and devices that had been used by the colonizers to weaken the land claims of local people. Those forms of resource use that do not result in visible, permanent occupation – including pastoralism and shifting cultivation – were threatened by big development schemes like the state farms in Tanzania, Ghana and Mozambique. Ideology, a lack of understanding of rural livelihoods among the ruling elites, concerns about building the nation and promoting economic development, and a desire to seize an asset that was the source of much political power all shaped the attitudes of African governments towards land.

From the late 1980s, political and economic liberalization swept across the African continent. Structural adjustment programmes in the 1980s and transitions to multiparty elections in the early 1990s brought about radical shifts in relations among states, markets and citizens, and greater reliance on the private sector in the promotion of economic development. Governments moved away from state-centred models of agricultural development, and sought to attract foreign investment by revising land legislation, providing tax breaks and introducing new legal protections.

Liberalization resulted in increased investment flows into African agriculture. Despite major diversity in crops and contexts, the new wave of agricultural investments presented important differences compared to the situation in the colonial era. It was less about establishing large plantations, and more about controlling value chains supplied by local farmers – in line with the approach already followed by colonizers in some parts of Africa. There were several reasons for this. The nationalization of colonial plantations in many newly independent countries highlighted the political risks associated with the plantation model. Increasing unionization of estate labour forces and stricter labour legislation also encouraged a move away from plantations.[31] Perhaps most importantly, agricultural value chains tended to concentrate commercial returns in processing and distribution, while primary production presented significant risks. This situation created incentives for agribusiness companies to focus on activities upstream (provision of inputs, seeds and machinery) and downstream (processing and distribution), and to leave farming to local growers.

Drawing on earlier evolutions in Europe and North America and on experiences developed by parastatals in Africa, agribusiness companies provided farmers with inputs on credit and then bought farm produce after harvest. A great diversity of these 'contract farming' arrangements allowed companies to outsource production risks, reduce labour and social security costs, and avoid tying up capital in land.[32] Within a few years, the historical pendulum between plantation and contractualized agriculture shifted towards the latter in relation to several important crops. Contract farming became widespread for crops as diverse as palm oil, cocoa, tobacco, tea, cotton, rice and sugar. In Kenya, where the colonizers had established extensive tea plantations, contract farming came to account for 60 per cent of tea production.[33] Similar shifts from plantation agriculture to contract farming took place in the international tobacco industry, for example.[34] For farmers, the potential for higher and more stable returns came to the detriment of control over key farming decisions: growers had to produce to detailed specifications from the companies.

Today, global processors and traders, transnational super-market companies and consumer goods manufacturers based in Europe and North America source agricultural produce from hundreds of thousands of farmers worldwide. This has provided new livelihood opportunities for many African farmers, facilitating access to more lucrative markets and creating new sources of income. But structural forces have shifted negotiating power between different segments of global value chains in ways that are unfavourable to African farmers. In colonial times, agricultural value chains were 'producer-driven', with much control in the hands of the colonial plantations. But agricultural value chains have now become 'buyer-driven', led by transnational firms specialized in processing and distribution.[35] While farming is carried out by a very large number of producers worldwide, processing and retail are increasingly concentrated. A handful of traders and processors control a huge share in global trading of commodities like grains, palm oil and coffee. And in the United Kingdom, the top four supermarkets account for about 80 per cent of food sales.[36] The growing concentration in downstream segments of the value chain, coupled with corporate control over brands, patents and information, means that negotiating power is increasingly in the hands of large companies.[37] Also, advances in transport and communications enable companies to move sourcing to different parts of the world, which further undermines the negotiating power of farmers.[38] Transnational firms tightly coordinate their supply chains to ensure quality, timeliness and reliability of deliveries. In this prevailing pattern of integration into world markets, African farmers may have kept the land, but their control over farming decisions and their share of value added tend to be limited.[39]

Overall, policy-making after independence has brought significant changes to African economies and societies. Commercially oriented farmers in many parts of Africa have become increasingly integrated in international value chains. But there are important continuities in Africa's long-term historical trajectory. Evolutions over the past few decades have entrenched the continent's integration in world markets mainly as an exporter of commodities and raw materials, continuing an international division of labour that dates back to colonization. Economic relations with the outside world have continued to be mediated by foreign – typically Western – companies. Much land legislation has consolidated some of the key features of colonial law, including with regard to the central role of government in land relations and to the qualified protection of local rights. State farms have been privatized, but governments have continued to be fascinated by large-scale, 'big push' development projects. The important role that African governments play in facilitating today's land deals, including through the widespread use of land expropriations for a public purpose, is a continuation of this historical trajectory. Africa presents much diversity of contexts, and it is important not to generalize. In some countries, political liberalization in the 1990s led to a new wave of land laws that strengthened the legal protection of local land rights – for example in Mali, Mozambique and Tanzania.[40] But as will be discussed, shortcomings in implementation have limited the impact of these progressive reforms. In much of Africa, control over land remains largely in the hands of the government – and, in some jurisdictions, in the hands of customary chiefs. Throughout this period, the ability of local farmers, herders and foragers to shape their own future remained limited.

## Agricultural intensification and 'land grabbing' from below

January 2011, Wassa Amenfi East district, in the cocoa belt of Ghana's Western Region. A scarcely visible path runs through the cocoa trees and leads to a settlement on top of the hill. Cocoa beans have been laid to dry on large wooden tables close to the village. This elevated place commands a beautiful view of the surrounding hills. In a clearance among the cocoa trees, villagers welcome us, sitting in a small circle. They are worried about recent developments that threaten their relationship with this land.[41]

These villagers are not from this part of Ghana. They do not own the land they farm. Shortly after independence, their forefathers

27

moved here from the country's Eastern Region to carve a role in the cocoa boom. They cleared the land to grow cocoa as sharecroppers. The land is owned by the 'stool' – a collective body represented by the paramount chief in the nearby Wassa Akropong, the main centre in the district. Over the years, villagers felt secure that the cocoa farms they established were theirs. They paid an annual rent for the land, and owned the trees they had planted. But this sense of security has now been shaken. A new regulation passed by the traditional council in Wassa Akropong requires all sharecroppers to survey the land and sign new fifty-year leases. The rule aimed to bring clarity to land relations in the area. But in the village, there is confusion as to whether the fifty-year period begins from the settlers' first arrival on the land, or from the time of the survey. The settlers have been farming for over forty-five years, and the retroactive application of the new rule would mean that their land rights are soon up for renegotiation. Farmers are worried about the prohibitive cost of surveying, and about the steep upfront fee that the chiefs may demand for a new lease. Years ago, land fees were purely symbolic, and were often paid in the form of drinks to show respect for the landowning authority. Nowadays, 'drink money' is paid in cash, and involves large sums that are beyond the reach of many.

Access to land in this area has undergone major changes over the years. Once plentiful, land has become scarce, and competition fierce. The district population has been growing fast. In the settlements around Wassa Akropong, villagers see their land being eaten up by the expansion of the town. Elsewhere, galamsey miners – small-scale, artisanal miners, often migrants from northern Ghana – are taking up much land and leaving devastated landscapes in their wake. Many galamsey miners strike deals with local landowners, and the sharecroppers have the land taken away from under their feet. Also, landholdings are increasingly concentrated. Some 'smallholders' have a lot of land, others have very little, and many have none. Some villagers have farms of 14, 16 or 20 hectares. A local leader says proudly that he has 40 hectares. But many farmers juggle with multiple plots of just a few hectares each. Women tend to have smaller plots than men. Youths struggle to find any land to sustain their new families. In some villages, it is difficult to get even one hectare. In the village of Amanikrom a young man eager to farm could only get a fifth of a hectare. So the landless youth work their way up by starting as labourers or sharecroppers. In the past, sharecropping attracted migrants only from other parts of the country. Today, young members of the landowning family have to resort to sharecropping too. Meanwhile, much land is in the hands of absentee landlords who work in Accra and use part of their wages to pay for agricultural labourers.

The changes happening in Wassa Amenfi are in line with social transformations that are sweeping across the African continent. Over the past few decades, demographic growth, movements of people, encroachment from expanding urban centres, integration into world markets, wages from formal employment and pressures from non-agricultural land uses have all profoundly transformed land relations in many parts of rural Africa. Similarly to developments in Wassa Amenfi, competition for higher-value land has dramatically increased in much of the continent.[42] Where in the past farmers and herders could access land by giving traditional authorities token contributions like drinks or nuts, markets for commercial land transactions have emerged, and land prices have skyrocketed. In coastal West Africa, old agreements that decades ago enabled migrants to access land are now being renegotiated by the new generations.[43] And in Mali's Inner Niger Delta, a seasonal floodplain of strategic importance to pastoralists in the region, the Fulani chiefs responsible for managing resources, the *jowro*, used to collect symbolic fees in the form of cola nuts. Today they extract substantial cash payments, and herders are increasingly forced to tend livestock owned by urban elites who can afford cattle and fees.[44]

Growing inequality in landholdings is also not unique to Wassa Amenfi. Across the continent, the integration into agricultural value chains and the commercialization of land relations have evolved hand in hand with growing social differentiation in rural areas.[45]

Many farmers have used ingenuity, wealth and social relations to improve their lot. They have invested in new farming techniques and expanded production. They have migrated into areas with higher agricultural potential, and toiled their way through upward social mobility.[46] Other farmers have struggled to keep the pace, and are locked into subsistence agriculture on ever smaller plots. Some have little or no land and engage in farming as casual labourers. Many are leaving farming altogether – it is too much hard work for too few returns. Where land scarcity is compounded by lack of alternative livelihood options, customary or religious norms have been rediscovered to exclude women from the land.[47] And as resources are squeezed and farming intensifies, herders increasingly find strategic livestock corridors encroached upon by the expanding cultivation.[48] There are multiple 'rural worlds' in Africa's countryside[49] – from the dynamic farmers successfully integrated in global value chains to those who make a living as farm labourers, through to pastoralists whose mobile ways of life are being threatened by changing economies and societies.

Access to wages from formal employment is an important source of investment in this increasingly commercialized agriculture, but also a driver of the growing inequality.[50] As the case of Wassa Amenfi shows, people earning wages in town reinvest part of their income in farming. This investment may increase agricultural productivity, but also inequality – because families without wage employment cannot invest in the same way. In the well-documented case of Kenya's Machakos district, where farming has intensified in response to demographic growth, people with wage incomes purchased land, hired labour and invested in farm improvements like terracing. As a result, productivity increased.[51] But so did inequality, because those without access to wage income faced declining productivity. In Machakos, incomes and landownership became more concentrated.[52] Similar processes of agricultural intensification and social differentiation have been documented in many parts of Africa.[53]

And it is not a purely rural phenomenon. In many African cities, there are people with money to spare who see land in rural and peri-urban areas as an asset that will increase in value. Politicians, army generals, former liberation fighters, high-level government officials and business people have been acquiring rural land for many years. In addition, economic growth and urbanization in many African countries have led to the emergence of middle classes also interested in rural land as a means to store value and generate complementary income. While operating at different scales, national elites and growing middle classes have the money, connections and information to navigate the official systems and succeed where many rural people cannot – that is, buying land on the informal market and registering it in their name. In Sanankoroba, a rural municipality not far from the capital of Mali, Bamako, the number of title deeds increased exponentially between 1996 and 2005; most of these land titles were held by civil servants and business people based in town, not by local farmers.[54] The picture is similar in Ghana's Eastern Region, especially where proximity to the capital Accra makes commercial agriculture an appealing option.[55] In a globalized world, cross-boundary movements of people add a new international dimension to this rush for land. In countries with substantial diasporas overseas, such as Senegal or Ghana, international remittances have enabled migrants or their families to acquire land or consolidate their existing landholdings.[56] The increasing value of land and the lack of a level playing field between competing claimants make land a natural arena for strategies of accumulation. As the new absentee landlords take the land, some of the gains are redistributed through networks of patronage, with lower-income people connected to the land acquirers receiving financial benefits for their roles as land allocators, intermediaries, drivers, security people or farm labourers.

In these contexts of profound and rapid change, the content of customary rules and the nature and distribution of customary rights are often hotly contested, with different groups putting forward competing interpretations, and with power relations between those groups shaping evolution in the content and application of customary law. Assertive customary chiefs are reinterpreting their guardianship powers as those of owners. The fragmentation of extended family units and the weakening of collective decision-making fora erode the mechanisms traditionally used to ensure the accountability of customary authorities. In Mali's Inner Niger Delta, the *suudu baaba*, a body representing the extended family, is traditionally responsible for choosing the *jowro* among its members, and for holding the *jowro* to account in case of misconduct. Today, the nature of the relationship between the *jowro* and the *suudu baaba* varies in different locations. But it is not uncommon for members of *jowro* families or better-educated individuals to style themselves as *jowro* despite their lack of any formal endorsement by the *suudu baba*. And in some places, the *suudu baba* no longer functions on a regular basis, and its ability to hold the *jowro* to account has been greatly eroded. This weakened accountability enables some *jowro* to allocate land to outsiders for personal gain.

Agricultural commercialization, growing social differentiation and the erosion of customary institutions have been accompanied by growing land disputes. In Wassa Amenfi, disagreements over boundaries, multiple transactions for the same land by different family members, and contested sharecropping agreements are recurring sources of conflict. Many disputes are taken to the High Court in Tarkwa. Some farmers in the area now use witnesses when they transact land. But witnesses can be corrupted, and in some cases a witness summoned to court supported both sides of the story. Again, these evolutions are in line with wider trends. In many parts of Africa, land disputes are on the rise. Competing claims over land may assume wider socio-political connotations. Indigeneity – descent from the first occupants, and the basis for land access under customary systems – is being redefined in narrower terms to exclude groups that settled decades ago.[57] In the most extreme cases, land disputes and political manipulation of indigeneity have been linked to armed conflict. Land issues were among the root causes of the devastating wars in the Great Lakes region, Côte d'Ivoire and the Mano River basin.[58]

The upshot is that local land relations in Africa have changed profoundly over the past few decades. Competition for higher-value land has been growing for a number of years. Landholdings have become more concentrated and social differentiation among small-scale producers has increased. Local elites and urban groups have manipulated legal processes and customary systems to seize land. These processes of 'land grabbing' from below are very different from the large-scale land grabs triggered by colonial and post-independence policies. They do not involve spectacularly large land deals, though their cumulative impact on land access for poorer people in rural areas can be substantial. They result from deep-rooted socio-economic changes, more than deliberate government policy. Rural and urban groups, settlers and first occupants, farmers and pastoralists, men and women, youths and elders are the protagonists of these land struggles.

But like the land acquisitions perpetrated by colonial and independent governments, the long-standing processes of growing land concentration have profound implications for the features and outcomes of today's land rush. At one level, the growing competition for land in many parts of Africa challenges prevailing discourses about the availability of 'empty land' on the continent, which underpin public decisions favouring large-scale land allocations to commercial operators – although many of today's large deals target areas that are used less intensively. At another level, today's transnational land deals enter local arenas characterized not by united, undifferentiated 'communities', but by highly stratified groups with widely diverging interests, where land relations are hotly contested along fault lines that are rooted in history and are not always easy to understand for government officials and incoming investors. Differentiated and contested local arenas mean that the deals will tend to produce differentiated outcomes – with some groups being better placed to capture the benefits or at least partake in the crumbs, and other groups losing out. The existence of powerful local constituencies that stand to gain from the deals – for example, customary chiefs who can use their land prerogatives for personal gain – is an important factor that facilitates today's large-scale land acquisitions.

In much of rural Africa, land has formed the object of accumulation and dispossession strategies for a long time. However, economic and political considerations made African land unattractive to foreign investors. For a long time, local and national groups, not transnational corporations, were the main players in Africa's land arena. In the mid-2000s, interest in Africa's land from outside players increased substantially. In global value chains, the historical pendulum between large plantations and contractualized production shifted again, with many companies rushing to sign large land deals for plantation agriculture in Africa. International geographies have also shifted, in line with intervening changes in the global economy. While Western companies remain a big player in Africa's agriculture, emerging powers like China, India and Brazil have become increasingly involved. The global rush for Africa's lands was unleashed, triggering a profound reconfiguration of local land dynamics and of international relations among sovereign states and transnational corporations.

# 3 | Scale, geography and drivers of the land rush

*How much land has been acquired, and where?*

London, June 2010. A five-star hotel towers over a busy street in the central neighbourhood of Kensington. Men in dark suits outside the main door stub out their cigarettes and walk towards the conference room in the basement of the hotel. Dozens of senior officers from agribusiness companies, pension funds and asset management firms are gathered in the conference room for a 'Farmland Opportunities Day'. The event is part of a three-day corporate conference on global agriculture. Throughout the day, speakers from companies that operate large farms in Europe, Latin America and Africa highlight the commercial opportunities that lie in land and agriculture. Their message is clear: changing agricultural commodity prices and technological innovation in farming and logistics have changed the face of agriculture. Today, farming is an attractive business opportunity. At a panel session devoted to 'end investors', a few pension fund managers from Europe and North America discuss why they are assessing options for investing in companies that run large farming operations, much like the ones represented here, or even in farmland directly. Coffee breaks in the elegantly draped area next to the conference room provide opportunities for networking between companies and investors.[1]

This world of high finance and big corporates might seem light years away from the everyday life of villagers who grow crops and graze livestock in rural Africa. Compared to the realities of farming in Africa, the remotely controlled tractors and computerized farm management systems showcased by some speakers at the conference seem to come from a different planet. But in recent years, these two worlds have increasingly come into contact. A new wave of land acquisitions has been unfolding, with agribusiness companies aiming to develop large-scale, mechanized farming in Africa. And new farmland funds have been launched in the world's leading financial centres, with the explicit aim of acquiring vast areas of land worldwide. Just a few years ago, corporate events on farmland would have been unlikely to prove so popular. Today, they are an easy win. Farmland has become a much-sought-after global commodity.

Sustained media reporting about land deals in Africa, first for biofuels, then for food production, has played a critical role in raising public awareness of the growing interest in Africa's land among corporate players. Media attention has also helped to promote public scrutiny in an arena characterized by a chronic lack of transparency. Since the reports started flowing, non-governmental organizations (NGOs) and campaigning groups have mobilized public opinion, campaigned for change in policy and practice, and named and shamed 'land grabbers'. In June 2012, delegates attending another corporate conference on agricultural investment were met with protests by activist groups outside the London hotel that hosted the event.[2]

The many corporate events, media reports and activist campaigns reflect an ongoing shift in global agriculture – a shift that will have profound implications for rural people in Africa, a shift where the fault lines between corporate modernizers and the defenders of small-scale farming are deep and entrenched. But despite the many studies published in recent years by development agencies, think tanks and academia, the scale, geography and drivers of land acquisitions still form the object of intense debate and widespread misperceptions. Does the level of international attention reflect the real scale of the land rush? Is the pace of the deals accelerating, or slowing down? Is Africa indeed the focus of much of the action? Who are the land acquirers, where do they come from and what motivates them? In this chapter, I look at the evidence concerning these questions. The picture that emerges challenges some common perceptions.

Before going any farther, it is worth clarifying what a 'land acquisition' is. In the minds of many, acquiring land means buying it. In Africa, the land rush mainly involves long-term leases; outright land purchases are rare. This is a direct consequence of the law prevailing in most African countries, because much land in Africa is owned by the state and private entities can only hold use rights or leases. In practice, the leases can have very long durations – up to a century. And while the contract may restrict the ability of the lessee to transfer the land, there are ways around these legal restrictions. An investor may sell its shares in the company that holds the lease. So in effect many deals are transferable. Long-term, transferable deals blur the distinction between a purchase and a lease, though the lessee will eventually have to return the land to the lessor when the lease comes to an end. It therefore makes sense to consider a lease as a land acquisition – even though, strictly speaking, landownership does not change. All publicly available assessments of the scale of the land rush treat both purchases and leases as land acquisitions. I will follow the same approach.

Let us start from a discussion of scale. Prevailing discourses about the land rush point to a phenomenon of massive scale, with some estimates suggesting that more than 200 million hectares of land – 'an area the size of Western Europe' – have been acquired worldwide since the year 2000.[3] But figures about scale are contested. Estimates of how much land has been acquired vary widely, partly because of the different ways in which they are produced. Multiple data sources reflect different ways to conceptualize land deals, and different circumstances that lead to information about a land deal being included in a data set, or excluded from it.

Most of the estimates of scale that have been circulated are derived from varying combinations of two types of sources: international reviews mainly based on media and research reports, perhaps cross-referenced with in-country sources, and systematic national inventories based on official government records. These two types of sources capture different realities, which partly

Mali and Senegal are important recipient countries according to media or official sources (see Figure 3.1). Cameroon, Zambia and Tanzania are also known to have attracted much investor interest, and these countries feature among the Land Matrix's 'top ten' recipients in Africa; but systematic inventories based on government records are not yet available for these three countries.

With a few important exceptions, however, the figures gathered through the national inventories tend to be lower than those based on media reports (see Figure 3.1). In Mozambique, for example, media sources arrived at more than ten million hectares acquired between 2008 and 2010,[21] while a national inventory for the period 2004–09 calculated a figure closer to 2.7 million.[22] The Land Matrix figure is even lower (see Figure 3.1). On the other hand, some countries have attracted substantial investor interest but have experienced less intensive scrutiny from international media. Ghana is a case in point (see Figure 3.1). This is perhaps due to the fact that, in Ghana, many deals are signed by local chiefs, rather than by the central government. These local negotiations are more difficult to track. In Liberia, national inventories include the renegotiation of long-standing plantations, which partly explains the discrepancy with media figures (see Figure 3.1). Also, in line with public perceptions, the size of some land acquisitions can be very large. Verified deals for mega-farms include a 220,000-hectare project in Liberia and two 100,000-hectare projects in Ethiopia and Mali.[23] But national inventories indicate that the average size of individual deals is much smaller than that suggested by media reports.[24]

Scarcity of reliable data and a fast-evolving situation require caution in reaching conclusions about the scale of the land rush. But the gap between figures based on media reports and figures based on official records suggests that public perceptions may have overestimated the aggregate scale of the transnational deals signed so far. The roughly one-to-four ratio between cross-referenced and reported deals included in the Matrix seems to confirm this finding. So does the gap between the aggregate scale of deals cross-referenced by the Land Matrix (some fifty

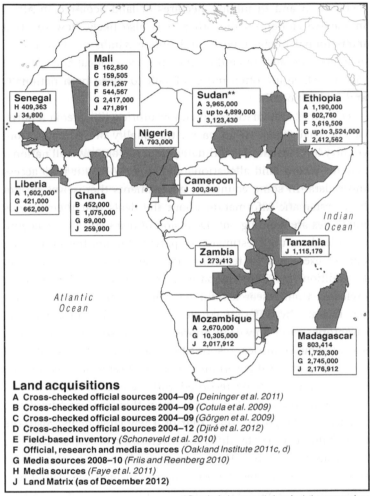

**3.1** What we know about the scale and geography of land acquisitions in selected African countries

million hectares worldwide over more than ten years, including deals outside agriculture), on the one hand, and assessments of scale produced by studies that relied on media reports from the databases run by GRAIN (56 million hectares of agricultural deals worldwide in one year alone) or the International Land Coalition in attracting investment may refer to the usually larger land areas featured in the memorandum of understanding.

Another issue is that, while national systematic inventories can give a good sense of how much land has formed the object of deals, they say little about the scale of operations on the ground. Signing a deal for a 100,000-hectare plantation is not the same as establishing that plantation in practice. In fact, there is much evidence to suggest that the scale of operational activities is much smaller than that reflected in the contracts. In large deals, implementation usually begins on a small scale, and is phased up to full capacity over relatively long periods of time. And many approved deals have had little implementation, owing mainly to greater-than-expected challenges on the ground or to difficulties in financing, but also to the speculative nature of some land acquisitions.[28] In fact, many deals have never been implemented, or else implementation was discontinued. In other cases, companies have had to scale down their original ambitions, and the plantation turned out to be smaller than planned. A World Bank report found that, in Mozambique, some 35 per cent of the land acquired was not used, and an additional 15 per cent was not used to the extent required by investment plans.[29]

The gap between reported and actual deals, and between the land area transacted and the limited degree of implementation should not give ground for complacency. There are three reasons for this. First, the deals matter even if they have not yet been fully implemented. As the implementation of the deals progresses over time, the fuller impacts will start to be felt. And deals that are not implemented still exacerbate land pressures and create opportunity costs. This is because alternative land uses are prevented or delayed. The government cannot allocate the land to another use and local people are restricted from using the land even if the company does not develop it – although in the case of some unsuccessful ventures villagers are encroaching upon the land leased to the company. Many contracts do allow the government to terminate the lease if the company does not invest. But these provisions are rarely implemented. In practice, the land acquired can remain idle for years, in whole or in part, even in successful ventures.[30] And where projects fail, the land is usually not returned to local landholders. Governments will seek other investors to take the project forward. This process may take a long time, during which the land is subtracted to alternative uses.

Second, the pressures that the deals create on local land relations are shaped not only by the aggregate land area acquired, but also by the quality and location of that land. In Ghana, much agricultural investment is concentrated in the centre and north of the country, where population densities are lower and there is greater potential for agricultural intensification. But despite the rhetoric of bringing 'marginal' lands into production, investors often target the best land in terms of soil fertility, irrigation potential, infrastructure development or proximity to markets. For example, land acquisitions in Mali and Senegal appear to have been heavily concentrated in the irrigable areas of the Ségou Region and the Senegal river valley, respectively.[31] Initiatives to support 'agricultural development corridors' in Mozambique and Tanzania suggest that investor interest concentrates along strategic transport and communication axes.[32] Investors are also drawn to lands in peri-urban areas. In such strategic locations, competition for land has been growing for a long time, as a result of population pressures but also of the increasing involvement of urban elites in rural and peri-urban land markets. So the acquisition of even relatively small land areas can greatly exacerbate pressures on the land.

Third, transnational land deals for plantation agriculture are not happening in a vacuum. In many places, land pressures have increased as a result of multiple processes – from demographic growth to land acquisition by local and national elites, through to developments in mining, petroleum and conservation. Processes of 'land grabbing' from below were discussed in Chapter 2. Data presented farther below suggests that national players account for much recent land acquisition. Here, it may be useful to briefly discuss pressures from extractive industry developments.

2009.[35] This may reflect greater discretion due to fear of adverse publicity among investors previously bent on grand announcements. But it probably also reflects changes in the volume of transactions. The financial crisis in the West restricted access to finance for companies planning operations in Africa. This had a major impact on biofuels ventures, many of which were highly dependent on bank loans. Several investments have been discontinued because of financing difficulties – for example, in Ghana, Mozambique and Tanzania. Similarly, asset management firms launched ambitious farmland funds but struggled to raise capital from investors (pension funds, endowments, rich individuals). For example, an investment management firm dumped plans for a $387 million farmland fund it first announced in 2008.[36] These financing difficulties may ease in the medium term, giving renewed momentum to the land rush. But a growing number of failed investments has also persuaded many that establishing plantations in Africa is not as easy a ride as some initially thought. And there are signs that governments too are becoming more cautious in allocating large areas of land to outside investors. This is due to the manifest failures in the implementation of earlier projects, but also to the resistance met by the deals at local and national levels. Some governments enacted formal or unofficial halts to large land deals, for instance in Mozambique and Ethiopia.[37] In Tanzania, the government announced maximum ceilings on the size of the land deals – 5,000 hectares for rice and 10,000 hectares for sugar cane, for instance.[38] In a departure from earlier lax attitudes towards contract management, some governments have terminated deals because companies did not honour their investment commitments – for example, in Mali and Mozambique.[39] In Mali, there is much uncertainty as to the future of many land deals following the political instability in the country, and many foreign investors have pulled out.

But despite these reversals, new transnational deals are being signed. Corporate conferences on opportunities in farmland investments continue to be organized. Memoranda of understanding and public announcements about new farmland investments that have not (yet) translated into leases can still provide a measure of the strong interest of global players in acquiring land. This greater interest may concretize into new leases in future, and as such it provides an indicator of the growing pressures on land in the coming years. The transformations in the global economy that have triggered the land rush will continue to make land acquisition an appealing commercial prospect. And profound transformations in national societies mean that land acquisitions by nationals are likely to continue for years to come. On the ground, the consequences of the deals concluded a few years ago are only now starting to be felt. New conflicts are emerging as the deals start being implemented at scale. The land rush and its implications are likely to stay for the next few years. They must be taken very seriously in both policy and practice.

## Who is behind the deals?

It is easy to get lost in the building of the European Parliament in Brussels. Within a single day, the parliament hosts many events on issues ranging from research and development in the pharmaceutical industry through to decentralized governance in fisheries. Lobbyists, journalists and nervous-looking speakers negotiate their way through security checks. As I try to find my way around, a stream of people converging towards a lobby area is of precious help – I follow the crowd and I am lucky enough to end up at the right event. In the plenary hall, the parliament's Committee on Development is holding a public hearing on 'food security in developing countries'.[40]

The parliamentarians are sitting in the inner circle of benches. Behind them, numerous participants populate the hemicycle, NGOs and trade unions among them. Interpreters behind large windows translate discussions in several of the many official languages of the European Union. Presenters in rapid succession – European Union commissioners, high-level United Nations officials, representatives of farmer organizations from lower-income countries, NGOs and researchers – tackle the main food security challenges confronting the developing world today – from

51

commodity speculation to distortions in international trade through to, of course, large-scale land acquisitions. I sit on the panel discussing large-scale land acquisitions, and raise a few issues about the scale, drivers, features and early outcomes of the land rush. But there is one point that attracts much attention. It is about the geography of the deals. While much public debate has focused on the role of companies from the Gulf and East Asia, evidence shows that Western companies are a major player in the global rush to Africa's lands. This point may be a truism to many, but it seems to cause surprise in the audience. It prompts assertive requests from the chairperson for me to disclose the names of the European companies involved. That would be a very long list.

While empirical studies on the global land rush have received much attention, there are still big gaps between research findings and public perceptions. The geography of the land rush, and particularly the geographical origin of the land acquirers, is an area where misperceptions have been particularly rife and enduring. Months before the parliamentary hearing, a coalition of European advocacy groups published a report that exposed the role of European companies in land acquisitions.[41] But at the time of the hearing, the news did not seem to have been fully digested. Many commentators were still looking east. Knowing who is behind the deals and what motivates them is critical. Not only because the public has a right to know, both in the countries that are most directly affected by the deals, and in the countries where the final products are marketed and sold. But also because, without that understanding, it is very difficult to develop effective responses. Policy measures are bound to prove inadequate if they fail to address key players and fundamental drivers. And it is impossible to hold companies to account if it is not clear who they are in the first place. So I now turn to investigating the main players in the land rush.

*'Land grabbing' starts at home: the role of national and regional players* In the global land rush, land acquisitions by transnational

corporations have dominated the headlines. But this does not reflect the real trend. Public debates about transnational deals have diverted attention from another important source of pressures on the land. In many parts of Africa, villagers are feeling the squeeze not because of land acquisitions by global capitalists, but because of growing land concentration within the national society. Empirical research shows that nationals account for a major share of the land being acquired. A World Bank study covering the period 2004–09 found that nationals accounted for 97 per cent of the land area acquired in Nigeria, and for half or more in Sudan (78 per cent), Ethiopia (49 per cent) and Mozambique (53 per cent).[42] Similarly, in Senegal, acquisitions by nationals account for 61 per cent of acquired land areas according to one inventory.[43] Nationals have been acquiring land also in countries that have received less interest from international investors. A study from Benin, Burkina Faso and Niger documented significant levels of land acquisitions, and found that over 95 per cent of the investors involved in land deals were nationals, including professional farmers and urban groups like civil servants, traders and politicians.[44] While the average size of these plots (85 hectares) was tiny relative to some international deals, these farms were still considerable relative to average plot sizes in the area.[45] Also, the aggregate land area acquired through many small deals can be larger than that involved in fewer, larger deals – as suggested by the findings of the World Bank study. The diaspora – local nationals living overseas – is also a big player in land acquisitions.[46] It is difficult to quantify the scale of this phenomenon. But some data from Ethiopia suggest that the role of migrants overseas is significant. Land contracts published by the Ethiopian government in 2011 included several leases involving the diaspora (six contracts out of twenty-three), though the aggregate land area acquired by international migrants was small (less than 5 per cent of the total).[47]

So the land rush is not only or even primarily the result of the activities of big companies, or of deals developed in the international corridors of power. It reflects longer-term processes of capital accumulation and social differentiation within the national societies concerned. Urban groups have acquired growing landholdings in rural areas. Politicians, government officials and business people based in town have used their entries into the state apparatus and forged alliances with customary land management authorities to seize control of rural land. The involvement of national elites in the rush for land is perhaps the single most important reason for the pervasive lack of transparency surrounding the deals. Access to land registries for researchers and scrutinizers is constrained, not so much because of the big transnational deals that the government may have signed, but because of what an analysis of the registry would reveal about how much land has been acquired by the people in power. Growing land concentration has been driven by processes rooted in rural areas too. As discussed in Chapter 2, more dynamic farmers have been able to increase their landholdings at the expense of other groups. And in many places, customary chiefs have reinterpreted their land management responsibilities as rights of ownership. Effectively, many chiefs act as large landowners, rather than as custodians of common lands. These processes of growing land concentration from below may be less glamorous than the large deals concluded by transnational corporations. But their impact on land access for rural people is very substantial.

Of course, it is often difficult to disentangle national and international players. The role of the diaspora illustrates this. In some cases, international migrants acquire land directly. In others, it is the family left behind that uses the remittances received from a relative overseas to secure or expand its landholding.[48] Trends in foreign investment also blur the divide between local and foreign nationals. Transnational companies typically operate through local subsidiaries. Nationals may facilitate land access for foreign investors, acting as intermediaries or partners.[49] In Ghana, a 7,000-hectare biofuel project I visited in the Brong Ahafo Region was set up by a local national in collaboration with a group of Italian consultants, who later identified an Italian company willing to invest money in the project. The local national went on to run the project as the company's manager. Nationals may also acquire land in the hope of transferring it to foreign companies for a big mark-up. Strategic positioning seems to be an important consideration in land acquisition by nationals. A much-publicized, large deal in South Sudan reportedly involved a partnership between a local national – a former army commander who secured control over a large piece of land – and a former Wall Street banker.[50]

Where foreign investment is involved, a significant share of it comes from within Africa.[51] For example, South Africa is an important investor country. It is home to major players in the agribusiness, energy and pulp and paper industries. Yet land in South Africa is a loaded issue. After the end of apartheid, the country adopted an ambitious land redistribution and restitution programme. Progress has been slow, but the programme has now started to bite in rural areas. In late 2008, I visited Pietermaritz-burg, the 'capital' of South Africa's forest industry. Progress with the land restitution programme was forcing companies operating large tree plantations to rethink their business model, as much of their land was being returned to communities dispossessed during apartheid or was under claim. Back then, there was much discussion about different models for possible partnerships with the new landowners – from joint ventures to locally negotiated land leases. But some companies were also turning their eyes to acquiring land and setting up new plantations in neighbouring countries. A pulp and paper company went on to initiate a 150,000-hectare plantation project in Mozambique's Zambezia Province, but later abandoned this venture out of concerns about the likely adverse impacts on local groups and the environment.[52] Other industries have been active too. South African sugar companies have responded to the increase in global demand for sugar and ethanol by taking over privatized state farms or acquiring land in several southern and eastern African countries.[53] And beyond the big corporates, South African commercial farmers who sold or may sell their land as part of the redistribution or restitution programme, and those that have been squeezed by the greater concentration and corporatization of South Africa's farming sector, are also looking elsewhere.[54] AgriSA, a body representing the commercial farmers, signed a major land deal in the Republic of Congo, and is exploring options in other countries.[55] These negotiations may reflect a real interest in acquiring land abroad. But they may also represent a negotiating chip vis-à-vis the South African government – a warning that, if the land reform goes too far, the commercial farmers may move elsewhere.[56]

Much as for relations between nationals and non-nationals, the border lines separating players from within and outside the continent are blurred. Effectively, some African countries act as strategic transit countries through which investments from outside the region are channelled into Africa. South Africa is of increasing interest to companies who want to tap into the country's expertise in African agriculture and extend their reach into popular recipient countries like Mozambique, Tanzania or Zambia. Some European companies seeking to invest in African agriculture have bought shares in, or set up joint ventures with, South African companies.[57] South African consulting engineers have been involved with contracts to build sugar mills and ethanol plants for a range of operators in different parts of Africa.[58] Mauritius is also emerging as a strategic transit country, because of its favourable tax regime and the sizeable number of bilateral investment treaties it has with other African countries, which protect investments in these third countries.[59]

*Us and them: all about China and the Gulf?* Much public attention has focused on the role of Middle Eastern, North African and East Asian investors in the rush to Africa's lands. A reader following discussions in the Western media may be forgiven for thinking that the 'land grabbers' are not us, in Europe or North America – they are them, the governments and companies of China, South Korea, Libya and the Gulf. These are the ones taking up much of Africa's land, and planning to import agricultural produce from countries that could hardly feed themselves. Over time, these perceptions have been nuanced, as researchers and journalists have turned their spotlight on the role played by European and North American companies. It is now time to undertake a critical assessment of the real scale of Asian and Middle Eastern involvement in the land rush.

Some Middle Eastern operators have been active land acquirers, mainly out of government concerns about ensuring national food security. It is not difficult to see where these concerns originate from. In the Gulf, the population is expected to double from 30 million in 2000 to nearly 60 million by 2030, but cereal agriculture is in decline; dependence on food imports, now at 60 per cent of total demand, will grow as a result.[60] Reliance on imports will also increase because of changes in national policy. In Saudi Arabia, the government started subsidizing irrigated agriculture in the 1970s, initially out of concern that the West would retaliate against the oil embargo through restricting their food exports to the Gulf. But this policy was recently reversed following concerns that water tables were dropping below sustainability levels. The subsidies are being phased out, and Saudi Arabia is planning to source food from overseas. And yet, recent developments have shaken trust in international food markets. In 2008, the prices of many cereals spiked dramatically. Some major food-exporting countries imposed restrictions on exports, which further exacerbated increases in food prices. These developments caused alarm. For countries in the Gulf, the price of food is a very important issue. Wealth and income distribution are extremely skewed. Oil-producing countries in the region have very high income per capita. But they also host large numbers of blue-collar workers, mainly migrants from South Asia, who live significantly below average income levels. Affordable food is critical to avoid social unrest and ensure political stability. Increases in food prices played an important role in the Arab Spring that swept some Middle Eastern and northern African countries in 2010/11.[61] Governments in the Gulf want to avoid a repeat.

As protests unfolded in northern Africa, some governments in the Gulf increased subsidies to help lower-income people to purchase food. But well before that crisis point, Gulf countries developed strategies to ensure reliable supplies of affordable food in the longer term. Acquiring land overseas came to be seen as a mechanism for doing this. Some governments adopted policies to support investments in agriculture overseas. Saudi Arabia's King Abdullah Initiative for Saudi Agricultural Investment Abroad is the best-known example. It supports agricultural investments by Saudi companies in countries with high agricultural potential. The scheme involves financial support for private operators, and strategic crops include rice, wheat, barley, corn, sugar and green fodders, in addition to animal and fish resources.[62] Over a period of several months in 2009 and 2010, representatives from the highest level of government in several Gulf countries travelled to talk about agriculture with their counterparts in a vast belt of countries surrounding the Middle East – from the Horn of Africa to Kazakhstan through to Pakistan. Agribusiness companies, sovereign funds and investment firms from Saudi Arabia, Qatar and some Arab emirates (particularly Abu Dhabi and Dubai) were widely reported to have clinched large deals in those countries. In Africa, countries like Ethiopia and Sudan, with their cheap and 'abundant' land and their geographical proximity to export markets in the Gulf, seemed ideal locations for this wave of investments.

Similar concerns about food security emerged in Gaddafi's Libya, a country also with vast oil wealth but limited arable land. But additional geopolitical considerations seemed to play an important role here. For a long time, Libya sought to increase political influence in the Sahel. A complex web of economic and political relations underpinned these efforts, including security issues, public and personal financial interests, and interstate patron–client relations. Negotiations involving Libya in large agricultural investments were part of this wider set of relations. In Mali, the Libyans signed their largest known land deal, a 100,000-hectare irrigation project in the Office du Niger area, now discontinued. But it would be a mistake to view Libya's land deal in Mali as a free-standing farming operation. Until war and instability changed political trajectories in both countries, Libya's involvement in Mali was pervasive. In a highly symbolic gesture, the construction of a new administrative citadel in Bamako – a majestic fusion of modernity and traditional Sahelian architecture – to host many of the Malian governmental institutions was financed by Libya. In fact, Gaddafi was personally present at the ceremony to inaugurate the citadel.[63] The knock-on effect that civil strife and political transition in Libya had on the occupation of northern Mali by jihadists and Tuareg rebels illustrates how closely intertwined the fate of the two countries had become as a result of Gaddafi's geopolitical ambitions and of Mali's interest in patronage from Libya. So while the contract for Libya's project in the Office du Niger area is now in the public domain,[64] the real motivations and the full terms of the deal may well involve untold considerations still to be uncovered.

The role of operators from Libya and the Gulf in the rush for Africa's land is borne out by evidence from multiple sources. A systematic inventory of land deals in Sudan found that Saudi Arabia was the largest investor country, accounting for about half the land area acquired by foreign investors.[65] Contracts and official documents also provide useful pointers. In 2011, a public notice issued by the government of Mauritania for the allocation of some forty thousand hectares of land to a company with Saudi links was widely circulated on the internet.[66] In addition to the agreement for Libya's investment in Mali's Office du Niger area, a contract involving a large deal by a company with Saudi links operating in Ethiopia has also come in the public domain.[67] Libyan interests are known to have been involved in other land deals too, for example in Liberia. These circumstances confirm the significant role played by operators from the Gulf and northern Africa in the global land rush. But, overall, public perceptions have overestimated the scale of this role. Available national inventories show that it is only in Sudan that Gulf countries account for a majority of foreign projects.[68] The much-debated King Abdullah Initiative has had little implementation so far, leading some analysts to talk of a 'big landgrab that wasn't'.[69] Reported negotiations in Kenya involving a deal with the Qataris did not go through. And while there have been reports that the Kuwait Investment

in Asia involving a total of 2.5 million hectares.[74] China is the main foreign land acquirer in Cambodia and Laos, chiefly for rubber and rice plantations.[75] Relations between China and countries in the Mekong region are complex and multifaceted, and strategic considerations about geopolitical influence are at play. In Africa, the intensity of the relationship is lower. Beyond media reports, hard evidence of a key role played by China in the rush for Africa's land has so far been difficult to come by. In fact, there is growing evidence to disprove some of the earlier claims made about China's direct role in the acquisition of farmland in Africa. A study on Chinese involvement in Mozambique's agricultural sector found little evidence to support earlier claims about large Chinese land deals in the country. Instead, Chinese involvement focused on technology development and demonstration centres, mainly in a development aid mode.[76] Similar conclusions were reached by a study on Chinese agricultural operations in Senegal: fieldwork initiated to examine China's land deals found evidence of none, and focused instead on the operation of a joint China–Senegal training centre, which China supported as part of its diplomatic aid package by Senegal's request.[77]

To be sure, there are various examples of deals signed by Chinese companies. In Ethiopia, contracts disclosed by the government in 2011 included a 25,000-hectare deal with a Chinese operator,[78] though this deal has now been cancelled. A Chinese deal is also known to have been signed in Mali, involving a 20,000-hectare sugar cane plantation and processing facility.[79] This latter project is the extension of a joint China–Mali venture that has been running in Mali's Office du Niger scheme since the 1960s. A few additional deals have been documented in other African countries. An inventory of China's agricultural investments in Africa found deals for a total of 463,800 hectares.[80] This figure seems considerably smaller than what would be suggested by public reporting on the role of China in the rush for Africa's land. Also, a closer look at the largest deals in this list suggests that even this more conservative inventory is likely to overestimate the scale of China's involvement. The list includes a 100,000-hectare deal concluded by the government of Libya in Mali, where Chinese companies have provided construction services and led research and development. This deal translated into a land lease for 25,000 hectares, and has now been discontinued. The list also includes the above-mentioned 25,000-hectare deal in Ethiopia, which has been cancelled, and a 60,000-hectare deal in Senegal that is understood to involve contract farming rather than land acquisition.[81] Removing these deals alone would bring the total below 300,000 hectares. The remainder of the deals on the list include not only commercial ventures, but also demonstration farms established through aid programmes. This is hardly evidence of China's supposed leading role in the rush for Africa's land. There is no doubt that China is an increasingly important player in African agriculture, and that it has been involved with some land deals on the continent. But public perceptions have overplayed China's role in the rush for Africa's land. Efforts to identify the main acquirers of land in Africa must focus elsewhere.

*New kids on the block: India, Brazil and South-East Asia* Relatively few commentators have looked at the role of South-East Asian companies. Yet operators based in Malaysia, Indonesia and Singapore have signed very large deals in Africa. Much of this concerns palm oil. In South-East Asia, palm oil operations have come under growing scrutiny for their contribution to deforestation. Land prices in Africa are considerably lower than in South-East Asia. So some South-East Asian companies are expanding operations to Africa. In Liberia, two leading companies from Singapore and Malaysia signed two massive oil palm deals for 220,000 hectares each.[82] And a trader listed on the Singapore stock exchange concluded a deal for a palm oil plantation of up to 300,000 hectares in Gabon.[83] These three deals alone account for a very large land area. And the deal in Gabon alone could affect nearly as much land as the total land area acquired in Africa by China, according to the figures discussed above.

Brazilian firms have been looking to Africa for similar reasons – increasingly constrained room for agricultural expansion at home, and cheaper land prices in Africa. Hard evidence of any significant number of deals signed by the Brazilians in Africa remains elusive. But Brazilian companies have explicitly manifested interest in acquiring land, for example in Mozambique – a Portuguese-speaking country that is conveniently located for exporting soya to China. In August 2011, there was much speculation around media reports about discussions between a Brazilian business association and the government of Mozambique concerning 6 million hectares of land in Mozambique.[84] Media reports suggesting that an actual land allocation had been promised were denied by the Mozambican government, but a Brazil–Mozambique–Japan triangular cooperation project called ProSavana does exist that is expected to involve land acquisition, and prospecting is under way. No land leases have as yet been issued for ProSavana, and it remains to be seen whether Brazilian involvement will reach anywhere near the scale discussed in public debates. But some large Brazilian agribusiness and energy companies have expressed interest in running food and biofuel plantations in Mozambique.[85] This is a process that has been building up over the past decade. A few years ago already, for example, a leading Brazilian sugar producer acquired a controlling stake in a Mozambican company that grows and refines sugar.[86]

The role of Brazil in the land rush is not limited to the acquisition of land by Brazilian companies. Brazilian firms and research institutes have provided technical support to land deals led by investors from other countries. Some European and North American farmland investments in Africa involve leveraging agricultural know-how from Brazilian expertise,[87] building on the perceived success of Brazil's development of large-scale, mechanized farming in the vast savannah area known as the *cerrado*. Brazil is not just looking to export capital to Africa – it is exporting a model of agricultural development. While Brazil hosts both small and large-scale farming sectors, it is its experience with large-scale agriculture in the *cerrado* that exerts greater international pull. The *cerrado* experience, which was supported over the years by the Japanese cooperation, is today at the heart of the South–South cooperation scheme underpinning ProSavana. There is good reason to believe that Brazil's involvement with African agriculture will tend to increase in the future.

India is an important but largely under-reported acquirer of land in Africa. The activities of Indian company Karuturi, which has leased 100,000 hectares in the Ethiopian regional state of Gambella, have received much public attention.[88] But few have realized the full scale of India's involvement in the rush to Africa's lands. Among the contracts disclosed by the Ethiopian government in 2011, eight (out of twenty-three) were with Indian companies, with the main crops including soybean, rice, cotton and palm oil. These contracts accounted for a staggering 71 per cent of the aggregate land area acquired through the deals disclosed.[89] The disclosed contracts account for only about 30 per cent of the land area acquired, according to an inventory carried out by the World Bank, which covered a longer time frame.[90] So it is possible that Indian contracts featured particularly prominently in the official release. But even so, the contracts disclosed point to the very major role of Indian companies in land acquisitions in Ethiopia. This role has been blessed by high-level meetings between the governments of the two countries.[91] India's role in land acquisitions is also borne out by evidence from other African countries. In Madagascar, a 230,000-hectare deal involved an Indian company, though this deal seems to have been discontinued.[92] A study carried out in 2011 suggested that more than eighty Indian companies had invested about $2.4 billion in buying or leasing plantations in Africa, for instance in Ethiopia, Kenya, Madagascar, Senegal and Mozambique.[93] And according to one data set of deals signed from January 2005, India is the third-largest land acquirer in Africa.[94]

Ongoing shifts in the balance of global economic power mean that emerging economies in India, Brazil and South-East Asia are playing an increasingly important role in African agriculture. Some Indian and South-East Asian companies have already become major players in the global land rush. But to identify the real leaders in the transnational deals affecting Africa's land, we need to look west.

*A new shift in the pendulum: the central role of Western companies in land acquisition* The players discussed so far are relative newcomers to Africa's land arena. China has had operations in Africa since the 1960s, including a China–Mali joint venture for sugar cane in the Office du Niger area that is now being expanded. Gulf countries invested in irrigated farming in Sudan in the 1970s, with the plan of transforming the fertile lands along the Nile into the breadbasket of the Middle East. But by and large, the interest and involvement of operators from Asia and Latin America in African land deals was limited until recent years. By contrast, many Western companies have been heavily involved in Africa's agriculture since colonial times. It was Western settlers and companies that pioneered large land acquisitions in Africa for colonial plantations over a century ago. But from the 1960s onwards, many Western companies moved away from the plantation model, and concentrated on activities upstream (agrochemicals, seeds and machinery) and downstream (processing and distribution) of agricultural production.

Today's land rush signals that a new shift is under way. Companies mainly from Europe, but also from North America, have been leading players in recent land acquisitions in Africa. They are different from the companies that led the deals in colonial times. Some of those companies went on to become major conglomerates – and in many cases they have moved away from plantations. Many of the Western companies involved in the land deals today are smaller companies that have emerged over the past few years on the back of growing expectations that African agriculture can generate good returns. Some companies have no track record with tropical agriculture, and thin capitalization in relation to their ambitious business ventures – though the crowd also includes some big energy companies with considerable financial muscle that have moved into biofuel agriculture. And then there is finance – the direct involvement in land deals of asset management firms that channel large sums invested by pension funds, endowments and rich individuals.

As usual, reliable figures about scale are difficult to come by. One study found that Europe and North America accounted respectively for 40 and 13 per cent of all land acquired in Africa between 2005 and 2011.[95] In other words, over half the total land area acquired was taken up by Western companies, with European firms accounting for much of the action. According to that study, the United Kingdom, the United States and Norway were the world's first-, second- and fourth-largest acquirers of Africa's land.[96] These figures and rankings may turn out to be at the higher end. The uncertainties surrounding data sets of this kind have already been discussed at length. But even so, the central role of Western companies in land acquisitions seems undisputable. That role is evident in some recipient countries. Take the case of Tanzania. Companies from Sweden, the Netherlands and the United Kingdom have all launched and then abandoned plans for ambitious biofuel plantations close to the coast in the centre and south of the country.[97] In the southern highlands, a Norwegian company has developed large tree plantations for wood and carbon credits,[98] and a merchant bank based in the United Kingdom runs a 2,500-hectare farm to grow improved potato varieties for sale to smallholder farmers.[99] In the east of the country, an American company reportedly requested over 300,000 hectares of land for a combination of food crops and biofuel feedstock.[100] This diversity of ventures offers a microcosm of the involvement of the West in African land deals. Biofuels, trees, carbon credits and finance have been the engines of that involvement.

For a long time, public debates about 'land grabbing' focused on the production of food crops for export. Land deals are often discussed with regard to the need to feed a planet that will host 9 billion people by 2050. So it may come as a surprise to see just how much land acquisition has actually been driven by biofuels. Data from the Land Matrix suggest that biofuels account for 66 per cent of the land acquired in Africa between 2000 and 2011, with the rest being split between agri-food, timber concessions and mining ventures.[101] Another study found that biofuels accounted for 63 per cent of the total land area acquired for plantation agriculture in Africa between 2005 and 2011.[102] The borderline between food and fuel is blurred, as the same crop may be used for both (sugar cane and palm oil, for example) or the same plantation may involve multiple crops. Weaknesses in quantitative data sets mean that these figures must be taken with a robust pinch of salt. But both figures do point to biofuels as being a critical driver in the land rush. They challenge the prevailing discourse that links land deals to the need to feed the planet. They suggest that the rush for Africa's land is mainly driven by energy demand, particularly in the West. The biofuels boom has added renewed momentum to 'colonial' crops like palm oil, and promoted crops that do not have a long history of plantations in Africa, such as jatropha. Western companies have dominated biofuels investments in Africa.[103] For example, large-scale palm oil developments – rehabilitating and expanding colonial plantations, or establishing new ones – have been led by British companies in Liberia, by French and United States firms in Cameroon, by Portuguese companies in Sierra Leone, and by Italian companies in Congo-Brazzaville.[104] Jatropha projects have been initiated by Dutch companies in Tanzania,[105] British companies in Tanzania and Mozambique,[106] Norwegian companies in Ghana,[107] and Italian companies in Senegal and Ghana.[108] Sugar cane is also a popular crop, with activities led by companies from the United Kingdom, for example in Mozambique;[109] from Switzerland, for example in Sierra Leone;[110] and from Sweden, for example in Tanzania.[111] A number of these deals have now collapsed.

Tree plantations for pulp and paper, timber or biomass energy are another protagonist in today's land rush, often in conjunction with carbon credit schemes. Globally, tree plantations are expanding fast – at a rate of 2.5 million hectares per year from 1990 to 2005.[112] This expansion is likely to continue in future. The trend is partly driven by the expansion of biomass energy capacity in some major energy-consuming countries, for example through the actual or planned construction of new energy plants fired with woodchips and wood pellets in some European countries.[113] Carbon markets reflect a profound change in the conceptualization of the relationship between people and nature. By providing a revenue stream that complements cash flows from the sale of wood, carbon credits create new economic incentives for tree plantations. Western companies have been at the forefront of both tree plantations and carbon credit schemes. Scandinavian companies are a particularly big player in this field. For example, Norway is home to companies that run large tree plantations and carbon credit schemes in Mozambique, Tanzania and South Sudan.[114] A Swedish ethical investment fund has developed thousands of hectares of tree plantations in Niassa Province, in the north of Mozambique, in a project that was launched with good intentions but has reportedly become embroiled in local conflict.[115] Energy companies have also concluded land deals and explored the feasibility of tree plantations in the global South. For example, a company based in the United States announced the acquisition of a forty-nine-year lease on 5,000 hectares of land in Ghana for a biomass energy plantation, and plans for similar plantations in Madagascar, Mozambique and Tanzania.[116]

Finance is the other main reason why the West tops the list of the land acquirers. Interest in developing-country agriculture as an investment opportunity has gained significant traction among financial operators. Some investment funds trade agricultural commodities such as wheat or corn, aiming to buy and sell at the right time to make money from fluctuations in prices. 'Farm to fork' strategies are also popular, with funds buying shares in companies across the agricultural value chain – from growers to traders, processors and distributors.[117] In this context, investments in farmland are on the rise. In early 2012, a quick search revealed sixty-six funds investing in farmland, and the sector was projected to grow fast.[118] An estimated $14 billion in private capital was committed to investment in farmland and agricultural infrastructure as of early 2012, and analysts expected this figure to double or even treble by 2015.[119] Many investment funds include farmland in their property portfolios, but a growing number of specialized farmland funds are now emerging. Western companies have played the leading role in this growing 'financialization' of agriculture. Two separate surveys found that most investment funds involved with farmland investments worldwide were based in Europe and North America.[120]

The growing role of emerging economies like China, India, Brazil and South-East Asian countries in Africa's agriculture has received much public attention. But this should not distract public opinion and policy-makers in the West from the important role that Western companies are playing in the global land rush. Much land acquisition in Africa is led by companies based in Europe and North America. Business opportunities linked to demand for energy and consumption goods in the West, and efforts profitably to invest capital held by Western companies and savers, are important drivers of the land rush. The interest of European parliamentarians in knowing more about the land rush and about the role of European companies is a promising sign that this message is reaching institutions that could regulate these matters, including in relation to the activities of investors overseas.

## *The business case for 'land grabbing'*

At the corporate conference in Kensington, the Farmland Opportunities Day was opened by a guest address discussing the potential of Africa as the future breadbasket of the world. The chief investment officer of an asset management firm involved with land deals in southern Africa articulated the business case for investing in farmland. I was expecting a dry presentation about yields and returns. Instead, the presentation focused on the big picture: the United States is in decline, China is on the rise, but the future lies in Africa. Analogies were drawn with the rise and fall of the Roman Empire. But outside this conference venue, most investors would demand a more cogent business case before allocating their capital to risky agricultural ventures in Africa. To sell their business plan to potential investors, the companies clinching the land deals would need to provide a few more specifics. So what is the business case for the deals? What motivates companies to get involved with Africa's agriculture? And why large plantations, when many companies have sourced produce from local farmers for decades? The answers to these questions may be long-winded, but the basic idea is very simple. It has to do with what motivates business worldwide. Companies are in search of good ways to generate returns. And many believe that there is good money to be made from agriculture. This belief has to do with changes in the global food and agriculture system. It is worth reminding ourselves of a few fundamentals.

First, there is the prevailing narrative about food demand. By 2050, the world will host more than 9 billion people. Demand for food will increase more than proportionally, owing to the additional effect caused by growing incomes on changing diets in emerging economies.[121] Rapid urbanization expands the share of the world's population that depends on food purchases. Growing resource scarcity and declining increases in agricultural productivity will constrain the ability of supply to keep up with demand.[122] Most analysts believe that the era of relatively low and stable agricultural commodity prices is over. It must be borne in mind that, from the early 1980s to the early 2000s, food prices were on a long-term trajectory of decline. This reflected the expansion of agricultural frontiers and agricultural trade, increasing concentration in the retail sector that created economies of scale and squeezed producers, and innovation in production. With prices so low, farming was not an attractive investment proposition – it is a notoriously risky business owing to environmental factors (weather and pests, for example), and the returns were too low. But the food price hike of 2008 shook the assumption that the world will continue to experience low food prices. Maize and wheat prices doubled between 2003 and 2008.[123] Food prices dropped after the summer of 2008, as Western economies dipped into recession. But by 2011, global prices had again reached the levels of 2008, though price volatility also increased,[124] and prices were down again in 2012.[125] The Food and Agriculture Organization of the United Nations predicts higher prices in the medium to longer term.[126] And higher prices mean better prospects of commercial returns from farming. Besides this global picture, domestic food markets are changing fast in many parts of Africa. Increasing

71

urbanization and sustained economic growth in many African countries are swelling the ranks of urban middle classes that can provide an important consumer base.[127] Although reliable statistics are scarce, evidence suggests that a significant number of today's land deals mainly target domestic markets.

But it is not just food. Nor is it just market fundamentals. In fact, the land rush is not primarily about food or market forces. Global demand for bioenergy is also on the rise, and, as discussed, two separate data sets indicate that biofuels investments account for the majority of land areas acquired in Africa. The growing demand for bioenergy partly reflects demand for energy to fuel growth in emerging economies like China and India. But it also reflects important non-market forces, namely policies in some major energy consumer countries that promote renewable energy. There has been much discussion about the role of Middle Eastern and East Asian governments in promoting agricultural investment overseas. We have already discussed the oft-quoted examples of Saudi Arabia's King Abdullah Initiative and of China's Going Global strategy. But policy support plays a role across the board, including in the 'market economies' of the West. While Europe does not have a policy that specifically encourages land acquisitions overseas, European land acquirers do respond to policy incentives.

In Europe, demand for biofuels is fuelled by legislation that requires specified shares of energy to come from renewable sources. The 2003 Biofuels Directive, now repealed, established a biofuels consumption target of 5.75 per cent of all petrol and diesel used for transport in the European Union, a target to be met by 2010.[128] In 2009, before this deadline expired, the directive was repealed and replaced by a more comprehensive Renewable Energy Directive, which is currently in force. This latter directive requires increasing the share of transport fuels from renewable sources to at least 10 per cent by 2020.[129] Effectively, these targets create guaranteed demand for biofuels. Since the mid-2000s, European firms have responded with significant investment in the farming of biofuel feedstocks, not only in Europe, but also in Africa. Climate change mitigation is often presented as the rationale for legislation pro-moting biofuels, although whether biofuels do help to mitigate climate change has proved controversial. In practice, there are other reasons why European governments are supporting biofuels. Promoting energy security, particularly reducing dependence on oil, is a pressing concern, given the fluctuating oil prices and the heavy reliance of Europe on a small number of oil producers in Russia and the Middle East.[130] European governments see a change in the way energy is sourced as more politically palatable – and perhaps more realistic, at least in the short term – than bold reductions in energy consumption. This is where biofuels come in handy. Increasing the share of biofuels in European energy consumption enables Europe to make progress towards the stated policy goals on climate change and energy security, without, however, incurring the sacrifices that would be involved in radical changes to consumption patterns. Sadly, there are few votes to be won on a 'reduce consumption' ticket.

Diverse combinations of changing market fundamentals and deliberate policy measures explain the renewed interest in African agriculture among business players in major land-acquiring coun-tries – from Europe to North America through to India, South-East Asia and the Gulf. But why the shift away from small-scale farm-ing? Why acquire land, instead of getting local farmers to grow crops? There has been much debate about whether small- or large-scale farming is more productive. Broadly speaking, small-scale farmers tend to present higher productivity per hectare, because they are more motivated than wage labourers, and because if other livelihood opportunities are limited they can cheaply deploy more labourers per hectare. But large-scale farming tends to have greater productivity per unit of labour, thanks to the higher level of mechanization. In mechanized farms, few workers can run very large plantations – so output per labourer is very high.[131] In prac-tice, crops and contexts are different; the comparative advantage of small- and large-scale farming can change over time, for instance as a result of technological innovation; and there is no one-size-fits-all model of agriculture that works best everywhere and at all times. Small-, medium- and large-scale farming coexist and work together in many places. But the global land rush signals that a shift towards large-scale farming is under way. Today, powerful forces favour land acquisitions for large plantations.

The first is about speculation. Many investors and companies are increasingly interested in acquiring farmland as a strategic economic asset. Many believe that there is money to be made, not only – or not so much – from agricultural production, but from increases in the value of the land. African governments are allocating land on the cheap – as will be discussed, land fees are often low, and in some cases they are not charged at all. Most analysts expect land values in Africa to rise owing to growing scarcity, productivity increases driven by agricultural investment, and higher returns from farming caused by rising agricultural commodity prices. In fact, historically, farmland values have tended to increase in developed countries too. In the United Kingdom and the United States, farmland prices have outperformed stock markets in the past few years.[132] Today, farmland investments in developed countries are low-risk but also low-return, because prices are already high and unlikely to increase much. In Africa, risks are higher, but potential for land values to rise is much greater. An official from an asset management firm involved with land deals in Africa was cited as saying:

> In South Africa and sub-Saharan Africa the cost of agriland, arable, good agriland that we're buying is one-seventh of the price of similar land in Argentina, Brazil and America. That alone is an arbitrage opportunity. We could be moronic and not grow anything and we think we will make money over the next decade.[133]

In addition to generating returns, acquiring land also helps investors to diversify risks away from traditional assets like equities and bonds, and to hedge against inflation. In times of great uncertainty on financial markets, these advantages are important considerations. And it is not just land. Many land deals grant the company long-term rights over water – another critical and increasingly valuable resource. Another asset manager reportedly said that the real value of the deals is not so much in the land itself, but in the water rights that are transferred together with the land leases.[134]

Statements made by asset managers must be taken with a pinch of salt. Asset managers may have a good sense of how to make returns, but they do not necessarily have money to invest. They must work hard to persuade those with capital – from institutional investors such as pension funds to wealthy individuals – to put money into the funds that the asset managers have established. In selling these investment packages, the *perception* that money can be made is as important as the actual profitability of an investment.[135] So the prevailing narratives deployed by asset managers about the appealing prospects of returns from land and water are better seen as advertisement than as dispassionate analyses. But there are good reasons to believe that increases in the value of the resources acquired are a critical consideration in the business model of many land acquirers – not only financial investors, but also agribusiness companies that are primarily interested in agricultural production rather than land per se. The low level of implementation of many land deals is partly due to the real challenges linked to establishing large farms in remote areas. But it also reflects a widespread speculative motive and strategic considerations, as many companies seize control of far larger areas of land than they are able to cultivate. A World Bank study found that some companies were acquiring larger land areas than they could farm in an attempt to 'lock in very favourable terms of land access and eliminate future competition'.[136]

Beyond speculation, other important forces are at play too. In recent years, developments in global agriculture have favoured a shift towards large-scale farming. Changing agricultural commodity prices are shifting the distribution of risks and returns in global value chains. Higher prices boost returns from farming, meaning that becoming directly involved with agricultural production now pays much better than it used to. Higher and more volatile agricultural commodity prices also increase the risks that processors and traders face in relation to the security of their supplies. Companies that trade in agricultural commodities or that manufacture goods from those commodities are increasingly faced with the risk of not being able to source the supplies they need. As a result of these shifts, many companies – including both well-established processors and new entrants in the industry – are directly taking up farming in order to both increase profits and secure supplies. These moves constitute an acceleration in trends that have been developing for several years already, whereby companies traditionally focused on downstream activities have strengthened their control over their supply chains to respond to transformations in global agriculture. For example, quality, safety and traceability requirements have become stricter, partly as a result of standards imposed on suppliers by large supermarkets in the global North. Today, a company must be able to show where its products come from and whether they comply with standards imposed by legislation or buyers.[137] Traceability and compliance are easier to ensure if the company directly controls farming activities, or sources supplies from a few large producers.

Features affecting farming operations also push towards large-scale plantations. Large agribusiness companies tend to control new, more profitable crop varieties through internal research and development, and through patenting. The norms of the World Trade Organization have extended to most countries the application of international conventions to protect intellectual property rights, and have provided effective mechanisms to sanction violations. Technological innovation has also made it easier for companies to manage large farms, for instance through remote sensing and sophisticated farm machinery. On the other hand, to operate at scale, companies that source from local farmers would need to work with large numbers of suppliers, in contexts where farmers are often dispersed, farmer organizations are weak and rural infrastructure is poor. The transaction costs and logistical challenges can be prohibitive. Relatively low yields and high transportation costs also constrain the commercial viability of sourcing from small-scale farmers. And where agricultural investments target areas with low population density and weak farming capacity, sourcing supplies from small-scale farmers may not be a viable option.

In addition, the land rush is associated with crops that lend themselves to large plantations, such as sugar cane, cereals and palm oil. This creates powerful incentives that favour large land deals. Let us look at this issue in greater detail. Scale economies in farming play out differently for different crops. Maize can be farmed on a large scale through mechanized techniques, for example, but cocoa is labour intensive and thus best grown on a smaller scale. Also, economies of scale upstream (for example, in accessing capital) or downstream (in processing, for instance) may be transmitted to agricultural production. For example, sugar cane and palm oil are highly perishable after harvest and must be processed within hours. This requires tight coordination and close geographical proximity between farming and processing, and creates an incentive for processors to take direct control of farming. By establishing a plantation close to the processing facility, the company would secure supplies that can be used within hours. And recent developments have pushed towards larger plantations. Today, a single processing facility for palm oil can absorb produce from up to 70,000 hectares of land.[138] Also, in remote areas, companies may have to build roads, power and water infrastructure; these costs can be absorbed only by large projects. Large processing facilities and ancillary infrastructure require considerable investment, and without secure supplies the factory risks operating below capacity and not being viable. Many corporate officials doubt that small-scale producers can provide the necessary volumes. Also, quality, timeliness and reliability of supplies are easier to attain if the company directly controls farming. Indeed, where a company sources from smallholders, security of supplies is jeopardized if farmers sell to competing processors that offer higher prices ('side-selling'). Many companies feel that at least a share of supplies must be guaranteed by a plantation placed under their direct control. Lenders and investors would otherwise not put money into the project.

Finally, the nature and scale of the investment now flowing into agriculture also favour large-scale farming. Investors – pension funds and rich individuals, for example – are increasingly attracted by the prospect of good returns from agriculture. Asset management firms have set up investment funds to help these investors channel their vast capital into agriculture. These investors and investment funds are more likely to put money in farmland and agribusiness than in small-scale agriculture. Investment opportunities in small-scale farming are few, small and dispersed, compared to the large sums that a fund would need to invest relatively quickly. Fewer large investments are easier to assess and manage than many small ones. Information about important aspects of small-scale agriculture is lacking – for instance, about producer organizations, credit ratings and supply chains. It is easier to buy shares in large, publicly listed agribusiness companies, for which information is available. Public listing on stock markets also makes divesture easier, because the investor can sell the shares.

So the land rush is to a large extent the story of a restructuring of the global food and agriculture system in ways that favour large- over small-scale farming. Structural factors, not just individual agency, are at play. The aggregate effect of the changes in global agriculture is a growing concentration of power in corporate hands. But for individual companies, business options are shaped – and restricted – by the distribution of risks and returns in agricultural value chains, and by concerns about security of supplies, transaction costs, bankability, traceability or compliance with standards. These evolutions increase pressures towards large-scale farming. They tend to squeeze small-scale farmers – by putting downward pressures on their profit margins, by eroding their control over farming decisions, by directing capital towards their large-scale competitors, or by displacing them altogether through the emergence of large-scale plantations. The signing of large land deals is a manifestation of these processes. As a Ghanaian scholar put it, the land rush 'is not the result of dubious and unethical land deals between governments and private corporations, but arises from intensive global market competition, which leads to the exit of smaller producers and market pressures for new scales of production related to technical innovations and logistics'.[139] Changes in Ghana's pineapple industry exemplify how global structural factors and evolving power relations can translate into rapid change in production patterns on the ground.[140]

Pineapple cultivation in Ghana spread from the mid-1980s as a result of policy changes brought about by structural adjustment. Exports to Europe boomed in the 1990s and early 2000s. Up until then, pineapples from Ghana and the Côte d'Ivoire dominated the European market, and small-scale producers accounted for much of Ghana's production – many of them based in the hilly Akuapem South District, some forty kilometres north of Accra. In 2004 and again in early 2005, I travelled to the district, met some pineapple farmers and visited a processing facility that prepared sliced fruit for export to Europe. Some farmers were growing pineapples on their own land, others were migrants leasing land from local villagers. Most farmers were cultivating up to a few hectares. The pineapple boom sent land prices skyrocketing, but also raised big hopes for better livelihoods. A farmer-owned cooperative helped growers with inputs and marketing. On the surface, the prospects looked good for local farmers. But just as my visits were taking place, a global restructuring of the industry profoundly changed the lives of Ghana's pineapple farmers.

In the 1990s, a North American company operating plantations in Costa Rica patented a new pineapple variety called MD2. The new variety was sweeter, more yellow and more rounded than the Smooth Cayenne variety cultivated in Ghana. In the mid-2000s, a marketing campaign led to a rapid switch to MD2 in European consumer preferences and supermarket orders. Exports from large plantations in Costa Rica made rapid inroads into European markets. Ghana's share of the European market shrunk, and large quantities of Ghanaian pineapples remained unsold. Producing the new variety required large capital investments in cooling and packing facilities that were beyond the reach of Ghanaian smallholders. Suckers for the new variety were also more expensive. Many small-scale producers were driven out of business, and the farmer cooperative ceased operating in 2007. Only the most dynamic small-scale producers are still active. In recent years, attempts to revive the Ghanaian pineapple industry have been led by large commercial plantations controlled by European and North American companies, which have introduced the MD2 variety. Large land deals have been signed to set up these plantations. Migrants who had leased plots for pineapple farming have now lost the land to large-scale exporters, and are becoming agricultural labourers on commercial estates.

The story of Ghana's pineapple industry shows how competitive pressures from changing global market conditions can cause rapid transitions from small- to large-scale farming. Today, there are powerful forces that favour large plantations, and the land rush is a reflection of those forces. But this does not mean that large plantations will necessarily succeed. Many ventures established with the recent wave of land acquisitions have now collapsed. Some industry commentators have raised concerns about the level of debt and exposure to illiquid positions (land being more difficult to transfer than shares, for example) that some processors have taken on as a result of business strategies involving land acquisition for farming. Nor does the existence of powerful forces favouring large-scale farming mean that small-scale producers are doomed. Small-scale farmers still account for the bulk of agricultural production in Africa.

Determination and imagination can address many of the factors that underlie the forces favouring large land deals. Many companies source their produce from thousands of family farmers worldwide – and some are scaling up these efforts. Some experienced industry players are going against the land acquisition tide. Unilever sold its oil palm plantation in Africa, and pledged to work with 500,000 smallholders worldwide.[141] Companies have secured supplies through increasing coordination in their value chain. They have developed solutions to the challenges of working with many dispersed smallholders, reducing transaction costs by sourcing from cooperatives or intermediaries. They have reduced the risk of side-selling as market prices rise by working with cooperatives, giving farmers an equity stake in the company, or linking farm-gate prices to the price of the final product – so that increases in the final price translate into higher prices for farmers. Some investment funds are investing in small-scale agriculture through innovative partnerships involving retailers in the North, inclusive companies and farmer cooperatives in the South, NGOs supporting farmers, and donors to fund NGO support. Development aid has been used to front the costs of strengthening farmer organization and capacity. The attractiveness of land and resources as an economic asset is reduced if governments properly charge companies for the resources they are given. Public provision of infrastructure such as roads, power and communications would offset pressures towards larger investments to absorb private shouldering of infrastructure costs. Development of 'soft' infrastructure such as databases and credit ratings for small- and medium-scale enterprises that work with family farmers would reduce the cost of investing in small-scale farming.

These interventions can help improve the profitability of investment in small-scale farming, thereby opening up a wider range of investment models beyond large plantations. But much depends on whether governments are prepared to take the actions needed to reverse the incentives that currently favour large-scale farming. The problem is that there is no political will to do this. In fact, many African governments have embraced the shift to large-scale farming, and are making land available to agribusiness on favourable terms. Policies in recipient countries, not just global market forces, have favoured the land rush. I now turn to discussing these issues.

# 4 | 'Land grabbing' in the shadow of the law

*How governments facilitate the land rush*

In August 2011, reports in the Brazilian media prompted lively discussions. According to the newspaper *Folha de São Paulo*, the government of Mozambique was discussing offering 6 million hectares of land to Brazilian companies for the cultivation of soya, cotton and cereals.[1] The Mozambican government subsequently denied having offered land, though a cooperation scheme involving Brazil and Mozambique does exist that is likely to involve land acquisition.[2] This was not the first time that large land offers caught the public attention. In 2009, the Ethiopian government was reported to have earmarked 1.6 million hectares of land, extendable to 2.7 million, for investors willing to develop commercial farms.[3] And in May 2011, at the end of a two-day India–Africa summit held in Addis Ababa, the then Ethiopian prime minister invited Indian companies to invest in the country and reportedly launched this challenge: 'We have three million hectares of unutilized land. This land is not used by anybody. This land should be developed.'[4]

The story of African governments offering land to foreign investors illustrates three factors that have played a critical role in facilitating the global rush to Africa's land. The first is the fascination of many government officials with large-scale, mechanized agriculture. The *Folha de São Paulo* cited the then Mozambican agriculture minister as saying: 'We want to repeat in Mozambique what [Brazilian farmers] managed to do in the *cerrado* 30 years ago.'[5] The subsequent rectification by the Mozambican government also mentioned the *cerrado* as an experience to learn from.[6] In Brazil, public research led to breakthroughs that enabled the cultivation of soils previously considered unsuitable for agriculture. This resulted in the massive expansion of large-scale, mechanized farming in Brazil's *cerrado*, a vast savannah area. The poverty reduction outcomes were below potential owing to the high levels of mechanization.[7] But today, the perception that large-scale plantations are needed to modernize African agriculture is widespread in government circles, and many officials in Africa see the *cerrado* experience as a promising model. On the other hand, governments have little faith in small-scale farmers and pastoralists, whose production systems and ways of life are seen as backward and unproductive.[8]

Delicate political considerations compound these perceptions. Export promotion is a central part of agricultural modernization strategies that translate into large land deals. But with rapid urbanization under way in many African countries, governments are well aware that politically vocal urban groups will need growing volumes of cheap food. When world food prices spiked in 2008, riots erupted in many African cities. New protests followed subsequent increases in food prices. In September 2010, hikes in the price of staple foods triggered riots in Maputo and other Mozambican towns, for example.[9] While food price hikes are rarely the real cause of these disorders, they can catalyse discontent that has deeper socio-political roots. Governments know this, and are keen to avoid new riots. In their eyes, large-scale farming holds the promise of higher food volumes at lower prices. Yet it is hard to reconcile the perceived benefits of large-scale farming with hard facts. Large-scale agriculture generally has a poor track record in Africa, with the exception of southern Africa, where there is a historical legacy of settler farming. And even where large-scale farming has been successful, its poverty reduction impacts have come under scrutiny, not least because mechanized farms tend to create few jobs.[10] Because of its labour intensity, small-farm development can not only increase agricultural productivity, but also help reduce poverty in rural areas.[11] And yet the fascination of those in power with large-scale mechanized agriculture continues to be a powerful driver of large land deals.

The second factor facilitating the land rush that is illustrated by large land offers from African governments is the widespread perception that much land in Africa is 'empty'. The statement attributed to the then Ethiopian prime minister, cited above, speaks volumes about how ingrained these perceptions are at the highest level of government. But they are also common among investors. In this 'empty land' narrative, the equation is simple: African countries have abundant land but little capital and know-how to develop it; companies from richer countries need land and can provide the necessary capital and know-how; the result is a win-win that delivers both development and commercial returns. But perceptions of land availability in Africa are misplaced. Driving through countries like Ghana, Mali or Mozambique does give the impression of immense empty spaces. In Africa, population density varies considerably. Rwanda has 307 people per square kilometre, far more than most European countries. But in Mozambique, population density is much lower – 23 people per square kilometre. In Mali, it is a mere 9 people per square kilometre.[12] Yet the picture changes substantially when only land suitable for agriculture is considered. In Mali, much of the land is barren, and the population is concentrated along the River Niger and in the lusher south of the country. Large land deals do not target the Malian desert either – they are heavily concentrated in the Office du Niger area, where irrigation potential is higher.[13] Simplistic use of statistics on population density belies the growing scarcity of higher-value lands in much of rural Africa.

And there is more. Global statistical databases and satellite imagery suggest that land is underutilized in some African countries.[14] Even setting aside forests and protected areas, there is much potential for more intensive use of the land. But global studies tend to overestimate the extent of this potential. Some data go back to the mid-1990s and do not fully factor in intervening changes such as land degradation. More importantly, satellite-based studies underestimate the land areas used by shifting cultivators and pastoralists. If a piece of land is used for grazing or left fallow, satellite imagery would not reveal much evidence of current use. Yet, in much of Africa, fallow and grazing play a crucial role in local land use systems and livelihood strategies. They can account for a large proportion of local landholdings. Also, the resolution of the satellite imagery used in these global studies is not high enough to adequately capture land use on the ground. Where higher resolution has been tried, for instance in Mali, much local land use became evident that had previously been invisible.[15]

There is a time dimension too. Many countries targeted by the land rush are experiencing sustained population growth, and population density is projected to grow dramatically over the next few decades in countries like Ghana, Mali, Mozambique and Tanzania. It is true that urbanization is also increasing, so population changes may not be concentrated in rural areas. But there is widespread evidence that demographic growth in many parts of rural Africa has already increased competition for more valuable land and resources – between herders and farmers, first occupants and 'migrants', elders and youths, and men and women, for instance.[16] The realities of growing competition and conflict for rural land in Africa are a far cry from the 'empty land' narrative that prevails in government and investor circles. Despite claims to the contrary, valuable lands are likely to be used or at least claimed by local groups. Very large land deals are bound to involve some squeeze on existing rights, even where the intensity of current resource use is low. And even where land seems available, important resource constraints may be dictated by water scarcity. There is potential for agricultural intensification in parts of Africa. But robust scepticism is needed when governments or companies make general statements about land being empty or underutilised.

An important political dimension underlies the claims that land is 'unused' and ready for allocation. The degree of political control over land deals varies across countries. For some governments, allocating long-term leases is a mechanism to consolidate their control over areas where their authority has so far been limited. This process is not unique to very large land deals. Research from

Laos showed that government programmes to resettle people from 'degraded' highlands to the lowlands and to improve tenure security in the new settlements served as mechanisms to consolidate state control. People who had until then had limited contact with state institutions now came to depend on those institutions for land access and legal recognition. By handing out certificates of temporary use rights, the government was effectively reaffirming its pre-eminent control over the land.[17] Large land deals enable similar strategies on a grand scale. Here too, reasserting control over the national territory is an important consideration. In Ethiopia, where state direction of the deals is particularly pronounced, many leases are concentrated in peripheral regions populated by ethnic minorities – such as Gambella, close to the border with South Sudan. For a long time, the integration of these regions into the national economy and the reach of the central government have been weak. Today, the Ethiopian government is taking steps to more fully integrate these peripheral regions into the national economy. The land deals are part of this strategy, together with the sedentarization of transhumant herders. Justified in the name of better service provision in rural areas, the villagization policy of concentrating rural people in fewer, larger settlements is also instrumental in consolidating central authority in marginal rural areas.[18] The 'empty land' discourse provides a powerful narrative to legitimize these political strategies.

The real issue is not that land is not used, but that the ways in which local people use the land may be treated as unproductive and backward, and that the claims of rural people to their land may not be properly recognized. Even where the land is not used to its full potential at a given point in time, this does not mean that it does not belong to anybody. The widespread conflation of perceived productive use and existence of tenure rights brings us to the third factor that facilitates the land rush, and that is illustrated by the story of governments offering land to foreign investors. This factor has to do with the law. The reason why African governments can offer land on such a huge scale is that, according to many national laws, they own it. And in many countries, the protection of local land use rights is conditioned to proof of visible productive use. This legal context is rooted in legislation passed by both colonial and independent governments. It contrasts with the customary rules applied by local people, which typically vest landownership with the clan, lineage or family. As a Ghanaian lawyer noted in 1897: 'According to native ideas, there is no land without owners. What is now a forest or unused land will, as years go on, come under cultivation by the subjects of the [customary chiefdom] or members of the village community [...].'[19]

But the land rights established by these customary systems are often not fully protected by national law, and in any case they are rarely recognized as ownership. Also, local rights are often not protected in the absence of visible land use, for example through cultivation. So land used for grazing, forest areas used for gathering wood and forest products, and land reserves that the village may have set aside for future generations, may be treated as empty and without owners. The same goes for land under fallow, and land used for cultivation on a seasonal basis. Much land that rural people claim as theirs by virtue of customary systems is vulnerable to being allocated to commercial operators. This 'empty land' rhetoric echoes the notion of 'vacant land' that was used by European colonizers to 'lawfully' appropriate Africa's resources.

In addition to control over land, multiple bodies of national and international law regulate other important aspects of the land rush – from the rules that liberalize trade and promote investment through to water law. The law contains multiple levers that can be used in different directions – to protect or undermine local rights, for example. But, overall, many norms facilitate large-scale land acquisitions and make it more unlikely that the deals will benefit local people. When faced with growing pressures from incoming investment, legal options for local landholders are few and weak – or else progressive laws are not properly implemented. In practice, people, governments and companies rarely go to court to enforce their rights. But even when not formally enforced, legal entitlements influence the way in which the costs, risks and benefits of a given investment are shared among the parties. Using a powerful metaphor developed over thirty years ago, legal claims cast a 'shadow' that can influence the nature and outcome of negotiations among different actors.[20] In the global land rush, the shadow of the law grants little protection to rural people.

### 'We are also sons of this country': how national law makes rural people vulnerable to dispossession

Much discussion about 'land grabbing' has focused on deals for plantation agriculture. But in many parts of Africa, mining is also exacerbating pressures on land. In the rural municipality of Sanso, amid the scrublands of southern Mali, a gold mine has brought much change to people's lives. Some villagers took up jobs in the mine, and the mining company contributed development funds to the neighbouring villages. By some indicators, living conditions in the municipality are better than in most other parts of the country.[21] Here, people have schools and a health centre. But the mine and ancillary infrastructure have also swallowed up valuable land, and some villagers felt that they received modest compensation.[22] The commercial cultivation of cotton, once an important source of livelihood in the area, was reported to have shrunk.[23] And the villages around the mine squabbled over the distribution of the development funds. One village claimed primacy because it hosts the seat of the municipality, another because the mine carries its name and because of its pre-eminence under customary land tenure.

It is November 2008. The hot season is still months away, but the sun is already scorching. The courtyards between the clay houses in the village are strangely quiet. Gathered in the local school, villagers are discussing an unusual topic. They are talking about the law – what it is, and what rights it gives to them. Lecturers from the faculty of law in Bamako facilitate the discussion. They drove some three hundred kilometres to run legal literacy trainings in the villages surrounding the mine. Law students are also in the group. They came to get first-hand exposure to the challenges of making the law work for the rural poor.

For villagers, awareness of rights can be a powerful tool. After an earlier training session, a participant said: 'we now know that we are also sons of this country, and that we have rights to claim'. And the law does give villagers some important rights. It entitles them, for example, to compensation for losses suffered as a result of mining operations. Getting adequate compensation can make a difference to living conditions and the sense of justice. But on most issues, the law is not on the side of these villagers. The land that farmers have cultivated for generations legally belongs to the government. Villagers say that, before the mine came, government officials made this very clear to them. And it was law reforms that brought the mine here in the first place. In 1991 and again in 1999, the government revised mining legislation to make the country more attractive to foreign companies. After the reforms, gold mining boomed, Mali became the third gold exporter in Africa, and public revenues started flowing. The mine in Sanso opened in 2001 as part of this trend. But the legal rights of villagers have not kept pace with these rapid changes. Malian jurists spoke of local communities as 'the forgotten of Mali's mining legislation'.[24]

Over the past twenty years, African governments have enacted similar reforms in different countries and economic sectors. They have vied to attract foreign investment in mining, petroleum and agriculture through reforming their legislation on investment and natural resources. Donor assistance and conditionalities have facilitated these reforms: the World Bank supported the revision of Mali's mining legislation in the 1990s, for example. Today, a combination of colonial legal heritage and neoliberal law reforms has gone a long way towards opening up Africa's resources to foreign capital. But it has failed to protect the rights of some of the world's poorest people.

Villagers in Sanso are not the only ones not to own their land. In Africa, landownership is influenced by historical legacies rooted in the colonial experience and in post-independence politics. Largely following the colonial patterns discussed in Chapter 2, most African governments claim ownership of much rural land. In fact, in some countries land is nationalized altogether. In Mozambique, for example, all land is owned by the state.[25] Other countries have enabled or even promoted private landownership. Mali is an example. But for full ownership rights to be recognized, villagers would need to navigate costly and cumbersome land registration procedures. Very few are able to do this. Few of the people who lost land to the mine in Sanso had land titles.[26] Elsewhere in the country, the little registered land is in the hands of companies and urban elites.[27] Most rural people do not own the land they claim. This situation is in line with wider trends across the African continent. With a few country exceptions, private landownership is rare even where it is legally recognized, particularly in rural areas. According to the World Bank, only between 2 and 10 per cent of the land in Africa was held under formal tenure as of the early 2000s, mostly in urban areas.[28] Because in many jurisdictions all untitled land is owned or otherwise held by the state (including in Mali[29]), governments end up controlling much rural land even where the statute books devote numerous provisions to regulating private ownership. Villagers may feel that the land they have used for generations is theirs. But, legally, it belongs to the government, and it is the government that has the power to decide on its allocation.

On land owned by the state, the villagers of Sanso, and many rural people across the continent, hold qualified use rights. Since the 1990s, some countries have taken steps to strengthen the protection of these rights, including by legally recognizing customary rights – the main mechanisms through which people access land in rural Africa. For example, progressive legislation in Mozambique and Tanzania legally recognizes customary rights, and allows local landholders to formally record these rights. Mozambique's legislation enables the registration of collective landholdings. And recognizing the difficulties experienced by many people in registering their land, Mozambican law explicitly protects local rights even if they are not formally registered. It also requires investors to consult local communities before obtaining land leases from the government. In Tanzania, 'village lands' account for the vast majority of the country's rural lands, and responsibility for their management is devolved to village authorities. And while customary land rights often enjoy weaker protection than titled property, legislation in Tanzania and Mozambique grants customary rights the same legal status accorded to other land rights.[30]

Other countries also passed progressive land laws protecting customary rights, for example Uganda, Namibia and Niger. Innovative legislation in Madagascar abolished the presumption of state ownership and introduced low-cost systems to record rural land rights.[31] In line with this wider context, successive lawmaking in Mali strengthened the legal protection of local land rights. After independence, customary rights were first recognized by a Land Code introduced in 1986, but only so long as the state 'does not need the lands on which they are exercised'.[32] In 2000, a new Land Code strengthened that legal protection, although customary rights have weaker protection than titled property. And a law passed in 2001 protects the traditional rights of pastoralists, including their rights over the 'home areas' and the right to move livestock for transhumance.[33]

On paper, this recent wave of law reforms has gone a long way towards strengthening local control over Africa's land. But in practice, it has had relatively little impact. Despite the reforms, local rights remain weak and insecure, partly because of gaps in legislation.[34] In Mali, more than ten years after the adoption of the Land Code, the decree necessary to implement the provisions protecting customary rights is the only statutory instrument that is yet to be adopted. By contrast, the decree regulating the transfer of rights over the state's private land estate was adopted soon after the Land Code was enacted.[35]

The law also undermines local rights in more explicit ways. Tenure reform has usually been cautious. With a few country exceptions such as Madagascar and Niger, governments have been reluctant to relinquish their ultimate ownership of the land. Following a pattern dating back to colonial times, in most cases customary rights are protected as use rights only, and this protection is typically conditioned to proof of visible productive use.[36] Some forms of resource use are not deemed to meet this requirement and are thus excluded from legal protection, despite their importance to local livelihoods – including fallow lands, pastoralism, foraging and, more generally, land set aside for future generations. In many rural societies in Africa, these forms of land use can account for a very large share of customary landholdings.[37] And even where local rights are protected, national law typically enables the government to expropriate land for commercial projects. This is commonly the case in extractive industries. Mali's Mining Code of 1999 requires the consent of landholders for mining operations, but then clarifies that, if consent cannot be secured, land can effectively be expropriated.[38] For people in Sanso, the legal options to contest the land takings were always limited. Expropriation of local land rights is also a common practice in agricultural investments. A World Bank study documented widespread use of compulsory acquisition in the global land rush.[39] The law makes this relatively easy: public-purpose requirements are often loosely defined, and in some cases they explicitly include private investments. In Tanzania, for example, village land can be expropriated for private investments of unspecified 'national interest'.[40] Where land is taken, compensation payments may be inadequate to restore livelihoods, and no compensation may be paid for loss of rangelands or land reserves where no visible improvements exist.

In addition, the implementation of progressive legislation protecting local rights has tended to fall below expectations. In Mozambique, many local consultations carried out by governments and investors involve one-off meetings with local elites; women tend to be excluded; and the result is a report, not a binding contract that would enable communities to hold the investor to account for the promises made.[41] In practice, an orchestrated consultation report signed by a few community members may be enough for local people to permanently lose their land. Similarly, in Tanzania local consultations for a biofuel project led to villagers manifesting their consent to transferring village land to the land estate managed by the government. But research suggests that villagers were provided with information about the benefits, not the costs, of the investment; they did not fully appreciate that their consent involved a permanent loss of the land; and as in Mozambique, these consultations do not lead to binding contracts between companies and villagers.[42]

A recurring problem in much of Africa is that implementation is not assisted by the resources and political will that would be required for these laws to have an impact. In fact, much legislation protecting local rights is framed in ways that make application very difficult. Where legislation requires establishing complex bureaucracies and procedures, its chances of success in resource-constrained countries are slim. Several years since the enactment of Tanzania's Land Act and Village Land Act in 1999, only 850 villages have obtained a certificate for their village land under the Act, out of an estimated total of 11,000–14,000; and estimates of the number of certificates of customary right of occupancy that have been issued under the Act range anywhere between 14,000 and 165,000, out of an estimated potential total of 8 million.[43]

As a result of these trends in national law, control over Africa's land is usually in the hands of governments, and villagers tend to have weak land rights. This is the case in countries that have adopted progressive legislation, where local rights remain fragile once land becomes attractive to commercial interests. But the problem is more acute in the large number of African countries that have not changed the fundamentals of their land legislation since the 1960s or 1970s (Cameroon, for example), and in countries that have legislated in ways that consolidated government control (such as Ethiopia).

Government control and weak local rights are even more pronounced in water legislation. Over the past two decades, law reforms across the world have abolished or eroded private water rights, and have brought water resources under state ownership or control. Water rights are then allocated by government authorities through administrative processes, with exemptions made for domestic use or use below specified quantities. This legal regime aims to enable flexible water use planning and to promote efficient and sustainable water use. But it means that, even where people hold legally protected rights to a piece of land, they usually do not have any rights to the water flowing through that land.

National law empowers the government – as the legal owner of land and water – to allocate resource rights to commercial operators. In Mozambique, the government can issue long-term leases, and comparable systems exist in Mali and virtually all other African countries. Economic liberalization may have entailed a shift towards recognizing private enterprise as the driver of economic development, but the state retains a central role in making natural resources available to private operators. This legal context creates real risks that local people are marginalized in decision-making and dispossessed of their land. Negotiations between governments and companies usually happen behind closed doors. Only rarely do local landholders have a say in those negotiations. In these circumstances, the gap between legality (whereby the government may formally own the land and allocate it to investors) and legitimacy (whereby local people feel the land they have used for generations is theirs) exposes local groups to the risk of dispossession and investors to that of contestation.

Governments have made extensive use of their powers over land. Most deals in Africa involve long-term land leases on state-owned land, rather than outright purchases. To attract investment, governments have been prepared to allocate land in return for low or even no fees. It is true that recent concerns about 'land grabbing' have partly reversed a trend towards the easing or removal of restrictions on the acquisition of long-term land rights by foreign nationals. In 2011, the Democratic Republic of the Congo introduced legislation whereby only Congolese citizens or companies that are majority-owned by Congolese nationals are allowed to hold land.[44] But many African governments have made efforts to facilitate land access for large plantations, whether run by foreigners or nationals, allocating large areas of land for little or no fees.

Take the case of Tanzania. Here, in contrast to many other African countries, much of the country's land is under the control of village authorities, rather than the central government. This legal regime provides stronger protection to local rights than what is available in some other African jurisdictions. But the law also establishes legal routes that can be used to erode local control and enable investors to access land. The first such route involves obtaining from the central government a 'granted right of occupancy' on 'general land' – that is, the land area that is under direct management by the central government. This route is the most commonly used for agricultural investments. But only an estimated 2 per cent of the country is classified as 'general land', so this legal route typically involves first transferring land from 'village land', which is managed by village authorities, to 'general land'. The need for this transfer and the associated bureaucratic hurdles would tend to protect local land rights. Also, a compulsory transfer would have to be justified by a public purpose and accompanied by payment of compensation. But, as discussed, the law explicitly states that investments of national interest constitute public purpose. Reforms currently under discussion aim to facilitate these compulsory acquisitions by eliminating administrative bottlenecks. Also, the definition of 'general land' is different in the two relevant national laws, despite the fact that these laws were adopted on the same day. While Tanzania's Village Land Act of 1999 draws a neat distinction between village and general land, the Land Act of 1999 defines general land as also including those parts of village land that are 'unoccupied or unused'. The law does not define what constitutes use or occupation, but these concepts are usually interpreted as requiring evidence of visible 'unexhausted improvements' – in other words, crops, buildings or fences. This interpretation undermines the rights of pastoralists and foragers, whose resource use often does not result in visible improvements. It also undermines local rights to fallow land and to land reserves set aside for future generations. On the basis of this legal inconsistency, land that villagers consider to be part of village land under one law might be deemed to be 'general land' instead, and could be allocated to commercial investors under the other law.

The second legal route developed to facilitate access to land for investors in Tanzania involves obtaining a 'derivative title' from the Tanzania Investment Centre, which is the government agency mandated with promoting investment. Given the small share of the land under direct central government control, the Centre sought to establish a 'Land Bank' to promote investor access to village lands. The Land Bank is effectively a database of land deemed to be 'available' for allocation to investors. As of 2005, over 2.5 million hectares of land were included in the Land Bank,[45] but the initiative has since lost steam. The original idea was that title on these lands would be vested with the Centre, and that the Centre would then sublease plots to investors. But this has not happened. Effectively, the Land Bank operates as a source of information, rather than of derivative titles, and it is not clear whether the database is being regularly updated. Finally, evidence suggests that some investors are acquiring land in Tanzania through subleases from parastatal agencies.[46] In practice, acquiring land can still be a long and difficult administrative process for prospective investors seeking opportunities in Africa. But the possibility of obtaining large areas of land on the back of deals with the central government and in exchange for little by way of monetary payments creates a powerful incentive that favours large land deals over alternative investment models that involve sourcing produce from local farmers.

There are important exceptions to the dominant role of government in land allocations. In Ghana, for example, part of the land is owned by the state, but most belongs to customary chiefdoms, extended families and individuals. A few years ago, two Ghanaian experts estimated that 80–90 per cent of all undeveloped land in Ghana is held by these private entities.[47] Ghana's Constitution recognizes customary law as a source of law, and the role of customary chiefs in land administration.[48] So land deals in

Ghana are commonly signed with customary chiefs rather than the central government. And even where national law places control over land squarely in the hands of the government, investors usually seek some engagement with local groups to secure support for their activities. Very often, this means talking to customary chiefs and local elders. Even where it is not formally recognized, customary law continues to shape relations between chiefs and their constituents, and through those relations the outcomes of negotiations between investors and local groups.

In principle, the involvement of customary authorities would give local landholders greater control over decisions affecting their land. In practice, this is not necessarily so. In Ghana, where customary authorities play a primary role in land allocations, legislation emphasizes the fiduciary obligation of chiefs and family heads to perform their functions for the benefit of their community or family.[49] However, customary chieftaincies enjoy considerable latitude in the exercise of their natural resource responsibilities. Evidence suggests that these requirements may have little impact on land relations within the community. Customary systems are often deeply inequitable, entrenching major differentiation along status, age and gender lines. Also, as discussed in Chapter 2, the current wave of agricultural investments is entering local arenas where rapid socio-economic change has had profound impacts on local tenure systems. The content and legitimacy of customary rules and institutions are increasingly contested. The traditional mechanisms to hold customary leaders to account have been weakened in many parts of Africa. In these contexts, negotiations between companies and chiefs can become an additional avenue for the dispossession of local landholders. There are many reports of customary chiefs giving away collective lands for personal gain, with local people losing land and getting little compensation.[50] Much like national laws that vest ownership with the government, customary systems dissociate the authority to make decisions on land allocations, which is vested with traditional authorities, from the adverse impacts of loss of land, which are felt by local landholders. In fact, because chiefs

In the shadow of the law

97

can get higher and easier-to-collect revenues from commercial operators than from small-scale farmers, they have a monetary incentive to dispossess their own constituents.[51]

As pressures on Africa's land increase, important features of the national and customary law that regulates control over land and resources facilitate exclusion. Other bodies of national law are also at play. The law governing investment is a case in point. Over the past two decades, African governments have taken steps to attract foreign investment. Measures include investment liberalization, namely the easing or lifting of government approval requirements on foreign investment; investment facilitation, for instance through simplifying administrative procedures and establishing 'one-stop' agencies to help investors to obtain the necessary permits from government departments; investment protection, as investment codes prohibit discrimination between national and foreign investors, restrict the power of the government to expropriate investments, and allow foreign investors to bring disputes to international arbitrators, rather than national courts;[52] and investment incentives, including low corporate tax rates, tax exemptions and holidays, and capital allowances. Recent years have witnessed some government moves to regulate or restrict foreign investment.[53] But the bulk of policy-making in Africa remains focused on investment promotion.

While some earlier investment codes applied only to foreign investment, the most recent generation of codes tends to apply to both nationals and foreigners. But the emphasis is typically on large-scale investment, to the exclusion of investment by small-scale rural producers. Minimum-size requirements make this explicit. For example, the Tanzania Investment Act of 1997 applies only to investments above $300,000 for foreign investors and $100,000 for domestic ones, and Mozambique's investment legislation applies to investments approved by the government, with a minimum value of $5,000 for nationals and $50,000 for foreigners.[54] These thresholds are prohibitive for the vast majority of rural dwellers. Elsewhere, investment legislation contains no minimum value but requires government approval as a precondition for access to the protection, facilitation and incentives provided. Therefore, these benefits are unlikely to apply to investments made by small-scale producers, which collectively account for the bulk of agricultural investment in Africa but, individually, tend to be for relatively small monetary values and not to involve government approval.[55] Small-scale producers are in effect excluded from the benefit of investment legislation. It is true that many are not integrated into the formal economy and as such pay little tax – so tax incentives would not be relevant to them. But there is no reason why legal measures to protect investment should not benefit small-scale producers, for example.

Investments above the minimum size or otherwise approved would benefit from the measures irrespective of whether they involve large plantations or source agricultural produce from small-scale farmers. But tax incentives for activities typically associated with the establishment of mechanized plantations, such as the common exemption of large-scale investment from the customs duties that would be payable for the importation of machinery, tend to favour large-scale, mechanized farming. Against this backdrop, safeguards for the screening of the commercial viability and the social and environmental impacts of proposed investments remain weak. Environmental legislation adopted in much of Africa since the 1990s requires environmental (and sometimes social) impact assessments to be carried out before an investment project is approved. In theory, impact assessments provide an important safeguard for local interests that may be affected by the investment, especially where they include local or public consultation requirements.[56] However, the application of this legislation has suffered from major shortcomings. Some land deals started to be implemented without the required environmental permits, while others only had inadequate impact assessment studies.[57]

Centralized government control, weak local rights and safeguards, and a bias in favour of large investments in natural resources all undermine the position of local groups faced with incoming investments. The law – as formulated or implemented

– gives local landholders very little control over their resources and over decisions that can so profoundly affect their lives. It reinforces the major power imbalances that tend to exist among local landholders, national elites, governments and transnational corporations. As a result, it makes local people vulnerable to dispossession. Both national and statutory law remove control over land from the people who use the land for farming, herding or foraging. Under both systems, the power to allocate land to commercial operators is vested with authorities other than local land users themselves – namely, the central government or customary authorities. Also, investment codes favour models of large-scale investment that exclude local groups.

One may ask why these exclusionary features are so pervasive in Africa's legal systems. At one level, the features respond to the perceived need for African countries to attract investment as a way to promote economic development, create employment and generate public revenues. But benevolent choices are only part of the story. These features are rooted in the colonial legacy and reflect Africa's continued integration into the world economy mainly as a supplier of commodities. They also suit the interests of powerful groups in national society, for whom land is an important source of wealth and power. This leveraging of land for wealth and power can take different routes, which are reflected in the different approaches that African governments have followed in their land policies. In the few countries where the ruling elites own much land and are interested in extracting value from agricultural activities, such as Botswana, governments have established effective systems to record and protect land rights.[58] But in most African countries, land is mainly used as a vehicle for extracting value in more indirect ways – namely through political and economic patronage. The central role of the state in land relations enables elites to control resources through their control over state institutions, and to maintain their grip on political and economic power by using resource allocation as a tool for patronage and enrichment. In this context, attracting foreign capital provides national elites with opportunities for business activities, political patronage and personal gain. And keeping local land rights in check facilitates the deployment of these strategies. Despite much diversity, important features of national legal systems respond to concerns other than securing the land rights of rural dwellers, and other than enabling these groups to have control over their own lives.

## *International law at two speeds: universal rights and different rules*[59]

Rome, October 2011. At the headquarters of the Food and Agricultural Organization of the United Nations, the Committee on World Food Security is holding its 37th session. The Committee is the global forum for discussing food security issues. On the agenda is the negotiation of the Voluntary Guidelines on the Responsible Governance of Tenure of Land, Fisheries and Forests in the Context of Food Security. Government delegations are busy hammering out the details of a text that many saw as an international response to the global land rush. Non-governmental organizations, farmer associations and development agencies concerned about 'land grabbing' are here in numbers. In reality, the preparation of the guidelines started well before the land rush came to international attention, and the text deals with many issues beyond large-scale land acquisitions. But perhaps inevitably, the provisions concerning land deals have attracted particular attention. The guidelines are not binding, but their negotiation resembles in many ways those to develop multilateral treaties: delegates contest competing draft texts, and check with their capitals whether proposed language is acceptable. A sign, perhaps, of the awareness among government negotiators that the issues at stake are sensitive and important. And of how intertwined control over land and concerns about state sovereignty are in government circles. The negotiation makes good progress, but the guidelines are adopted only months later, in May 2012, after another round of negotiations.

The Voluntary Guidelines provide progressive guidance on a wide range of important land tenure issues. With regard to agricultural investments, the guidelines encourage governments to protect all legitimate tenure rights, to establish safeguards against dispossession, to require local consultation and independent impact assessments before project approval, and to support investments by and with small-scale farmers.[60] The Voluntary Guidelines are not the only source of guidance for governments or investors. The past few years have witnessed major developments in international principles, guidelines and standards on responsible investment. In 2011, the United Nations Human Rights Council endorsed the Guiding Principles on Business and Human Rights.[61] The Organisation for Economic Co-operation and Development, a grouping of rich countries, revised its Guidelines on Multinational Enterprises.[62] The International Finance Corporation, the private sector arm of the World Bank, revised its Performance Standards, which regulate social and environmental safeguards in investment projects supported by the Corporation.[63] The United Nations Special Rapporteur on the Right to Food developed principles on large-scale land acquisitions.[64] Commodity-based certification schemes like the Roundtable on Sustainable Palm Oil and the Roundtable on Sustainable Biofuels have developed standards through multi-stakeholder processes.[65] The World Bank and United Nations agencies proposed Principles on Responsible Agricultural Investment that have attracted much lively debate,[66] and in October 2012 the Committee on Food Security followed up by launching a two-year process of public consultation to develop principles for responsible investment in agriculture.[67]

Today, there is plenty of international guidance for governments and investors that want to 'do the right thing'. This is certainly a positive development. But voluntary guidance can go only so far. Even if all individual investment projects were to comply with international guidance on responsible investment, the global land rush would still exacerbate pressures on resources. In this context of increased resource competition, the structural features of 'hard' law – who has what enforceable right to what resources – coupled with varying abilities to exercise rights, matter more than guidance on the desirable course of action. Entitlements that can be credibly enforced through legal processes, not general statements of principles, determine the shadow that the law cast on social relations – and on negotiations between companies, government and local groups. After all, many investors would object if protection of their assets was provided by voluntary guidelines alone, rather than by enforceable entitlements. The problem is that, as economic globalization has deepened over the past twenty years, the balance of the legal entitlements created by international law has experienced change at variable speeds.

On the one hand, a body of international law regulating trade and investment flows has developed effective arrangements to liberalize trade and facilitate foreign investment. Multilateral, regional and bilateral trade agreements have done much to liberalize cross-border trade. A booming number of investment treaties, now totally over three thousand worldwide,[68] and growing use of international arbitration have significantly strengthened the legal protection of foreign investment against adverse interference by governments – though in recent years a new generation of investment treaties and greater deference to state sovereignty in some arbitral awards have signalled that a rebalancing of the rights and obligations of investors and states may be under way. Host government concerns about attracting foreign investment and home government concerns about protecting the assets of their companies operating overseas have been the main drivers of rapid legal developments in international investment law.

On the other hand, international human rights law affirms universal rights linked to human dignity. In large agricultural investments, human rights law would protect the rights of people affected by the deals. Yet the legal arrangements established to claim and enforce human rights remain less effective than those provided by international trade and investment law. It is true that new human rights treaties have provided new avenues for people to hold their government to account, at least on paper. For instance, a 1998 protocol established the African Court on Human and Peoples' Rights.[69] International human rights bodies have clarified the normative content and practical implications of state obligations under existing treaties.[70] Greater clarity has also been achieved on the human rights responsibilities of business operators.[71] And although the number of international human rights cases dealing with land rights remains relatively small, people adversely affected by natural resource investments have increasingly resorted to international human rights courts to protect their land, exercising fundamental human rights such as the rights to food or to property.[72] But despite this flurry of legal activity, international human rights law is still far from offering people a degree of legal protection comparable to that which international law accords to foreign investment. For the vast majority of the rural population, international protection is still undermined by shortcomings in substantive rules and legal remedies. For them, challenging adverse host government action before international human rights bodies remains very difficult. Admittedly, investment law also does not offer absolute sanctuary against determined host state action that adversely affects an investment. But investment treaties, contracts and arbitration have gone a long way towards protecting investment and imposing discipline on the arbitrary exercise of state sovereignty. The resulting legal regime is more geared towards enabling secure transnational investment flows than it is towards ensuring that these flows benefit local people in recipient countries.

Take the case of legal safeguards against expropriation. Investment treaties and the extensive jurisprudence of international arbitral tribunals have consolidated the protection of foreign investment, including through wide-ranging safeguards against unfair treatment and expropriation and through direct access to international arbitration as a means to challenge adverse government action. Expropriation clauses contained in investment treaties typically require public purpose and non-discrimination for the taking to be lawful. They also tend to include specific compensation requirements and standards, so that investors would be entitled to compensation at internationally agreed standards even where national law is deficient. Although compensation standards under investment law continue to form the object of much debate, many investment treaties anchor compensation amounts to market value, often requiring 'prompt, adequate and effective' compensation. Specific standards on how to determine market value may also be included. And even where an investment treaty does not refer to compensation and valuation standards, 'most-favoured-nation' clauses would enable investors to claim more favourable compensation arrangements that may be provided by another treaty.[73]

Compared to these exacting standards, international human rights law provides weaker protection to local landholders who may have their land expropriated to pave the way for agricultural investments. The human right to property is affirmed in the Universal Declaration of Human Rights, but it is absent from the International Covenant on Civil and Political Rights and from the International Covenant on Economic, Social and Cultural Rights. These covenants are the cornerstones of global human rights treaty law. So the protection of the right to property largely depends on regional human rights systems. In Africa, the African Charter on Human and Peoples' Rights affirms the right to property but does not require states to compensate right-holders for losses suffered – it merely requires compliance with applicable law. In many African countries, the national constitution protects the right to property and requires compensation for expropriation. A breach of constitutional rules would also violate the requirement of the African Charter to comply with applicable law. But the Charter does not address gaps in compensation requirements that may exist under national law. In addition, Convention No. 169 of the International Labour Organization recognizes the rights of indigenous and tribal people to their land and natural resources, but only one African country has so far ratified this convention.[74]

Disparities in treatment between foreign investment and local rights affected by it are not limited to substantive rules. International legal remedies against alleged violations also differ in important ways. International human rights law allows right-holders to challenge before international bodies state action deemed to violate human rights. Examples include the

African Commission on Human and Peoples' Rights and the African Court on Human and Peoples' Rights. But international human rights law typically requires petitioners to first try all available remedies under national law. This may involve several degrees of appeal. Also, petitioners can usually bring disputes only to the African Commission on Human and Peoples' Rights; it is the African Commission that then decides whether to bring the matter to the African Court. Only where a state has issued a special declaration can petitioners access the Court directly; and only four African countries, including Mali and Tanzania, have issued this declaration to date. The road to the African Commission and the African Court is long and difficult.

For foreign investors, on the other hand, access to international remedies is usually more straightforward. The general rule is that disputes must be settled by national courts. But states can and increasingly do allow investors to bring disputes to international arbitrators through provisions in national investment codes, international investment treaties, or contracts with investors. There are many different systems of investment arbitration. A prominent forum is the World Bank-hosted International Center for the Settlement of Investment Disputes, which was established through a multilateral treaty in the 1960s and has gained much currency since the 1990s. Other systems include the International Court of Arbitration of the International Chamber of Commerce, and the London Court of International Arbitration. Disputes are usually settled by a panel of three arbitrators appointed by the parties – often, one arbitrator appointed by each party, and the chair appointed by the two arbitrators. Where arbitrators decide in favour of investors, they can award large amounts of public money in compensation. Use of international arbitration has grown exponentially in recent years. The vast majority of the investment treaties currently in force provide for international arbitration, although a few countries have more recently signalled that this may be changing. Many investment codes also provide for arbitration, and so do some publicly available contracts for land deals. And well-advised investors will structure their investments in ways that maximize legal protection. So they often channel the investment through a company incorporated in a third country that has a robust investment treaty with the host state – a treaty that allows investors to bring disputes to international arbitration. In contrast to human rights law, many investment treaties allow investors to access international remedies without going through domestic remedies first – though some do require this and others require trying domestic remedies for a minimum period of time.

Another important difference in remedies relates to the nature and enforceability of the outcome of international disputes. If human rights petitioners win the case, the ruling may have limited legal or practical force. The African Commission on Human and Peoples' Rights issues only non-binding decisions. The African Court on Human and Peoples' Rights issues binding judgments, but only about half the African states are parties to the Court's protocol. So the Court is inaccessible for people in many countries. And even for the judgments of the African Court, enforceability against a government's determined resistance is ultimately dependent on political action, not legal redress. On the other hand, arbitral awards are legally binding. In practice, enforcing awards against determined host government resistance can be difficult. But arrangements for enforcing awards are generally more effective than those provided by human rights law. By virtue of some widely ratified multilateral treaties, where governments are unwilling to pay up, investors can seize assets that the host state holds abroad – though immunity rules may restrict this option. In addition, governments are often under pressure to comply with awards in order to keep attracting investment.

In addition to the development of international law, the increasing globalization of the world economy has been accompanied by the growing importance of transnational legal relations – relations that involve the national law of different countries. The rise of transnational litigation as a means to hold companies to account, whereby people who feel wronged by foreign firms sue the parent company before the courts of its home state, provides new opportunities to defend the rights of those affected by large land deals. In the United States, for example, the Alien Tort Claims Act of 1789 grants jurisdiction to federal courts over 'any civil action by an alien for a tort only, committed in violation of the law of nations or a treaty of the United States'.[75] Based on this legislation, courts in the United States have been prepared to hear cases involving violations of internationally recognized human rights overseas, irrespective of whether the parties are related to the United States. In other jurisdictions, transnational litigation is based on the general law of torts rather than a special statute. In the United Kingdom, for instance, the House of Lords ruled that it had jurisdiction, under specified circumstances, to hear cases brought by people who claimed to have suffered damage as a result of actions committed by companies operating overseas and controlled by British businesses.[76] But these cases were settled out of court after the jurisdiction finding, and were not decided on the merits.

Transnational litigation may enable people affected by large land deals to bypass shortcomings in the effectiveness or independence of courts in the host country, to get higher damages awarded, and to obtain judgments that are easier to enforce against companies. But it is easy to overestimate the significance of transnational litigation. Exacting legal and practical barriers restrict the availability of this option in most cases. Two legal barriers exemplify this. One relates to the fact that, formally, the parent company and the subsidiary operating overseas are separate legal entities. Courts have been prepared to pierce the corporate veil and hold the parent responsible for the acts of its subsidiaries only in exceptional circumstances. The other relates to the so-called *forum non conveniens* doctrine, which applies in some jurisdictions. Under this doctrine, a court can refuse to hear a case if there is a more suitable forum in another country. In this type of litigation, the most obvious forum to hear the dispute is the courts of the country where the investment – and the alleged violations – took place. Only in rare circumstances have courts set aside the *forum non conveniens* doctrine – for example, for English courts, where 'substantial justice will not be done in the alternative forum'.[77] In the United States, a court recently ruled that the Alien Tort Claims Act cannot be used to sue corporations – because the Act refers only to customary international law, which confers jurisdiction only over natural, not legal, persons. However, US courts have allowed many other suits against corporations, and a case to clarify this matter is now pending before the US Supreme Court. Restrictions on legal standing – the need to prove a direct interest in the dispute in order to be able to bring the lawsuit – may also get in the way. And in addition to this array of legal barriers, the practical difficulties, including financial costs, of launching transnational litigation will prove insurmountable in most cases.

To sum up, much progress has been made in developing the human rights obligations of states, clarifying the human rights responsibilities of companies and improving the effectiveness of international remedies for human rights violations. Innovative approaches to holding parent companies responsible for the actions of their subsidiaries overseas have been developed. But important gaps remain, and so do important shortcomings in the mechanisms to enforce human rights. Much is still left to the power of 'naming and shaming' human rights violators. In the rapid developments that have reshaped international law over the past few decades, it is in the area of investment law that more progress has been made with establishing mechanisms that have legal bite. In other words, international law has evolved at different speeds, with mechanisms to facilitate international capital flows developing faster than safeguards to ensure that those flows benefit – or at least do not harm – local people.

Investors do need effective safeguards against arbitrary treatment. There may be legitimate reasons to treat different rights differently. But as global interest in developing countries' natural resources increases, competing rights – those of rural people and those of international capital – are increasingly coming into contest. So differences in legal protection matter a great deal. In some recent cases in Latin America, for example, investors and

affected people have brought disputes about the same investment respectively to international arbitrators and human rights
bodies.[78] In situations where both land acquirers and affected
people resort to international law, lopsided legal developments
favour the interests of international capital over those of the rural
poor. And while large investment projects typically involve major
capital injections that require effective legal protection, in relative
terms affected people have more to lose from weak protection
than large investors – because the loss of a small plot of land can
make them vulnerable to destitution and loss of social identity.
Their human rights and dignity are directly at stake, and they
deserve legal protection at least comparable to that accorded to
commercial activities.

The development of international guidance like the Voluntary
Guidelines adopted in Rome is an important step forward. This
guidance provides an international reference that local groups
and the organizations supporting them can wield in their legal
and political struggles for justice. Properly implementing the
guidelines would go a long way towards addressing many of
the world's land tenure challenges. The voluntary nature of the
guidelines has attracted negative attention, as some commentators
felt that a non-binding document did not go far enough. And
indeed, voluntary guidance alone cannot redress the imbalances
that exist in hard law, which were outlined in this section. But
in legal terms, the formal nature of a document – binding or
otherwise – matters less than the effectiveness of the mechanisms
to enforce the entitlements that the document creates. Human
rights law is enshrined in legally binding treaties, yet the mechanisms that would enable citizens to enforce their rights against
persistent human rights violators present limited effectiveness.
The challenge ahead is harnessing both binding norms and non-
binding guidelines to increase political pressure for change in
policy and practice. And in legal terms, the challenge is to leverage
international guidance to increase pressure for legal reform that
can shift imbalances in rights and redress.

*What is in the contracts?*

Vientiane, Laos, February 2012. The picturesque tuk-tuks driving nimbly in the traffic echo the charming architecture of the temples and the colonial buildings. Yet, in the rush hour, the tuk-tuks look strangely out of place. Until a few years ago, bicycles dominated the streets of Vientiane. Today, the busy roads are full of shiny, expensive cars – a clear sign of the rapid changes that this country has experienced in the past few years. Growing levels of natural resource investments are translating into greater prosperity for people in the capital city. But there is evidence to suggest that people in rural areas are bearing the cost of these transformations.[79] Hydropower and mining are the focus of much of the action. But investment in agriculture has also been growing fast. While international debates about 'land grabbing' have focused on Africa, the land rush is happening in South-East Asia too.[80] Laos has attracted much interest from Chinese, Vietnamese and Thai companies – and a large number of land concessions have been signed since 2004.[81] Rubber plantations are popular in the mountainous north of the country. Contract farming schemes that involve sourcing rubber from local farmers are also common. Farther south, in the lowlands, there are eucalyptus plantations and sugar cane ventures. Many contracts have already been signed as part of a government strategy called 'turning land into capital'. But more recently, authorities signalled a change of tune. They announced a halt to new rubber and eucalyptus plantations until 2015,[82] though critics pointed to earlier moratoria that had been ignored. Advised by the United Nations, the government also sought to tighten up its contracts and impact assessments to ensure that any new investments would maximize pursuit of inclusive sustainable development. It is this more careful approach to 'quality investment' that brought me to Vientiane. Together with two colleagues, I was tasked with reviewing some of the contracts that the government has signed over the past few years for investments involving plantations, contract farming or combinations of both, and with helping rethink contractual practice and contracting processes.[83]

Interrogating the contracts is a key part of assessing how the risks, costs and benefits of an agricultural investment are distributed. Together with applicable national and international law, the contracts define the terms of an investment project. While many companies make bold promises about the contributions that their business will bring to local economies and societies, the contract reflects the 'real deal' underpinning the investment. Public scrutiny of the contracts can help answer important questions, such as: Are the company's promises of new jobs backed by specific legal obligations, monitoring arrangements and sanctions for non-compliance? What amount of public revenues does the fiscal regime provide to the government, and how are these revenues distributed over time? Does the contract specify the infrastructure that the company is required to build, the time frame for delivery and key parameters concerning the quality of the facilities to be provided? How does the contract regulate social and environmental harm such as loss of livelihoods and environmental degradation? The way in which the contract deals with these issues will say much about the nature of the investment and its potential to improve, or undermine, local livelihoods. In Laos, contractual practice has improved over time. There is still significant room for further improvement, however, and the government is now developing a more robust model contract to serve as a basis for any future negotiations.

Given the role of contracts in regulating agricultural investments, an important question is what is in the contracts for large land deals in Africa. The first problem is that very few people know. Negotiations typically occur behind closed doors. Only a few contracts are in the public domain. A couple of governments, namely in Liberia and Ethiopia, have posted their contracts online.[84] In Liberia, public disclosure of natural resource contracts is a legal requirement under legislation passed by the new democratic government to draw a line under a history of mismanagement and corruption allegations.[85] A few more contracts from other countries have been made publicly available by NGOs.[86] But these publicly available contracts constitute a tiny minority compared to the large number of deals that have been concluded over the past few years. This widespread lack of transparency makes it difficult for citizens to scrutinize public action and hold decision-makers to account. It creates a breeding ground for corruption and for deals that are not in the best public interest. At the local level, landholders are rarely consulted about the terms of the deal. Consultations carried out as part of social and environmental impact assessments are mainly aimed at canvassing local views about the impacts of a proposed project. They rarely provide a real opportunity for people to raise more probing questions about the project. And where governments and companies are legally required to consult local groups on whether the deal should be awarded, as in Mozambique, implementation has tended to fall short of expectations. Many consultations are aimed more at 'selling' the project to local groups than at consulting them on whether they think the investment is a good idea, let alone discussing the terms of the deal. This situation makes it more unlikely that the contract will reflect the aspirations of local people.

Over the past couple of years, researchers and activists have started looking into the few publicly available deals. Back in 2011, I wrote a legal analysis of twelve African land deals.[87] The sample was very small, though the contracts reviewed were quite diverse. The deals included host countries from East, West, central and southern Africa; very different land area sizes – from 500 to just below 200,000 hectares; a wide range of food, fuel, tree and agro-industrial crops; and diverse land providers (central and local governments, local landholders) and acquirers (nationals/ non-nationals, private/government, different regions of origin). Because each investment is typically regulated by multiple contracts but only one contract per project could be accessed, the analysis was presented as preliminary and incomplete. Other analyses have followed suit, usually with a focus on specific deals. In 2012, for example, a Cameroonian NGO published a report on a land lease for over sixty thousand hectares of palm oil plantation in Cameroon.[88] In the same year, a journal article examined contracts for carbon deals in Liberia, Uganda and South Sudan.[89]

A recent study from Mali contains a detailed discussion of the terms of one deal for sugar cane operations.[90] A picture of the contracts that African governments are signing up to is now starting to emerge. Unfortunately, there is reason to be concerned.[91]

Some of the contracts signed in the global land rush appear to be short, unspecific documents that grant long-term rights to extensive areas of land, and in some cases priority rights over water, in exchange for little public revenue and vague promises of investment and jobs. For example, a contract from Mali is six pages long and very unspecific about the investor's obligations – despite the considerable scale of the deal (100,000 hectares). Large contracts running over just a few pages have also been signed in Madagascar and Sudan. For contracts that involve allocating large areas of land and that are therefore likely to have major economic, social and environmental impacts, lack of specificity may undermine safeguards to ensure that risks will be properly managed and that expected benefits will materialize. This is not to say that a longer contract necessarily has more advantageous terms, for instance about taxation. But important aspects of the deal – from employment creation to safeguards for local food security through to social and environmental standards – are likely to be more tightly tied down.

While most of the leases reviewed involve payment of some land rental, amounts are often very low. A World Bank study found land rental fees to be significantly below the 'land expectation values' that the Bank developed through valuation methods based on the land's ability to generate returns. In one Mozambican case, the annual land fee was $0.60 per hectare, compared to an estimated land expectation value of $9,800 per hectare.[92] Acquiring land in Africa can be very cheap. And some contracts exempt the company from paying land fees for a few years. Yet others do not require payment of any land fees. In fact, a large contract from Mali explicitly states that land is allocated for free, though this contract also provides for higher-than-average water fees. Low or absent land fees may be compensated by investor commitments to contribute capital and develop infrastructure. The aim of attracting investment is a key consideration for host governments involved in land deals – more so than public revenues per se. Some contracts explicitly require the investor to develop irrigation infrastructure and to provide specified amounts of capital. For a country like Mali, where the irrigation potential is not fully exploited and government resources to expand irrigated areas are limited, the construction of irrigation infrastructure can be a major benefit.

Even so, transferring land below market prices seems problematic. It creates few incentives for investors to explore investment models that involve collaboration with local farmers, rather than large land acquisitions, and significant opportunity costs if the investment plan is not complied with. It also tends to encourage speculative acquisitions. Through the land deal, the company acquires long-term rights to the land, and in some cases also to other resources, particularly water. While restrictions on transfers of the lease commonly apply, they can be circumvented, so the deals are effectively transferable. For instance, the investor may sell its shares in the company that holds the land lease. Contractual devices can be used to restrict these indirect transfers, but they are rarely used in the few publicly available contracts. Increases in the value of scarce resources like land and water can generate substantial returns for the company if it decides to sell the project. Many expect land prices in Africa to increase in the future. As land values increase, it is business, not local landholders, that will reap the financial benefits. So while long-term leases leave landownership with the state or local chiefs, depending on the jurisdiction, in effect they privatize the economic rent that is likely to be generated by the growing scarcity of resources like land and water.[93]

In addition, contracts by which host country benefits are mainly in the form of investment contributions, rather than monetary payments, assume clear, enforceable investor commitments in the contract, and host state capacity to monitor compliance and sanction non-compliance. The latter is often limited, and in any case implies a cost for the host state. As for the former, subjecting leases to compliance with investment plans is common practice.

But the effectiveness of these provisions is undermined if investor commitments are formulated in vague terms. For example, several contracts contain little detail about job numbers and characteristics. As a result, promises of jobs would be difficult to enforce. Finally, several contracts contain little by way of social and environmental standards. Yet large land deals can have major impacts on society and the environment – from the displacement of local landholders to water pollution. As a result, there is a risk that local people internalize costs without adequately participating in benefits, and that environmental issues are not properly factored in.

Some contracts do feature better terms. With regard to land acquisition, for instance, a deal from Mali involved a sophisticated joint-venture arrangement whereby most of the land was allocated to a company controlled by the host government; a substantial share of this land was to be cultivated by outgrowers on the basis of a poverty reduction plan developed by the company; the foreign investor brought capital and expertise to develop processing facilities; and international social and environmental standards were applied owing to the involvement of a multilateral lender. In addition, some contracts concluded by the government of Liberia stand out for their more specific investor commitments on jobs, training, local procurement and local processing, for their more sophisticated provisions on public revenues, and for their tighter social and environmental safeguards.

These more sophisticated deals address many of the concerns raised in relation to the shorter contracts. But they can raise other types of concerns. The first is that the contract may provide investors with levels of legal protection that end up restricting policy space in the host country. For example, some more sophisticated contracts feature 'stabilization clauses' that could affect the ability of the host state to change the law governing the project. A contract from Mali contains a stabilization clause that provides that no new law or measure will be applied if it causes prejudice to the project.

Companies may seek to include stabilization clauses in the contract out of a concern that arbitrary changes in law will adversely affect their investment, particularly in countries where political risk is high. But broadly formulated stabilization clauses can restrict the ability of the host state to take action in the public interest. Indeed, measures to improve social and environmental safeguards can increase project costs or delay project implementation, and may therefore fall within the scope of a stabilization clause. Where a stabilization clause applies, and depending on the formulation of the clause, the host government would have to exempt the project from complying with the new measures, restore the overall economic balance of the deal, or compensate the investor for losses suffered. Where public finances are a concern, the obligation to pay compensation may make it more difficult for host governments to take action needed to protect people or the environment. Alternatively, exempting the investment project from the new measures would mean that similar investments would be governed by different rules, and might delay the application of those measures to a major share of economic activity for the often very long duration of the contract. This is particularly problematic in lower-income countries where the national legal framework setting social and environmental standards at project inception may not be well developed. Effectively, broad stabilization clauses can dilute the ability of the government to exercise its sovereign powers in pursuit of public interest goals.[94]

There are other concerns too. A legal analysis of a contract for palm oil operations in Cameroon found that the contract purported to prevail over national law in case of conflict, and that it allowed the company to pay employees according to 'minimum wage scales fixed on the basis of productivity and efficiency criteria'.[95] The study raised the concern that these two provisions taken together could be interpreted as allowing the company to pay employees less than Cameroon's minimum wage if this is required by efficiency criteria.[96] Finally, some contracts contain provisions that grant investors priority access to water – an issue that will be discussed further below; and commitments for the host government to provide trade protection to the goods produced by the project, or even to negotiate such protection at the regional level if regional integration treaties would otherwise require it to liberalize trade in the sector.[97]

Too few contracts for agricultural investments are in the public domain for analyses to reach any definitive conclusions. It is impossible to make generalizations from the small number of deals that have become available. The few available deals suggest that there is huge diversity in contractual practice. Some contracts are much better, or much worse, than others. Without substantially larger samples, general trends cannot be discerned. But the limited evidence that is emerging does provide ground for concern. Some publicly available contracts raise concerns because they appear not to have been properly thought out. They seem very different from the contracts for extractive industry developments that the same countries may have signed – they seem shorter, less specific, less sophisticated. Other deals are more sophisticated but can still raise concerns in relation to the far-reaching commitments that the government may have entered into. Given the relative effectiveness of international investment arbitration and related enforcement mechanisms, the fact that governments sign up to such stringent commitments in contracts having very long durations is a source of concern. And the fact that the deals are often signed without transparency of process, local consultation or parliamentary approval raises concerns about the lack of democratic control over decisions that will have major, lasting implications for livelihoods and the environment.

Even in the better-negotiated contracts, a government's capacity to manage the deals after negotiation is critical. Shortcomings in the implementation of some of Liberia's better-negotiated contracts, including with regard to compensation and consultation, have been documented.[98] The problem is that a well-written contract can achieve little if the government's willingness and capacity to monitor and enforce compliance are weak. In the absence of adequate contract management systems to ensure proper implementation, all that the contract really means, in effect, is that a large piece of land is allocated to a company –

while the legal provisions aimed at ensuring benefits for the host country will remain dead letter.

## Beyond the statute books

The law is more than written words on printed paper. It is also about how those words are interpreted, appropriated and applied by the norm users. The statute books give weak rights to rural villagers in Africa. But the law also offers many opportunities to protect local rights that are not used to their full potential. Today, there are growing signs that villagers are appropriating their legal rights to fight their corner. Over the past few years, for example, there have been growing reports of court cases filed by people affected by the land rush. In Cameroon, a local NGO filed a lawsuit to stop a large palm oil plantation, citing concerns about negative impacts on local communities.[99] In Uganda, thousands of people threatened with eviction by a land deal were reported to have filed a lawsuit with local courts,[100] and so were people affected by large deals in Tanzania.[101] In Mali, three villages affected by two separate agricultural investments in the Office du Niger area filed lawsuits with the Tribunal of Markala. At the heart of some of these actions are local-to-global alliances that are changing the arenas for citizens to hold their government to account. The lawsuits filed by villagers in Mali, for example, are supported by the Coordination Nationale des Organisations Paysannes (CNOP), a national federation of farmer organizations, in collaboration with a local law firm and with the transnational peasant movement Via Campesina. But the wave of lawsuits associated with the land rush might also reflect deeper changes in local perceptions and attitudes towards the law.

As a broad generalization, it is fair to say that, for many years, villagers in rural Africa have tended to see the law and the courts as remote and largely irrelevant institutions. For many years, they have been reluctant to involve outsiders in the settlement of their land disputes, preferring instead to resort to local systems that were seen as more accessible and legitimate – although in some places use of formal courts dates back a long time. And for many years, villagers have been reluctant to openly challenge established authorities in government or customary systems. Today, land is an increasingly contested arena in many parts of Africa. Often, the institutions that were traditionally entrusted with managing disputes have themselves become embroiled in conflict, and have lost the perceived legitimacy needed for the effectiveness of dispute settlement. It seems that, in response to these challenges, villagers are increasingly resorting to formal courts to settle their disputes. In Ghana, land disputes account for a large share of court backlogs. In the country's cocoa belt, where small-scale agriculture is commercial and intensive, discussing land with villagers immediately brings out disputes pending before the courts.[102] The new threats created by the land rush could accelerate these processes – they could increase the propensity of rural people to resort to the law as a means to defend their interests, including against customary and government authorities. An unintended consequence of the land rush might be a surge in active citizenship, with affected people supported by producer organizations, NGOs or diaspora groups increasingly using legal processes that they had until recently seen as distant from their needs.

Legal recourse strategies may well produce some successes. In Cameroon, the lawsuit against the palm oil venture reportedly led to a court order suspending the project.[103] But there is good reason to be sceptical about the emancipatory potential of these legal strategies. Judicial history in Africa is full of examples where better-resourced and -connected players have out-lawyered poorer groups, and obtained favourable judgments that gave a mantle of legitimacy to illegal acts of appropriation.[104] In the global rush for Africa's land, prevailing legal frameworks make local rights vulnerable to dispossession, and provide only limited opportunities for villagers to defend their rights. Once a piece of land becomes of outside interest, legal options for local people to defend their rights, negotiate a fair deal and hold governments and companies to account are severely constrained, not only by entrenched power imbalances, but also by the weak rights that villagers have under both national and international law. And while the land rush is unfolding fast, the pace of the reforms that would be needed in order to put in place the required systems is likely to be painfully slow – because of politics as well as technical challenges.

In addition, the practical implications of the law depend on the way in which legal provisions are interpreted and applied. It is widely recognized that the formulation of new laws is an eminently political process. But the implementation of an existing law is political too. The same norm can be implemented in different ways, and implementation may prioritize some norms over others. In mediating trade-offs, the implementation of a new law is shaped by power relations in the local, national or international society. Power disparities between land-acquiring companies and affected people are an obvious example. Companies and affected people have very different capacities to exercise legal rights, owing to differences in legal awareness, in their ability to navigate the necessary administrative and judicial procedures, and in the resources, relations and confidence needed to make the most of the law.[105]

Also, relations between companies and communities must be placed within a wider set of power relations that tends to be unfavourable to local interests. The 'idle land' narrative and the prevailing discourses that equate agricultural modernization with large-scale farming undermine the rights claimed by local groups. A government pursuing a vision of large-scale agriculture informed by these narratives may support the implementation of some norms – those that enable it to transact land, for example – and constrain the implementation of other provisions – those that would protect local rights. The latter norms may have been adopted under pressure from donors or citizens, and the political leverage that favoured their adoption may now have been eroded. The long delay in enacting the decree that is necessary to implement the provisions of Mali's Land Code on the protection of customary rights illustrates how administrative action – or inaction – can empty the content of progressive legislation. So does the introduction, in 2007, of regulatory and administrative bottlenecks on the delimitation of community landholdings in Mozambique, though these measures were then reversed in 2010 following national dialogue. In addition, the disappointing implementation of local consultation requirements in Mozambique and of devolved land management responsibilities in Tanzania, discussed above, shows just how difficult it is to translate progressive legislation into real change in a context characterized by major power imbalances.

Governments are not monolithic entities. Investment promotion departments may prioritize land allocations on a very large scale in order to meet ambitious investment promotion targets imposed from the top; government agencies responsible for land administration or environmental protection may adopt more cautious attitudes towards large land deals; while a ministry responsible for agriculture or rural development may be more versed in supporting small-scale farmers. Party politics may get in the way, for instance where opposition parties control local government bodies. Institutional rivalries may also be at stake, with competing ministries using the deals as a way to assert their authority: it is not uncommon for different government departments to sign contracts without much coordination. In Mali, for instance, some deals have been signed with the Ministry of Land and Habitat, others with the Ministry of Agriculture, and yet others with parastatal agencies that manage public irrigation schemes. Different levels of resourcing and high-level political support tend to influence power relations among government departments, and these power relations can affect the application of legislation – for instance, where the implementation of investment promotion norms is fast-tracked to the detriment of environmental impact assessment requirements.

The upshot is that, as competing claims come into contest, the law is more geared towards facilitating secure transnational investment flows than it is towards ensuring that these flows benefit people in recipient countries. There is a failure of governance, and the proliferation of market-based systems such as certification schemes reflects, at least implicitly, an increasingly widespread recognition of the inadequacy of legal frameworks.

This unfavourable legal context means that, often, there is only a 'fine line between coercion and informed consent'.[106] The law does not provide adequate space for rural people to have control over their own lives. There is a need to rethink the legal frameworks that regulate agricultural investments in Africa. There is a mismatch between the scale of the challenges linked to ensuring that recipient countries have appropriate legal frameworks, and the recurring policy imperative to attract as much foreign investment as quickly as possible.

In most cases, the legal recourse strategies developed by local villagers will at best deliver qualified successes. In Mali, advisers from CNOP, the producer organization involved with the lawsuits against the deals, have no illusions about the likelihood that the lawsuits will work. They see the legal process not necessarily as the solution, but as an important part of a wider strategy of mobilization and collective action.[107] Other public interest litigators in Africa also see court action as just one additional avenue for pressure towards accountability – for example, as court proceedings may enable NGOs to obtain secretive information, or may force government officials to render declarations under oath that could then be used to hold government to account.[108] This 'rights without illusions' approach,[109] which combines legal strategies with political action, is a promising route for the empowerment of local groups.

The balance of the legal claims that frame the land rush does not bode well for the likelihood that those deals will benefit local groups. Even investment projects that fully comply with all legal requirements can still push some of the world's poorest people into destitution. Positive experiences may still occur – but making them happen would typically require a company to go beyond what is legally required. While corporate social responsibility programmes are gaining momentum, the competitive pressures and investor expectations for returns, discussed in Chapter 3, create challenges for companies that seek to go beyond minimum legal requirements and to integrate inclusiveness in their core business model. More generally, imbalances in legal claims compound the power disparities that are exacerbated by evolutions in global agriculture, discussed in Chapter 3. And as was outlined in Chapter 2, imbalances in both law and power relations are rooted in a long history of dispossession and domination. Overall, the historical, socio-political and legal contexts in which the land deals occur make it more unlikely that the deals will respond to local needs and aspirations.

It is now time to examine the evidence about the outcomes that the deals are having on the ground.

# 5 | Winners and losers

*What do the deals mean for affected villagers?*

'I am unhappy about what happened, but there was nothing I could do. I do not own the land. The paramount chief does, and he leased it to the company.' A broad-brimmed straw hat shades much of the old man's face – only the white beard is exposed to the sun. As a migrant to the area, for ten years Samuel grew cassava, maize and yam on land given to him by the local chief.[1] Then, he says, a tractor came to plough the land. The paramount chief of Yeji, the main town in the district, had signed a forty-nine-year lease with a biofuel company now owned by an Italian investor. The deal involved plans to establish a jatropha plantation over some seven thousand hectares of land. Samuel says that he had to relinquish his farm, in exchange for 220 cedis from the company as compensation for his crops.[2] He still has a small plot planted with cassava inside the leased area, and knows that sooner or later the tractor will come to claim that too. When that happens, he says, he will just stay at home – he is too old to set up a new farm elsewhere. Sitting in his new office in Yeji, the manager of the company – a young, soft-spoken, internationally connected man from this town – says that the project involved the taking of cultivated plots and common land. But he stresses that the company invested much in community consultations, that the farmers who lost land are being compensated, and that the venture has created many new jobs for people who badly needed them. Like those of many other company officials I have met while researching land deals, his words suggest a genuine belief that the new plantation will be a force for good in the local community.

Yeji is a small town on the banks of the northernmost arm of Lake Volta, and is the capital of Pru district, in Ghana's central

Brong Ahafo Region. Travelling to Yeji involves a three-hour drive from Kumasi, the capital of the Ashanti Region and the seat of the powerful Asante king. In Pru district, the transition zone between the forest zone in the south of Ghana and the savannah zone in the north is ideal for a wide range of crops. Agriculture in the area is becoming more intensive. Fertilizer companies have set up shop in neighbouring Atebubu district, eyeing the many local farmers that grow maize and other food crops. The flat landscape facilitates the use of agricultural machinery. Along the road from Ejura, in the Ashanti Region, many tractors operated by small-scale farmers are working in the fields, refuelling at service stations or pulling trailers up and down the road – perhaps a legacy of the mechanized state farms that sprang up in the area back in the 1970s. Some farmers own the tractors, including through coopera-tives, others rent them from specialized firms. It is no surprise that this stretch of valuable land did not go unnoticed in the global rush for Africa's land. Italian and Canadian companies operate jatropha projects in Pru, while a South African company has set up a tree plantation for pulp and biomass in Atebubu. These projects are part of a recent wave of agribusiness developments that has spread across a large area spanning from central to northern Ghana. South of Yeji, in the central Ashanti Region, a Norwegian company signed a memorandum of understanding with the chiefs in Agogo for a 300,000-hectare jatropha plantation, though the actual lease subsequently issued was for a much smaller area – about thirteen thousand hectares.[3] And farther north, in Ghana's Northern Region, another Norwegian company holds some ten thousand hectares of land that it acquired to set up a jatropha plantation in Yendi district, a short drive from the capital of the Northern Region, Tamale. In all these cases, the advent of the new agricultural ventures involved deals with the chiefs, who allocated land to the company in exchange for promises of jobs.

There is still much that we do not know about what the rush for Africa's land will mean for affected villagers. Many land deals are recent and are only just getting established. Many involve investment targets spread over long time frames; implementing large investments inevitably requires time – to source the financing, build processing facilities, and scale up cultivation. In Mali, a large sugar cane project, now abandoned, involved the signing of a Convention of Establishment in 2007, but full implementation was going to be achieved only in 2017. And the full impacts of an investment may become apparent only a long time after full-scale implementation begins: in Ghana, the taking of land from farmers growing maize, yam or cassava to make space for commercial bioenergy projects raised immediate NGO concerns about what the shift will mean for the food security of affected villagers;[4] only time will tell whether, in the longer term, the jobs created by the project will enable villagers to buy adequate food. Finally, the time distribution of costs and benefits in large-scale investments is often uneven, so looking at short-term outcomes alone may result in a skewed picture: negative impacts – loss of land, for instance – are often felt first, while jobs, opportunities for local businesses and government revenues may only fully materialize at a later stage. For many recent agricultural investments in Africa, it is just too early to tell. And while much research has been carried out on land acquisitions, studies are of varying quality, and data remain patchy.

Yet a growing body of evidence is improving public understanding of what the land rush means for affected villagers. We now know more about the socio-economic implications of the deals at the local level than we did four years ago.[5] The trade-off between land and jobs that is at the heart of Ghana's new agribusiness ventures is a recurring theme of the land rush across the continent. The problem is that, in many parts of Africa, many people have lost the land on which they depended to access food and make a living, that the promised benefits have not always materialized, and that the people suffering adverse impacts and those reaping the benefits do not necessarily coincide.

*Negative outcomes* Reliable figures about how many people in Africa have lost land to the deals are impossible to find. There have been numerous reports of people being dispossessed in many parts of the continent – for example, in Ethiopia,[6] Ghana,[7] Liberia,[8] Mali,[9] Mozambique,[10] Uganda[11] and Tanzania.[12] Some of these reports provide figures of how many people lost land to individual deals. In Liberia, for example, the World Bank found that a rice project involved the relocation of 1,000 farmers (an estimated 30 per cent of the local population), and that an additional 1,500 farmers were at risk of being displaced by the continuing expansion of the plantation.[13] In Uganda, Oxfam reported that 20,000 people claimed to have been evicted from public land to make space for a commercial plantation.[14] As of April 2012, the Land Matrix reported figures on land dispossession for forty deals; of these, twenty-five involved the reported dispossession of more than a thousand people each.[15]

Figures on loss of land rights are often hotly contested – bold claims may prove exaggerated, while attempts by companies to play down the extent of dispossession may fail to recognize local land claims, or neglect far-reaching indirect impacts. On the whole, however, there are reasons to believe that publicly available information about land dispossession in Africa underestimates the aggregate scale of the impact.[16] This is all the more striking given that public perceptions are likely to have overestimated the scale of land areas acquired through transnational deals.[17] There are several reasons for this. First, it is very likely that some loss of land rights may not have been documented. The circumstances that trigger involvement of journalists, researchers and advocacy groups in specific land deals are still poorly understood, but information and opportunity are bound to play a role.[18] And while the impacts of some deals have been widely reported, other deals have received much less public scrutiny. Second, national law may not recognize that the land belongs to the villagers in the first place. As a result, many people may lose land without being formally dispossessed. The question of whether a family or community holds land rights that would need to be expropriated and compensated for is often conflated with the different question of whether the land is under current use. As discussed in Chapter 4, the law often conditions legal protection upon evidence of productive use, and some important forms of resource use are not deemed to be productive. So land that villagers are not visibly using at the time of the acquisition, perhaps because they use it for grazing or wood gathering, or because they have set it aside for future generations, or else because they have no standing crops owing to seasonal land use patterns, may be treated as 'empty', even though villagers may claim rights over it and the growing village population may increasingly need that land to sustain itself. Also, while attention has focused on physical displace-ment, people may lose land even if they are not displaced – for instance, where plantations take land used for cultivation, grazing or wood gathering, but villagers keep their home and part of their land. In fact, I have come across agribusiness ventures in Mali and Mozambique that avoided physically displacing villagers by allowing them to remain in the leased area – like islands in a sea of monoculture. In yet other cases, pastoralists did not lose their grazing grounds, but agribusiness developments blocked livestock corridors that were of critical importance for herds to access water and dry-season grazing. In all these cases, villagers may not be formally expropriated or physically displaced. But there is no doubt that their land access is squeezed, and the adverse impacts on local livelihoods can be substantial. In addition, the number of people who lose land to the deals will grow over the years if and when the contracts that have already been signed are fully implemented.

The intensity of the dispossession, not just its scale, shapes local outcomes. In some cases, loss of land has been accom-panied by significant disruption and trauma for local groups. In Mali, a large irrigation project reportedly resulted in the following outcomes:

The construction of the 40-km-long irrigation canal and adjacent road resulted in massive disruption in the region of Kolongo. Houses were razed, market gardens and orchards bulldozed, animal trails obstructed and the broad canal now divides single villages. A cemetery was unceremoniously unearthed in the village Goulan-Coura. Local people there were shocked to find human remains scattered about the construction site before the contractors then plowed them into the ground.[19]

In the more extreme cases, the land rush involves violence and human rights violations. Many deals are happening in contexts where governance is weak, or government is authoritarian – or security forces may not have been properly trained. In some instances, authorities have resorted to force in order to quell local resistance. In Mali, a project led by a private, nationally owned company was confronted with protests from villagers, who complained about the cutting of trees. It has been reported that the police suppressed these protests through beatings and arrests, with government sources arguing that local resistance was being fomented by groups based in Bamako.[20] A video documentary about another deal in the same part of Mali also featured testimonies of villagers claiming to have been beaten by security forces.[21] In Ethiopia, the NGO Human Rights Watch published two reports on evictions in different parts of the country. These evictions were linked to villagization programmes that, with the official justification of providing better services in rural areas, are sedentarizing pastoralists and clustering farmers in bigger villages. They were also linked to large dam developments aimed at generating power and making water available for irrigation. The Human Rights Watch reports argued that these policies were connected to large land deals, and found that the implementation of the policies involved arbitrary arrests and detentions, beatings and mistreatment, and governing through fear and intimidation.[22] While there is little evidence that Ethiopia's villagization programme is deliberately aimed at releasing land for large-scale agricultural investments, the two strategies appear to be indirectly linked, insofar as they both seem aimed, directly or indirectly, at strengthening central control over marginal regions.

Even outside the cases where violence is involved, the terms of land takings have proved a major source of conflict. Trends in national legal frameworks, discussed in Chapter 4, create a breeding ground for contestation, because ownership of the land is often vested with, or administered by, government agencies or customary authorities, and local land rights tend to be weak or qualified. Mechanisms that do exist under national or customary law to promote the downward accountability of decision-makers may not work as hoped. In Ghana, for example, evidence suggests that some chiefs sign the leases in exchange for payments, and simply tell the farmers – particularly migrant farmers with more tenuous land rights – not to return to their land after harvest; as a result, many farmers do not receive any compensation.[23] In Mali, where it is the government that signs the leases, the taking of houses and gardens for a large land deal led by a Libyan company reportedly involved no compensation at first. After protracted negotiations, a compensation package was promised, but as of late 2011 only 6 per cent of the compensation payments had been effected.[24] In Tanzania, a biofuel project paid compensation amounts that were seen as inadequate by some, and 60 per cent of those amounts were captured by local government bodies, rather than the dispossessed landholders.[25] Reports suggested that the project also affected more people than those who received compensation.[26] Similar disputes over compensation entitlements, amounts and distribution are a recurring feature of the land rush.

A common problem is that compensation to farmers is often paid for crops, not for the land. As discussed, depending on the jurisdiction the land may be legally owned by the government or customary authorities, often as trustees for their constituents, and villagers are expected to find alternative land elsewhere. But where land is increasingly scarce, customary authorities allocating land may charge a fee that the dispossessed may not be able to pay. The new plot may be less fertile, or located farther away than the one expropriated. Also, important losses may remain uncompensated – for instance, the loss of grazing land or forest resources where no visible improvements can be shown, or the loss of farmland with no standing crops at the time of the taking (if the project takes land during the dry season, for example).

In addition, governments often require the company to cover compensation payments, and some companies rely on lending to finance a large share of the investment, including compensation payments. If the company fails to secure the financing, expropriated landholders risk not receiving the compensation that they are entitled to. This arrangement exposes affected people to substantial business risks,[27] though lack of systematic data makes it impossible to establish how widespread this particular problem is.

Where the project does provide good compensation, one-off cash payments may allow a person, family or village to get by for a while, and, in the better cases, to invent a new livelihood. But, in the longer term, the ability of expropriated people or their descendants to make a living in the absence of alternative livelihood options will be significantly jeopardized. And in addition to its economic use, land also has an emotional, non-monetary value that cannot be reflected in compensation. Under all these circumstances, there are real questions as to whether a one-off cash payment for the loss of visible improvements can indeed 'fully' compensate people for the loss suffered, as is required by some national laws,[28] let alone restore people's livelihoods to pre-project levels, as is required by the standards developed by some international lenders.

The widely documented shortcomings in social and environmental impact assessment exercises mean that many adverse impacts on local livelihoods are not properly anticipated and mitigated at project design stage. In fact, impact assessments are often not carried out before project approval. In Tanzania, for example, an inventory exercise found that only about half the required impact assessments had been carried out. And where impact assessments are done, their quality is often weak, and documentation is rarely publicly available.[29]

*Positive outcomes* Thus, there is mounting evidence that the deals are having important negative effects on local livelihoods. The deals may also have some positive local outcomes, however. Local distribution of revenue flows is one example. A company may be required to pay periodic land rental fees, and some countries have developed arrangements to channel part of these payments back to the affected communities. In Ghana, rentals are collected by a government agency and distributed to local governments and traditional authorities, which are meant to use the money to promote development in the area. Although the rates are often very low,[30] aggregate amounts can still be non-negligible relative to the local economy. Some companies have also devoted resources to provide social infrastructure for affected villagers. An analysis of Land Matrix data found that, of a sample of 117 projects worldwide, 90 involved the provision of social infrastructure.[31] Social infrastructure may be provided in cash or in kind. According to company sources, the firm operating the 7,000-hectare plantation in Ghana's Pru district has set up a $20,000 community development fund that is managed by traditional authorities and replenished by the company with further annual payments of up to $10,000. And in Ghana's Yendi district, the company that leased 10,000 hectares of land for jatropha cultivation provided small dams for drinking water and a grinding mill. Roads and village markets are also common options for social infrastructure programmes. For companies, these corporate social responsibility initiatives are a way of shoring up local support for their business. And for rural people living in remote areas, a new clinic can save lives, and a new school offers the promise of better livelihood prospects. A new water point can save women having to walk long distances to fetch water. Women in Kpachaa, a village in Yendi district, had to walk 6 kilometres to the closest source of drinking water before the jatropha venture came, and they value the new facilities created by the company.

'Those who lost their land were unhappy about the project, but we were very happy to get the jobs.' Salifu, a young man who used to work as a farm labourer on the jatropha plantation in Ghana's Yendi district, smiles as he articulates this point.[32] The young villagers grouped around him nod in agreement. In international debates about the land rush, positions have tended to be polarized between those who argue that the deals will provide new livelihood opportunities, and those who fear that land acquisitions are a source of exclusion. But on the ground, the land rush is not the story of undifferentiated communities that together stand to lose – or to gain – from the deals. Because groups tend to be internally diverse, local impacts are often differentiated. The land deals can create both winners and losers.

Generally, those who stand to gain the most from the deals across the continent are national and local elites – business people who may have an equity stake in the project; government officials who may obtain personal benefits from the deals; politicians who can use the project to deliver on electoral promises of schools or clinics, and reward their supporters with jobs; and chiefs who receive substantial payments for personal gain. Local elites may have much to gain from the deals. For Ghana's customary chiefs, for example, land deals offer an opportunity to receive higher revenues than they would be able to extract from small-scale farmers. This can be a source of personal enrichment or, if the chiefs use monies for development projects, a way of consolidating the chiefly power base through patron–client networks. In contrast to numerous small-scale tenancies, fewer, larger and more formalized transactions make it easier for the chiefs to collect revenues. Allocating large areas of land to companies can also provide a means for the chiefs to assert their ownership of the land: being able to lease out the land without contestation, and perhaps even with the official sanctioning of the transaction from government agencies, implies a recognition that the chief has ultimate authority over the land in question. This is an important benefit, especially where customary landholdings, and the boundaries between them, are unclear or contested. In effect, allocating land to a company means staking a claim to radical title over that land.[33] The participation in project benefits by these local and national elites is an important enabler of the deals.

Some of the benefits trickle down to a wider group, for instance as women and youths gain jobs as casual labourers. But as Salifu articulated very well, the people who participate in the benefits may not be those who suffered adverse impacts. There are several reasons for this. Some villages may lose little or no land yet get many jobs. In Yendi, for example, the village of Kpalkore lost very little land to the jatropha plantation, but its youths took up many jobs. In contrast, villagers in Kpachaa lost more land to the project. In other cases, jobs may be taken up by people migrating from other parts of the country, or even from neighbouring countries, as migrants from poorer areas may be prepared to work for less.[34] Jobs may be taken up by youths, while it is often elders who control land – and therefore lose it to the project. Also, the more marginal farmers who lose land may become labourers on the new plantation. But many growers who have successfully run their own farms for a long time may not be interested in embracing the loss of independence and the radical lifestyle change that are associated with wage employment. They will lose the land, but not seek the jobs – though they might be interested in joining an outgrower scheme if the project involves one.

These distributive effects of the deals can benefit poorer and more marginalized groups. In Yendi, labourers working for the plantation included young men who had too little land to make a living as independent farmers, and women who preferred earning a salary from the plantation to working for free on their husband's land. The poorest of the poor, who have little land or resources to do their own farming, may get jobs that can make a real difference to their lives. Despite perceptions of an African agriculture dominated by a largely egalitarian smallholder farmer sector, as discussed in Chapter 2 many rural people have no farmland, or too little land to make a living from it, or else they may have land but no resources to cultivate it. These people work as farm labourers or caretakers on other people's farms, and may gain from employment opportunities that the land deals may bring. Research about Senegal's fruit and vegetables industry found that a shift in agricultural production from local growers farming under contract with agribusiness to large plantations run directly by agribusiness companies redistributed the costs and benefits of integration into global value chains in favour of poorer groups, who took up the jobs and did not have sufficient land or resources to be able to succeed as contract farmers.[35]

Wages may seem low by international standards, but they can appeal to local labourers. According to former labourers, the jatropha plantation in Yendi paid its farm workers 77 cedis per month (about $40 at today's exchange rate – but the cedi has lost value in recent times). This amount was higher than comparable average pay in the area. Villagers saw this as good money, and many say they would be happy to work again for the company. More skilled positions commanded higher pay. A tractor driver earned 150 cedis (about $75) per month, a substantial amount relative to the local economy. Other projects in Africa are reported to pay substantially lower wages – for instance, $15 a month in a project in Ethiopia, which if involving continued work would be well below the international poverty line.[36] Lack of reliable, systematic data makes it difficult to generalize. But, the practical implications of wage income on the well-being of the household would depend on the wider terms and conditions associated with employment, on how income and labour conditions compare to the multiple livelihood benefits that are often associated with multi-purpose land use on small-scale farms, and on how the new income is used.

Gender is an important but under-researched aspect of the land rush, and the gender outcomes of the deals are still poorly understood. In much of rural Africa, gender relations are a major source of social differentiation. Men and women typically access land in different ways. For women, access to land is often mediated through their male relatives or husbands. For example, a woman may cultivate a plot given to her by her husband, or may help her husband to farm his plot. This situation means that women tend to have more fragile land rights than men. If the husband dies or the couple divorces, for example, the wife could lose the land. Despite much diversity in local contexts, women also tend to have a weaker voice in decision-making concerning land. With some important exceptions, women tend to be excluded from customary authorities, and they are often excluded from local consultations about proposed land deals. This context makes women particularly vulnerable as outside interest in Africa's land increases, and there is some evidence to suggest that the deals have had particularly negative consequences for women.[37] For example, where land deals take land used for foraging, they affect women more than men – because women are often responsible for collecting wood, fruits, nuts and medicinal plants, whether for consumption or sale.

But sweeping statements about the vulnerability of women in the land rush should be avoided – not least because women are a very diverse group. Women with different wealth, income, age and status fare very differently in customary systems. Also, women may value opportunities for wage employment on plantations. In Kpachaa, a woman said that, when she took up employment as a farm labourer on the jatropha plantation, her husband was at first unsupportive – because she now had less time to help him on his plot. But she was happy to earn cash income that she had direct control over, and that gave her greater autonomy and negotiating power within the family. Women from other villages in Yendi also expressed appreciation for the jobs created by the company, even though most of them had been employed as unskilled farm labourers at the bottom of the wage scale. As discussed, women in Yendi valued the water points provided by the company, which significantly cut the distance they had to walk to fetch water.[38]

The benefits that local economies may receive from well-designed agricultural ventures led by operators with the necessary capital and track record are illustrated by a study of the long-term socio-economic outcomes of two agricultural investments in Zambia.[39] These ventures were initiated in the 1970s and 1980s. They were launched as parastatal companies involving joint ventures between the government and development agencies, and were privatized from the 1990s. In contrast to today's land deals, they were initiated with an explicit development objective, though commercial motives became prevalent following privatization. A sugar cane venture in Mazabuka district involves a nucleus estate

137

and 160 outgrowers on subleased land, for a total of about four thousand hectares. The experience is seen by many as a positive one. The outgrowers own about 13 per cent of the company, while another 25 per cent is owned by a district-level association of cane growers. Living standards among outgrowers are high relative to the Zambian context. Many outgrowers have modern housing, cars and consumer goods. Labourers on the estate also fare relatively well, in terms of salaries and benefits. Labourers working on the outgrowers' fields enjoy worse employment conditions and social protection, though they still fare well enough for the scheme to be fair trade certified. In Zambia's Mpongwe district, another long-standing venture involving large-scale mechanized farming of maize, barley, soybeans and more recently jatropha appears to have generated fewer business links with the local economy and no shared ownership with low-income groups. But substantial numbers of jobs have been created, though many are for manual seasonal workers. Training provided to the farmers seems to have had positive spillovers on the productivity of those farmers on their own fields. The venture accounts for a major share of the food consumed in the area and has probably been instrumental in keeping national food prices at accessible levels. That said, decades after their inception both projects are yet to fully cultivate the lands they were given, creating opportunity costs in places where land is becoming scarcer. In Mpongwe, court litigation has been instigated between the company and farmers who had encroached upon unused company land.

*How do the costs and benefits weigh up?* The discussion of the evidence thus far has highlighted both negative and positive outcomes, although the distribution of the benefits does not necessarily favour those most adversely affected. How do these positives and negatives compare? In any given locality, the net aggregate impact of an investment on livelihoods depends on the scale, quality and sustainability over time of the new livelihood opportunities created by the project, relative to the livelihood losses inflicted by it. Overall, evidence from different parts of

Africa suggests that the negatives tend to outweigh the positives. Take the case of employment creation. This benefit is often mentioned by proponents of large land deals. But there are several problems. The first is that the jobs created by the new agribusiness ventures tend to be far fewer than what would be required to offset livelihood losses from land dispossession. The pro-poor outcomes of the transition to large plantations in Senegal's fruit and vegetable industry, discussed above, owe much to the labour intensity of the crops involved in that experience: the plantations created many jobs. The findings of that research challenge some of the sweeping generalizations that are often made about the primacy of small-scale farming in terms of poverty reduction potential. But those findings would be of little relevance to the many recent land deals that aim to establish mechanized farms.

Some farming activities require use of many labourers. For example, jatropha cultivation can be labour intensive, because hand picking is a viable harvesting system, and because the harvesting season lasts for several months. So jatropha plantations like those in Yeji and Yendi can create many jobs. But for many crops and activities, businesses stand to gain from high levels of mechanization. So after the initial planting stage, the number of jobs is very small. Companies will need the villagers' land, but not their labour.[40] A comprehensive global study carried out by the World Bank found the jobs created by land deals to be generally few: 0.01 jobs per hectare for grains, 0.02 for tree plantations, 0.018 for soybean. Other crops had higher labour intensity: 0.42 jobs per hectare for jatropha and for rubber, for instance. In yet others, labour intensity varied depending on farming techniques: employment creation for sugar cane ranged between 0.15 and 0.7 jobs per hectare depending on whether harvesting was manual or mechanized. According to the same data set, investment per job created was very high, in line with the picture of highly mechanized farming that creates few jobs: $45,000 per job for grains, $200,000 for soybean, and a staggering $360,000 for tree plantations.[41] While data on employment creation remains limited, the World Bank concluded that the deals 'create far fewer jobs than are often expected'.[42] In fact, employment creation may be even lower than what is suggested by these World Bank figures. The figures are based on the business plans, rather than actual observation, and business plans attached to investment proposals may give an optimistic picture of employment and capital investment prospects. For example, the same World Bank report discusses the case of a project in Mozambique that was planning to create 2,540 jobs – but that at the time of the study had hired only thirty-five to forty full-time workers and some thirty seasonal workers.[43] The benefits of employment generation in the land deals appear to have been greatly overstated. In most African farming systems, small-scale farming can sustain many more people on the land than the few jobs created by large mechanized farms – although the spread of tractors among small-scale farmers in places like Ejura and Atebubu in Ghana suggests that, over time, the ratio between capital and labour may change in smaller farms too.

It is true that historical patterns of agricultural development have often been characterized by a declining share of the labour force being employed in agriculture. Space constraints prevent a proper discussion of historical trends in agricultural employment. But it is fair to say that, in Europe, a smaller proportion of the population work in agriculture today than was the case 300 years ago. Some argue that the fact that similar processes may be happening in Africa is only a natural part of economic development. But caution is needed with such simplistic comparisons, not least because the context of historical transitions in Europe presents important differences from that of today's land deals in Africa. As a broad generalization that cannot do justice to centuries of diverse historical trajectories, in Europe the Industrial Revolution provided employment opportunities to many of those who left rural areas. In England, the enclosures of common lands preceded the Industrial Revolution, and some historians argue that the availability of cheap labour played a role in facilitating industrial development; but in Scotland, for example, where the enclosures ('clearances') took place later, the

Industrial Revolution absorbed labour released from the country-side. Also, the expansion of the agricultural frontier in North America, Argentina, Russia and Oceania brought much new land under cultivation and provided new livelihood opportunities for European migrants. And the decrease in the proportion of the population employed in agriculture did not necessarily involve a transition to large-scale farming: small-scale agriculture remains vibrant in many parts of Europe. In Africa, industrial development is often embryonic at best, and emigration is constrained by tough restrictions in major destination countries. In the short term at least, those who lose the land they depend on have few alternative livelihood opportunities. The deals may compound existing processes of rural-to-urban migration, whereby large numbers of people flock to urban areas and swell a 'service' industry that ranges from petty trading to little or no stable occupation at all. With alternative livelihood options so limited, there is a risk that the more marginalized groups among those who lose land will see their livelihoods greatly undermined.

And it is not just about job numbers. The security of the new source of livelihood is also an important consideration. Even those who do get jobs effectively swap a permanent asset – land – for an often insecure economic activity. First, fewer labourers may be needed after the construction or planting stages. Secondly, many large land deals have now collapsed owing to financing difficulties or greater-than-expected challenges on the ground, and the new jobs have vanished together with the company. The deals may bring jobs, but also greater exposure to the fluctuations of international economic cycles, making local livelihoods more vulnerable. Growing numbers of villagers in Africa are experiencing the stark contrast between the bold promises and the wrecked livelihoods that large land deals can bring. In Tanzania, for example, the collapse of a jatropha plantation set up by a British company reportedly left villagers 'landless, jobless, and in despair for the future'.[44] Another jatropha venture in Tanzania, led by a Dutch company, reportedly had a similar fate.[45] In Mali, a South African company pulled out of a sugar cane joint venture that it had established with the Malian government, citing frustration for delays on the government side and concerns about the deteriorating security situation in the country. In Mozambique, a 30,000-hectare sugar cane plantation in Gaza Province has so far come to nothing, while a jatropha venture in Manica Province collapsed just as it started selling biodiesel to a major international airline. Projects that do not collapse may still face implementation challenges. Many known agricultural investments in Africa are behind schedule. Even in very large deals, it is not uncommon for only a few hundred hectares to have been planted. Success stories are still hard to come by.

Systematic data on failure and implementation rates are not yet available. But evidence suggests that these examples reflect a more general trend. A World Bank report that remains, in many ways, the most comprehensive study on the matter found that 'progress with implementation is surprisingly limited'. It also found that:

> In Mozambique, Tanzania, and Zambia, it was difficult to identify any projects operating on the ground. Among the projects that had started, the areas in operation were typically much smaller than those allocated. This lag in implementation was normally attributed to unanticipated technical difficulties, reduced profitability, changed market conditions, or tensions with local communities. [...] Investors may have underestimated the complexity of agricultural operations, particularly the challenges associated with clearing land, establishing internal infrastructure, and linking to markets. [...] [N]one of the biofuel operations in Mozambique were operating at the envisaged scale and all of them reported delays of at least three to five years.[46]

Where projects fail, people lose land without gaining durable benefits. The land is often not returned to local groups. Instead, the government seeks new investors to continue the project. The real 'idle land' in the 'land grabbing' arena is not the land claimed by local groups that is compulsorily acquired to make space for the deals; it is the land that investors take and fail to develop.

And while the Zambian experiences mentioned above provide insights on what the long-term outcomes of successful, inclusive investments might look like, a legitimate question is how many investments must fail and disrupt local livelihoods for every successful venture that can have positive long-term impacts.

Ghana is also going through the boom and bust of the land rush. In Yendi, the enthusiasm of villagers for the new jobs was short lived. The jatropha venture is no longer in operation, as the business was hit by financial constraints, although the company has now reinvented itself with a new focus on food crops and still hopes to continue the venture. The collapse of the jatropha project adversely affected the livelihoods of local villagers. Having taken the land, the company now had to dismiss the labourers. At peak, the plantation employed some four hundred people, mostly as seasonal workers.[47] By the time I visited the site in late 2012, only a handful of people still worked for the company, as managers and security guards. Failed projects can undermine local livelihoods. Not only because the jobs vanish. By the time the venture folds, the livelihood systems that supported villagers before the project may have been irreversibly turned upside down. In Yendi, some women complained that the shea trees they made a living from had been uprooted to clear the land for the planting of jatropha, although the scale of tree felling is contested. Many farmers who lost land to the biofuel project have now left the area: researchers estimated that the village of Kpachaa lost almost a quarter of its population.[48] The project also took land from urban dwellers who live in Tamale and who hired local labourers to run their farms. These absentee landlords have now left, and the casual labourers lost a source of income.

In Ghana's Pru district, the jatropha company was set up in 2008, and in 2010 it secured a memorandum of understanding with the local paramount chief for a land option of 46,000 hectares. After testing varieties, securing financing and formalizing a lease for 6,750 hectares, it has now planted some 1,400 hectares – that is, 20 per cent of the land area leased. Compared to many other recent agricultural investments in Africa, this seems good progress – though the company has yet to install its processing facilities and to generate any revenues. To date, the project arguably remains a fragile operation. Only time will tell whether it will prove successful in both commercial and sustainable development terms.

There are many reasons for the high failure rate in the recent wave of agricultural investments. All new businesses involve a risk of failure. In agriculture, this risk is particularly high owing to the uncertainties of weather, pests and other environmental factors, though modern technology has provided some insulation from ecological uncertainties. But additional factors increase the risk of failure. A vast literature suggests that some of the companies that have acquired land in Africa are new entrants with little track record, thin capitalization and high reliance on lending. Thin capitalization explains why so many biofuels projects have run into difficulties as the lending taps dried up following the economic crisis in the West. Also, many plantations involved ambitious plans for largely untested crops, like jatropha. Many have struggled with logistical challenges in delivering equipment and inputs in remote areas, and with difficulties in mobilizing the necessary management skills. In some cases, one wonders whether the company really had the intention or capability to cultivate all the land it acquired – as discussed, speculation and strategic considerations are also important drivers of the deals.

In addition, some of the recent land deals involve setting up mega-farms that seem unrealistically sized. Some contracts are for plantations above 200,000 hectares each.[49] There is no evidence as yet of a correlation between the size of the deals and the rate of failure. But creating a farm from scratch and running it successfully at that scale is a daunting task, especially in difficult environments presenting poor infrastructure, low levels of capacity and complex government bureaucracy. It is worth bearing in mind that, before the controversial land redistribution programme, the average farm size in Zimbabwe's commercial sector was below 2,000 hectares among what was considered to be the large farms, and just over 8,500 hectares in the agro-estate sector.[50] Worldwide, some mega-farms are commercially viable, for example in Latin America and South-East Asia.[51] But there is no track record of successful mega-farms in Africa. A few very large farms have existed in Africa since colonial times, but they tend to use only a fraction of the land they have been allocated. Of course, there is great variation in optimal farm size, based on crop and context. But as a general rule of thumb, efficiency tends to decrease beyond 20,000 hectares, because it then becomes more difficult for farm management to keep track of detail.[52] In the words of a leading agribusiness consultancy firm, 'decision making for very large units (in excess of 10,000ha) can become as remote as the command economics of post-war Communism'.[53] Operating very large land deals through subdividing the estate into smaller units can address some of these problems, but getting such ambitious projects running remains a challenging task.

The high failure rate of recent large land deals also owes much to the failure of governments to properly scrutinize investment proposals, where legislation empowers them to do so, and to widespread perceptions among new entrants in the industry that there was easy money to be made. Both factors are now changing, as some governments have become demanding and business operators more aware of the major risks involved. But, overall, the balance of the evidence on the local outcomes of large land deals in different parts of Africa is to date against the deals. People who stand to be directly affected have good reason to be concerned. The best evidence available to date suggests that, at the local level, large land deals for agricultural investments tend to be bad news for affected people. As a broad generalization, local livelihoods tend to be disrupted in ways that are not offset by the new agricultural venture – because of shortcomings in social impact assessments and compensation regimes, because of the mismatch between the livelihood opportunities lost and created, and because of the uncertainties about the viability of the new ventures in the longer term. And irrespective of the merits and demerits of the deals, the profound transformations in the very fabric of local societies that the cumulative impact

145

of land acquisitions can bring contrast sharply with the lack of control that rural people have over decisions that influence those changes. People who go through those transformations are rarely properly consulted about whether the deals respond to their aspirations. There is widespread evidence of the shortcomings of local consultations, when these are conducted at all.[54]

In this context, it is not surprising that many villagers in different parts of Africa are mobilizing. Growing discontent is finding its way both through formal channels like courts and democratic spaces, and through informal, more subterranean channels, possibly culminating in violence and conflict. In some places, villagers have established committees and associations for collective action. Local chiefs or opposition politicians have contested the legality or legitimacy of land allocations decided by local or central government bodies. National federations of producer organizations have convened farmer fora for local people to express their concerns and aspirations. Farmer mobilization has proved particularly effective where rural producers are close together and well organized – for example, in large irrigation schemes. In Mali, where most deals are concentrated in the irrigable Office du Niger area, producer organizations convened a high-profile farmer forum in the village of Kolongo, at the epicentre of large-scale land acquisitions. The forum called for a halt to land deals in disputed areas.[55] Court litigation, media campaigns and alliances with national and international NGOs, with religious leaders, with transnational social movements and with diaspora associations overseas have all been used as strategies to increase local leverage vis-à-vis companies and governments. There have been some partial successes, but also defeats – and some actions have resulted in favourable outcomes that were not at first anticipated.[56]

Here too, accounts of communities united against a deal may belie much local complexity. Social differentiation among and within groups means that communities are often divided about an investment project, which can result in patterns of both opposition and cooperation. Also, local responses to a large land deal are mediated by pre-existing tensions about land and authority. The history of struggles over land does not start when an investment project enters the local arena. Long-standing tensions may be reignited by the advent of the deal. In a large sugar cane project in Mali, opposition from some villages was partly related to local political and clan struggles that have opposed two lineages since colonial times. The municipal council led by members of one lineage supported the project, while members of the other family led local opposition to the deal, arguing that the council had 'sold out' community land on the cheap.[57] But irrespective of the diverse nature of local responses, large land deals have much potential to fuel conflict in rural Africa, a continent where land has already been a root cause of tensions and even outright war. If the wave of large-scale land acquisitions continues, land will become an even greater source of conflict in many parts of Africa.

April 2011, Washington, DC, headquarters of the United States Agency for International Development. A group of smartly dressed people populates a neatly arranged meeting room. Most have come to Washington for the annual World Bank conference on land and poverty. They are staying in the city one more day to participate in a round table on responsible agricultural investment. When the meeting starts, dialogue is constructive but perspectives are very different: NGOs and companies are sitting at the same table. Discussing a large land deal he was involved with, an investment banker says that the large number of jobs promised by the project 'can only be a good thing'. It is true that many rural people in Africa are desperate for better livelihood opportunities, including in the form of employment. But talk of job creation neglects the fact that, when an investment project arrives, people are already busy making a living from farming, herding, foraging, off-farm occupations or combinations of these. As the project is implemented, livelihood options are not created – they are transformed. The question is whether this transformation is for the better. Jobs *can* be a good thing – but assessing whether this is the case is much less straightforward than it might at first seem. The landless poor may benefit from new jobs for agricultural labourers,

147

but the deals may uproot pre-existing livelihood systems, often in irreversible ways. And the many failed or speculative deals cause suffering without bringing any benefits. To date, the local outcomes of many land deals provide little ground for optimism.

## Do land deals lead to a 'water grab'?

On this stretch of the River Niger, in central Mali, colourful pirogues bustle in all directions carrying people, sheep and goods. It is here that the River Niger meets the River Bani and feeds one of Africa's most spectacular seasonally flooded plains – the Inner Niger Delta. When I first visited the delta in October 2002, soon after the rainy season, the miracle of the seasonal flooding was at its peak. Bozo fishers were at work, hoping for a good catch. For a traveller coming from the surrounding dry scrublands, these vast expanses of water seemed like a mirage. With the rains, local farmers plant rice that they will harvest as the waters recede. During the dry season, the lakes turn into dusty plains where Fulani herders graze their livestock on the nutritious grass locally known as *burgu*. At this time, the delta hosts about half of Mali's national livestock, with cattle also coming from Burkina Faso and farther afield.[58] For the herders who, sitting in a circle, share with me sour milk in a wooden bowl, the delta is a source of life. It is here that, in the nineteenth century, the religious Fulani leader Sekou Amadou established a theocratic state and a sophisticated resource management system that, despite many important changes, is still applied today. A diverse mosaic of ethnic groups, each traditionally associated with different livelihood systems, depends on the delta. A walk across the bustling streets of Mopti, the main town in the delta, is a tour through this patchwork of cultures and livelihoods.

Upstream, the town of Ségou, on the southern bank of the River Niger, hosts colonial buildings that are a vivid reminder of a not too distant past. It was the French colonizers who built the Markala dam north of Ségou, created one of the largest irrigation schemes in West Africa – the Office du Niger – and forced farmers to settle on the scheme and grow cotton for the French textile industry.[59] After independence, rice replaced cotton as the main crop in the Office du Niger, and the Malian government and donor agencies expanded the irrigation infrastructure. Today, the Office du Niger hosts some eighty thousand hectares of irrigated land.[60] The parastatal agency that, through various incarnations, has managed the scheme since colonial times is based in the town of Ségou. The headquarters of the agency, also called Office du Niger, is an imposing white building in elegant Sahelian architecture located in the centre of the town. The extensive powers of this agency in shaping the lives of thousands of small-scale rice growers led some commentators to talk about 'a state within the state',[61] though institutional reforms adopted in the mid-1990s have redefined and partly democratized those powers. Productivity on small-scale farms in the Office area has increased sharply since the mid-1990s, but demographic growth and plot subdivision have resulted in an average farm size of less than two hectares.[62] For the government, expanding the irrigation infrastructure has become an imperative, yet there are limited public resources to finance the expansion.[63] To address this challenge, in 2008 the government issued an 'appeal to investors', calling on private capital to acquire land in the area and bring the irrigation scheme to its claimed full potential of 1 million hectares.[64]

Within a few years, the Office du Niger became a hotspot of the global land rush. Companies from South Africa, Libya, China and Europe have flocked in to tap into the area's potential. National entrepreneurs have also moved in. Nearly 900,000 hectares have formed the object of land deals since 2004, though, as discussed, only a small part of this involved definitive leases from the Office du Niger.[65] The political mobilization of local producer associations, concerned at losing their land to outsiders, resulted in high-profile farmer fora that called for a halt on the deals. As discussed in Chapter 4, villagers affected by the deals have also filed lawsuits to challenge two major investment projects. Opposition leaders in parliament have seized on the matter. But it was the military coup of March 2012 and the ensuing political instability in the country that put a brake on the pace of the deals. Many foreign investors have now pulled out, and much uncertainty surrounds the future of agribusiness ventures in the Office. But the full implementation of the deals signed so far could profoundly transform ecology and livelihoods not only in the Office itself, but also, via impacts on the water resource, downstream in the Inner Niger Delta.

No place in Africa can illustrate more powerfully the important implications of the global land rush for water resources. A land lease in a semi-arid country like Mali would be worthless if it did not ensure access to sufficient water for agricultural use. Land acquisitions in Mali were concentrated in the irrigable Office du Niger area. And water is an important driver of the land rush in the first place. Countries that have much land but little water – such as the Gulf states – have been among those signing the deals. Financiers interested in capturing increases in the price of land are also mindful of the gains that can be made from the water rights embedded in the land deals. It is impossible to assess what the land deals mean for recipient countries without properly under-standing their water dimension. There are two aspects to this. The first concerns water issues linked to individual deals – the 'micro' level. The second relates to the cumulative impact of numerous deals in a given location – the 'macro' level. Developments in the Office du Niger provide insights for both aspects.

At the micro level, an important issue concerns the commit-ments that governments enter into to make water available to the companies that lease the land. Some contracts relating to agricultural investments in the Office du Niger contain clauses that are capable of affecting water access for small-scale farmers. A deal for 100,000 hectares grants the company the right 'to use the quantity of water necessary for the project without restrictions' during the wet season,[66] and to use the water necessary for less water-intensive crops during the dry season. Another contract commits the government to provide water for irrigation and in-dustrial use for up to 20 cubic metres per second every day. This can be extended to 35 cubic metres per second if the company exercises an option to expand the plantation area within fifteen years. These contractual commitments to the company create a legal obligation for the host government to ensure that the water needs of the project are met. Effectively, this establishes priority rights for access to water. In fact, the contract for a sugar cane project explicitly states that the project regulated by the contract and a pre-existing sugar cane project would be prioritized if water became limited. Should a water shortage occur – owing, for instance, to drought or to over-commitment of the limited water available – government authorities would be contractually obligated to prioritize these two sugar cane ventures over other water users. Sugar cane is a thirsty crop. Thousands of small-scale rice growers, who account for the bulk of agricultural production in the Office du Niger, risked being left without sufficient water. Scope for dry-season cultivation of water-demanding crops like rice is already restricted by water scarcity during this season. Also, in times of crisis, prioritizing sugar cane over rice may result in food scarcity.[67] These concerns are all the more important if one considers the very long contract durations and the growing fluctuations in the water resource base due to climate change.

The cumulative impact of large numbers of land deals can also have profound implications for water use. The rise in large-scale irrigation projects in the Office du Niger area may impinge on water availability in the Inner Niger Delta. The environmental impact assessment carried out for a large sugar cane project in the Office noted that, although there is currently enough water to meet the water demands of different users in the area, the cumulative effect of numerous land acquisitions could create shortages vis-à-vis the multiple water demands of existing or planned users. That study also found that only measures to increase seasonal water availability, such as the construction of the Fomi dam upstream in Guinea, would ensure that water demand is met during the dry season in the longer term.[68] Others agree that the Fomi dam is critical for the viability of additional large irrigation projects in the Office du Niger.[69] It is worth looking further into this dam.

Fomi is one of three dams that the Niger Basin Authority –

the intergovernmental body that regulates the river basin – has been planning since 2008. The other two dams are downstream of the Office du Niger, in Taoussa (Mali) and Kandadji (Niger). Fomi is located in the highlands of eastern Guinea, which receive abundant rainfalls. This is where the River Niger originates. The dam aims to generate electricity and stabilize water flows for agriculture, fishing and navigation. Construction works are set to start in the course of 2013 and would involve a 'Build, Operate and Transfer' scheme, whereby a concessionaire will build the dam and generate returns through operating it for twenty-five years, before handing it over to the Guinean government.[70] The governments of Guinea and Mali have been strong supporters of this dam. It is not difficult to see why the Malian government is keen. The dam will increase water flows in the dry season, which – among other things – will allow extension of dry-season farming in the Office du Niger. Easing water constraints in the dry season will improve commercial prospects for agricultural ventures in the Office. But the dam in Fomi will also have negative impacts. One is that the dam will reduce water flows during the wet season. As a result, the flood plains of the Inner Niger Delta are expected to shrink.[71] According to some projections, the flood plains might be reduced by up to a half.[72] A squeeze on this scale could have disastrous consequences for the estimated one million herders, farmers and fishers who depend on the delta.[73] In the Inner Niger Delta, competition for resources is already intense. Over the past few decades, pressures on land, water and grazing have increased as a result of demographic growth, but also of an already shrinking resource base: the scale and duration of the flooding have already contracted owing to climatic fluctuations and to the earlier construction of another dam upstream, at Sélingué.[74] Already, when I conducted fieldwork in the delta back in 2006, concerns about the shrinking resource base were raised by mayors, customary authorities and pastoralists alike. Conflict over access to land and natural resources was endemic – for example, between competing customary authorities, between these authorities and elected mayors, and between fishers and farmers, on the one hand, and customary leaders and herders on the other.[75] Any further squeeze on the delta is bound to be felt.

The rapid unfolding of the land rush in the Office du Niger reflects strategic decisions about water management that will have lasting repercussions for livelihoods well beyond the areas immediately affected by the land deals. By signing many large land deals in the Office du Niger and by supporting the new dam in Fomi to make the deals viable, the Malian government put at risk one of its most precious resources, the Inner Niger Delta. Hundreds of thousands of farmers, herders and fishers risk losing out to plantations that will most likely support only a smaller number of jobs. Because of the close interconnection between livelihood systems and social identity, these changes will also profoundly affect local societies. There is nothing to suggest that people who have so much at stake have been meaningfully involved in these decisions. In fact, there has been very little public debate in Mali about the implicit strategic choice to shift water from the Inner Niger Delta to the Office du Niger, or about the full implications of this choice.

Where water is a trans-boundary resource, the cumulative impacts of land deals may have important international dimensions. The basin of the River Niger includes nine West African countries. A regional body to coordinate the management of this shared river basin, the Niger Basin Authority, has been in place since 1980. A Water Charter adopted in 2008 by the Niger river basin countries refers to the principle of 'equitable and reasonable' utilization of the shared river basin among the riparian countries.[76] But what this means in practice may be open to different interpretations, and is likely to involve political negotiation. The disconnection between the trans-boundary water implications of the land deals and the power of national governments, not regional bodies, to sign those deals may yet prove an important source of tension. Nigeria, which is the country farthest downstream and also West Africa's economic powerhouse, has raised concerns that the three new dams planned on the River Niger will reduce water flows.[77]

Despite the many specificities of the Malian context, the issues

153

raised by this experience resonate with developments in many parts of Africa. For example, governments from three countries that share the Nile river basin – Ethiopia, Sudan and South Sudan – have collectively allocated millions of hectares of land for irrigated agriculture. While exact estimates of increased water demand linked to the rise of large irrigation projects in Ethiopia are not available, important impacts on water availability downstream seem inevitable.[78] These developments risk straining relations among riparian states. In Mozambique's Massingir district, a large ethanol project raised concerns about water availability – with the trade-off here being between the new venture, involving irrigated sugar cane farming next to the dam, and pre-existing irrigated rice cultivation downstream, in the Limpopo river valley.[79] The rush for land has major implications for access to water – not only because the deals may give companies priority rights that disadvantage local farmers, but also because the cumulative effect of the deals on water abstraction may have far-reaching reverberations downstream, and because strategic policy choices may link the signing of the deals to major dam developments that can affect transnational watercourses. As a result, the socio-economic outcomes of the deals are not limited to the people who live in the project area. Directly or indirectly, the deals can affect a much wider set of interests, within the national territory and beyond.

Since the many land deals were signed in Mali's Office du Niger area, the political situation in the country has deteriorated. The occupation of northern Mali by an alliance of Tuareg rebels and foreign jihadists in early 2012 destabilized agribusiness developments in the Office du Niger. Several foreign companies have now withdrawn, and many investments have been put on hold. Between the rush for land and water, on the one hand, and political instability, on the other, the future of the Office du Niger and of the Inner Niger Delta looks more uncertain than ever.

### Changes in national economies and societies

Mozambique's Manica Province is a strip of land that runs north–south along the border with Zimbabwe. The mountains close to the border offer stunning views of the lush highlands in neighbouring Zimbabwe. In the province, population density remains relatively low, but pressures on land have been rising for a long time. Back in the 1980s, the government created a large eucalyptus and pine plantation that was encroached upon during the civil war. This plantation is still up and running, and has now been privatized. The peace accords of the early 1990s triggered a rush for land, with national elites acquiring leases from the government for speculation. Over the past fifteen years, land occupations in Zimbabwe have pushed some white farmers to move to Manica, setting up middle-sized plantations to supply international firms with tobacco and paprika; but lack of finance and infrastructure have brought most of these ventures to their knees.[80]

As the global land rush kicked off, demand for land in the province reached new heights. In January 2010, the cadastral officer in Chimoio, the provincial capital, provided me with lists of approved and pending plantation deals. Land leases signed annually in the province had risen from a mere 562 hectares in 2007 to 21,334 hectares in 2008 and 58,880 hectares in 2009. By any account, this is a staggering increase. The province was now home to many new agribusiness ventures, including sugar cane, jatropha and tree plantations run by British and Portuguese companies. Some high-profile projects have since collapsed. But pressures on land remain acute. As of January 2010, the government was examining applications for an additional 367,165 hectares of land in the province. South African commercial farmers have recently set up shop in the province, though many suffered the same fate as their predecessors from Zimbabwe and have now left.[81]

Manica is attractive to investors because of its fertile land and conducive climate, but also because it is located along the Beira infrastructure corridor – an axis of roads and railways that links the interior of Mozambique, Zimbabwe, Zambia and Malawi to the port of Beira, on the Mozambican coast. During Mozambique's protracted civil war, this road and rail link fell into disrepair. But completed and planned upgrades to the infrastructure are

155

now improving access to markets for crops produced in the landlocked Manica Province. A road going north from Manica to Tete Province, where mining operations led by Brazilian and Australian firms are set to make Mozambique a leading coal producer, increases the strategic value of transport infrastructure in Manica. Rapid developments in mining are also widely expected to increase demand for food, as immigration to take up jobs in the mines will create new markets for agricultural produce. These developments in agriculture, mining and infrastructure are rapidly changing this part of the world, and embody the profound transformations that Mozambique is going through.

In recent years, the Mozambican economy has grown at an average rate of nearly 8 per cent per year.[82] This makes it one of the fastest-growing economies in the world. Manica has been one of the fastest-growing provinces in the country, which recently led the Mozambican president, Armando Guebuza, to publicly praise the economic performance of the province.[83] The natural resource sector is an important driver of the country's growth. In addition to the mining boom in the northern Tete Province, recent discoveries of natural gas off the coast of northern Mozambique hold the promise of a new cash bonanza. However, aggregate agricultural production has displayed only slow growth in recent years, mainly driven by the expansion of cultivated areas, and agricultural productivity has remained stagnant.[84]

Some people are visibly benefiting from these rapid changes. In the country's capital city, Maputo, a construction boom is under way, with cranes and building sites set to transform the laid-back cityscape so far dominated by the tired colonial architecture. Maputo hosts a growing middle class interested in the amenities of urban life – shopping malls, restaurants and nightlife. Yet this rapid growth has yet to translate into real improvements in the lives of many rural people. Mozambique remains one of the poorest countries in the world. The United Nations recently placed Mozambique 184th, out of a total of 187 countries, in its annual global ranking based on the human development index.[85] The index measures performance against key indicators of income, education and health. The latest national poverty assessment does show significant improvements in non-monetary aspects of poverty, including health and education, mainly thanks to sustained government investment in service provision. But it also highlights the persistence of low consumption, including food consumption, in many parts of the country. In Manica, the prevalence of chronic malnutrition remains high (58 per cent), and the proportion of the provincial population below the official poverty line increased from 44 to 55 per cent between 2002/03 and 2008/09.[86]

Research on the socio-economic outcomes of the global land rush has focused on the impacts of individual deals on the people most directly affected – those who lose land to the project, or take up jobs with it. Case studies answer some important questions, but leave many others wide open. Land deals cannot be viewed in isolation. They are part and parcel of wider social and economic transformations that are changing the face of many parts of the continent. Processes of rapid if not inclusive growth are a recurring story in many African countries. In recent years, annual economic growth averaged 5.6 per cent in Ghana, 6.8 per cent in Tanzania, and a spectacular 8.5 per cent in Ethiopia.[87] Economic growth has continued even as the West dipped into recession, and is associated with important social transformations – increasing urbanization, emerging middle classes, and growing integration into the global economy. Are the deals playing a role in this economic growth?

To assess the socio-economic outcomes of the land rush in recipient countries, it is critical to understand the role that their cumulative footprint has played or could play in transforming economies and societies at the national level – or in particular areas within a country. After all, governments that allocate land to investors know very well that villagers will lose their land. But they believe that the contribution of these investments to economic growth will offset negative impacts. Typical theories about the main 'transmission channels' that link large-scale agricultural investments to economic change and in turn to positive social outcomes include the provision of new public revenues, which could be used for economically, socially or environmentally beneficial purposes; a catalysing effect for economic activities, for instance through increases in productivity or in exports, the development of strategic infrastructure or the creation of new opportunities for local businesses; and outcomes for national food security, for example by increasing the availability of food, reducing food prices, and generating incomes that can be used to buy food.

Yet very little is known about the cumulative impacts, both direct and indirect, of the land deals on macroeconomic aspects like economic growth, balance of payments and tax revenue, and whether and to what extent these translate into benefits for the poor, including those displaced by the deals. In particular, little is known about the indirect impacts of the deals: large-scale agricultural investments may create new opportunities for local businesses in the value chain, for instance as suppliers of goods and services – or they may crowd out local producers through increased competition for products and resources. Very few studies have taken geography, rather than individual projects, as the main unit of analysis – assessing the change that the cumulative number of land deals is causing in a given district or province, for example. 'Macro' changes tend to involve longer time frames than direct impacts at the local level: land takings may occur in the early stages of project implementation, but it will usually take longer for the cumulative effect of the deals to translate into significant changes in a country's balance of payments, for example. For the ongoing wave of land acquisitions, it is simply too early to tell. But while the evidence base is still thin, it is possible to develop preliminary considerations about a few 'transmission channels'. Overall, the best available evidence suggests that the operation of these transmission channels is far from automatic, and that hoped-for benefits do not necessarily materialize.

Take the case of public revenues. In theory, an investment can be an important source of revenues for the government – not only through fees and taxes paid by the company, but also through taxation on the income of the wage labourers employed by the project. In practice, reliable figures on the tax revenues generated by the deals are not available. With regard to taxes and fees payable by the company, governments have granted extensive tax incentives in order to attract commercial investments in agriculture. These incentives might bring more investments, but they also limit the potential for those investments to generate public revenues. As discussed in Chapter 4, many land deals involve no or low land fees, and corporate income tax rates can be low and subject to tax holidays. Also, a legal analysis of a small sample of contracts provided a cautionary tale about the extent to which the deals feature robust safeguards to ensure that any taxation due is properly paid: several contracts do not require independent audits and government oversight of the investor's financial accounts, and many do not establish safeguards against 'transfer pricing' – the practice whereby the project company's taxable profits are decreased through input purchases from, or product sales to, related companies at inflated or discounted prices, respectively.[88] So even where taxes are formally due, there is a risk that host governments will receive little in practice. But in investments that create many jobs, income tax paid by the workers can constitute a very substantial share of the public revenues contributed – even if wages and therefore individual tax contributions are low. This assumes that all revenues that a company deducts from wages are duly paid as taxes. Finally, any discussion of the importance of public revenues implies that these revenues are used in ways that maximize poverty reduction goals. The way revenues are spent is not a feature of the deals per se, but it should not always be assumed that the monies collected are used judiciously.

While the land deals are unlikely to result in a cash bonanza for the public coffers, they could still play a positive role by catalysing economic activities. Governments in Africa face important policy dilemmas regarding how to increase agricultural productivity and improve rural livelihoods. In many parts of Africa, agricultural productivity is lower than it could be.[89] Commercial investments in agriculture are seen as an important vehicle for helping drive increases in productivity. This is not just because the new venture may itself use more productive techniques. Training and on-the-job learning provided by a company may benefit other economic activities too ('spillovers'): employees may change employer, and seasonal workers may run their own farm in addition to providing labour for the plantation, so that new techniques learned on the job may be applied elsewhere too. Case study research from Zambia suggested that farmers providing seasonal labour to a plantation had higher productivity on their own farms compared to farmers that had not been exposed to agribusiness practices.[90] At scale, this increased agricultural productivity might have knock-on effects on local food markets or local employment – for example, if more people have to be hired for harvesting.

Agricultural investments may also create new business opportunities for local companies to supply goods or services to the project – for example, to move agricultural produce from the farm to transport hubs. Other local businesses may depend on the project in more indirect ways – for example, as a source of produce to sell. In addition, a successful investment project can have a positive 'demonstration effect', encouraging other investors to follow its path. A critical mass of successful investments may then trigger a positive cycle: infrastructure development and growing processing capacity associated with a large number of agricultural ventures may facilitate new agricultural enterprises. Outside the African context, for example, large-scale palm oil development in eastern Malaysia is now helping small-scale farmers to also become successful commercial growers, because a network of roads and milling plants has made it easier for small-scale farmers to sell their produce.[91] Investment in developing infrastructure can also make a difference to local economies. In Mali's Office du Niger scheme, where only about eighty thousand hectares of land have been developed for irrigation since colonialism, a single deal concluded by a Libyan entity promised the development of 100,000 hectares. While this deal was discontinued following political instability in both Mali and Libya, and while therefore this example does not provide evidence of how infrastructure development can make a difference, one can understand why governments may be attracted to such investment proposals. Finally, in more macroeconomic terms, the expansion of monetized employment may trigger a multiplier effect, whereby people spend or save earnings in ways that stimulate economic development.

These potential effects on agricultural productivity and business links seem one of the most promising routes through which the deals could benefit national economies. So far, however, there is little evidence that these benefits are materializing. Recent research by the Food and Agriculture Organization did suggest that foreign investment in agriculture has delivered macroeconomic benefits in countries like Ghana, Senegal and Uganda – for example, in terms of increases in production and yields, diversification of crops and, in some cases, higher export earnings.[92] But the research considered foreign investment in agriculture as a whole, including, for example, processing and contract farming arrangements, not just land deals for plantation agriculture. So while it confirms that foreign investment can play an important role in agricultural development, the research says little about whether large land deals are a desirable form of agricultural investment.

And there is also another side of the coin. Large land deals can undermine, as well as catalyse, local economic activities. In discussions about investment flows to developing countries, it is often said that investment brings economic benefits but creates social and environmental risks. But ill-thought-out agricultural investments can be bad not only for societies and the environment, but also for the economy. As discussed above, jobs may be created, but other livelihoods may be destroyed – and much depends on the balance between the two. Large-scale farming may out-compete local producers in accessing the best resources and in selling produce. The land rush may push up land prices and make it more difficult for local producers to access or retain land; large plantations may increase labour costs for small-scale farmers; and mechanized farming may drive down food and agricultural commodity prices to levels that are not sustainable for poorer

161

farmers. Many local producers may end up being driven out of business as a result. The multiplier effect is likely to be limited or even negative where the jobs created are few and predominantly unskilled and low paid, and the project undermines pre-existing livelihood strategies.

Part of the reason why there is to date little trace of wider benefits to national economies is that, as discussed above, so many land deals have now collapsed. Where a project fails or is delayed as a result of financing difficulties, greater-than-expected logistical and management challenges, commercial unviability or social unrest, it will produce none of the benefits – it cannot contribute public revenues or catalyse economic activities. But it can still impose significant losses on the host country and communities, for example in terms of loss of land and disruption of local livelihoods, and in terms of opportunity costs – because the land allocated or promised to an investor remains idle and cannot be put to alternative productive use.[93] These considerations are all the more pressing if one looks at the cumulative impact of the deals, rather than the outcomes of a single venture. Where many large deals fail or are severely delayed, the opportunity costs for the host country could be very substantial indeed.

One would expect the effect of the deals on national food security to be a prime consideration in assessing socio-economic outcomes. Yet this is an area ripe with paradoxes. The production of food and fuel for export is an important driver in many recent land acquisitions, but several major host countries are themselves food insecure and were even, until recently, recipients of food aid. This has prompted much public concern. A review of a small sample of contracts found that several deals provided very limited safeguards for local food security, including in times of crisis.[94] But another argument is that, if agricultural investment can bring major yield increases, it could benefit food security in both host and investor countries. Sharp increases in agricultural productivity, for example where land deals affect areas that had been subject to very low-intensity use, would mean that even the distribution of a small share of the produce on local markets might increase availability of food, bringing prices down, while wages might enable people to buy the food they need. Also, earning foreign exchange through agricultural exports is an important part of the strategy pursued by some of the African countries that have been signing large land deals. The calculation is that exports would help address foreign exchange crises and finance the importation of food as well as equipment for industrial development. Evidence on how these arguments and counter-arguments are playing out in the real world is still hard to come by. Nevertheless, reliance on international markets for food security can be a risky strategy in low-income countries: small drops in export prices and increases in food prices can have substantial negative impacts on households that, because of their low income level, are vulnerable to becoming food insecure with even minor shocks.[95] Gains may be made, but the risks borne by the poorer sections of the population can be high.

The prevailing technocratic discussion of economic costs and benefits misses the important changes that the land rush can bring to the very fabric of society if the deals signed to date are indeed fully implemented, and if the pace of the deals is sustained over time.[96] Indeed, while governments may focus their attention on economic statistics, the cumulative effect of the deals can have major implications well beyond economics. When a company acquires land, land use tends to shift from multiple, overlapping local uses – farming, herding, foraging – to monoculture. As a result, societies in which people farm their land or graze their livestock are transformed into societies in which control over land is heavily concentrated in few, large, corporate hands, and where people provide cheap labour to plantations. People who lose land become 'proletarians' (the classical Marxist notion used to identify those whose main resource is their labour power) or 'semi-proletarians' (if they retain a plot of land that is too small for them to make a living, so they will still have to depend on wage labour to survive).[97] But where land is becoming scarcer, there are already growing numbers of landless people, especially among the youth. These people may have continued access to common property resources, for instance for grazing or foraging, but little or no farmland of their own to cultivate. The unfolding land rush merely constitutes an acceleration in this longer-term process of social differentiation. Land concentration would tend to increase widening inequalities not only in wealth but also in political power. Because of the intimate connection between livelihood systems and sociocultural identity, these changes will have profound implications for the way people see themselves. For pastoralists, herding is a way of life as much as a production system. Requiring pastoralists to work as casual labourers on a jatropha plantation is not just about trading one job for another. Entire worlds – systems of traditions, values and beliefs – will disappear in the process.

This is not to romanticize traditional ways of life. Societies are already changing fast. Traditions, values and beliefs are continuously created, lost or reinvented. Younger people may have different values and aspirations from those of their parents and grandparents. A generational shift in culture and livelihoods appears to be under way, whereby young villagers value income-generating opportunities outside agriculture more than their parents did. Movements of people also change livelihoods, and bring new ideas about society, authority and legitimacy. It is not possible or desirable to freeze evolution in human societies. But insofar as change is fuelled by deliberate government action – namely, the allocation of large areas of land for monoculture plantations – it would seem legitimate to ask how far such action genuinely responds to a shared vision of national development, and how far the people whose ways of life are being so profoundly transformed have had an opportunity to be listened to about the model of development they aspire to.

Back in Manica Province, the future promises much change. The Beira Agricultural Growth Corridor initiative – a high-profile public–private partnership recently presented at the World Economic Forum in Davos – aims to promote commercial agriculture along the infrastructure corridor that runs through the province. Making explicit reference to the experience of large-scale agricultural development in the Brazilian *cerrado*, the 'Investment

Blueprint' for this initiative notes that, of the 10 million hectares of land along the corridor route, only 1.5 million hectares are currently being cultivated, mainly for subsistence agriculture. The Blueprint seeks to radically transform agriculture through 'clusters' that bring together medium-scale commercial estates, outgrowers, distributors of seeds and fertilizers, and market access infrastructure such as storage and wholesale markets. There is much potential for improving local livelihoods – but also for further increases in pressures on land. The biggest rush to land in Manica may be yet to begin.

## Transitions in the global food system

A pedestrian walkway runs along the coast, framed by the sea on one side and a wide avenue on the other. In the twilight, European expats jog in this oasis of calm. Manicured plants separate the walkway from the high-powered cars travelling up and down the multiple lanes of the large avenue. Beyond the avenue is a wall of skyscrapers of different heights and shapes. The glass windows look like many eyes overlooking the sea. The streets between the high-rises are crowded by scores of faces from South Asia, South-East Asia and eastern Europe.

A few decades ago, Abu Dhabi was a patch of desert land inhabited by Bedouin tribes and subject to a British protectorate. A legal dispute between the sheikh and a British petroleum company drilling for oil in the emirate became a textbook case of colonial attitudes towards local legal systems. The British arbitrator called upon to settle the dispute held that, while in principle local law should regulate the contested oil concession, no law could 'reasonably be said to exist ... in this very primitive region', and a 'modern law of nature' recognized by 'civilised nations', of which rules of English law were deemed to be a reflection, should be applied instead.[98] Much has changed since the time of the protectorate. The United Arab Emirates, of which Abu Dhabi is part, is one of the richest countries in the world. The commercial discovery of oil turned the fortunes of the emirate, and the Emiratis have managed to harness their newly found oil riches for economic development. As oil revenues started to flow, a construction boom ensued. Large numbers of unskilled migrants came to work in construction sites and in the service industry. Skilled migrants came to man ministries and corporations. Many Britons are now employees in Emirati companies and government agencies. Non-nationals constitute the vast majority of the country's population. Wealth has also brought some extravagant lifestyles: a luxury hotel on the coast features dome ceilings laden with gold, and hosts a vending machine that distributes gold against credit card payments.

But for all its wealth, Abu Dhabi faces a major challenge. Water is in short supply. Experts estimate that, on current trends, the emirate will run out of groundwater within forty years. Agriculture accounts for the greater part of current water use, though exact figures are disputed. Extensive use of pesticides has raised worries about the aquifers. Experts believe that only 1 per cent of the country is arable land. For a long time, agriculture was not a major concern for the Emiratis. In addition to an agribusiness sector, small-scale farms emerged through government provision of land and inputs that, from the early days of the independent emirate, were mainly seen as a form of social security programme – a way to provide people with the means to make a living. Heavily subsidized farming has brought advances in production, for example in the fruit and vegetables sector, but the country remains very dependent on imports for critical commodities such as cereals.

These days, food and agriculture have risen up the Emiratis' agenda. Concerns about the reliability of food supplies are now more pressing, as world food prices have become higher and more volatile, and as important producer countries have used or considered export restrictions on wheat and other critical staple crops. Concerns about the affordability of food are particularly acute because of the wide income inequalities in the emirate. The presence of a large blue-collar immigrant workforce makes access to affordable food an important part of the social contract, critical for political stability.[99] In 2011, the government announced a scheme to provide basic foods at subsidized prices. Other Gulf countries are grappling with similar challenges – scarce water, dwindling domestic production, high income inequality and a political imperative for national elites to ensure that the blue-collar workforce has access to affordable food.

While the West can secure its supplies through global traders that have a proven capability to shift agricultural commodities all over the globe, and that have substantial market power thanks to concentration in their segment of agricultural value chains, countries in the Gulf feel more exposed as the security of supplies becomes more uncertain.[100] As a response, several governments in the Gulf – including those of Abu Dhabi, Qatar and Saudi Arabia – have developed wide-ranging agendas to secure their food supplies in the longer term. Some governments are investing in technology to increase national food production and reduce their dependence on imports. In Qatar, the government recently announced ambitious plans involving desalinization, greenhouses and technological innovation in farming.[101] Outward foreign investment to produce food overseas and export produce to the Gulf forms part of these wider agendas. For example, Abu Dhabi has acquired land overseas to produce staple foods like wheat and maize, but also fodder for the country's livestock sector. Government-to-government deals or negotiations involving Abu Dhabi officials in Sudan, Egypt and Cambodia have received sustained media attention, with the government securing contracts, and private sector operators running the farms.[102]

Much has been made of the food security strategies of Gulf countries as a driver of land acquisitions in Africa. But, as discussed in Chapter 3, evidence suggests that public perceptions are likely to have overplayed the relative importance of operators based in the Gulf. In Africa, much land acquisition involving foreign investors is driven by European and North American companies, more than operators from Gulf countries. Without repeating that analysis, two points are worth exploring further here. They both concern the socio-economic outcomes of the deals.

The first point relates to outcomes for investor countries. By acquiring land overseas, governments may well improve the reliability of food supplies for their people in ordinary times. But food security strategies involving land acquisitions overseas are unlikely to work at the most critical times – that is, when global commodity prices increase sharply, as they have done in recent years. When price pressures become acute, countries that acquire land overseas to secure their own food security risk being disappointed. This is due not only to the high failure rate of recent agricultural investments in Africa, which points to the major challenges involved with establishing large plantations in difficult terrains. In many recipient countries, food is a very sensitive political issue. In 2008, food price hikes resulted in riots in several parts of Africa, mainly led by politically vocal urban groups. If a major food shortage occurs in future, the host government would come under tremendous political pressure to ensure national food security first. Some contracts for agricultural investments enable the investor to export a major share or even the entire production. But politically, it would be hard for investors to enforce these contractual provisions against a low-income country suffering from food shortages or even a famine. Legally, the norms of the World Trade Organization allow countries to impose restrictions on agricultural exports. In Africa, land itself is a politically and emotionally charged issue. These circumstances can undermine the long-term security of supplies that food-importing countries seek to establish through acquiring land in Africa. Risks include local contestation and conflict, the imposition of export restrictions, and the renegotiation and even outright expropriation of land leases.[103] Conventional risk management devices can themselves create new risks. For example, contract clauses that involve hard commitments for the government to give investors specified quantities of water may reduce commercial risks, but they may also create new risks of contestation. Diversification – spreading agricultural investments over multiple countries – can help to mitigate risks. But commodity price hikes could spark waves of renegotiations or export restrictions that affect several countries at the same time. Acquiring land overseas is not an effective strategy to ensure national food security.

The second point worth exploring further relates to the implications of the deals for the global food system. In this respect, it is important to note that the strategies developed by governments in the Gulf are far from unique. It is true that few countries today have policies that explicitly support land acquisitions overseas out of food security concerns. But across the world and throughout history, food and agriculture have constituted a privileged arena for government intervention. In ancient Rome, the grain dole for the urban populace formed the object of much political contention during the republican era, and became a mainstay of the political settlement under the empire. Since then, the political imperative to ensure that citizens have secure access to food and basic commodities at affordable prices has remained a recurring concern for governments in different parts of the world, even though the specific objectives and modalities of government intervention have varied considerably.

The 'market economies' of the West have also experienced much policy intervention in food and agriculture. In Europe, the Common Agricultural Policy has long involved extensive public intervention in agricultural markets that, on paper at least, aimed to balance multiple goals – increasing agricultural productivity, ensuring fair living standards for farmers, stabilizing markets, assuring availability of supplies, and ensuring reasonable prices for consumers.[104] With specific regard to today's land rush, the important role played by European legislation on renewable energy in indirectly creating new incentives for land deals has already been discussed.[105]

Despite the absence of rigorous measures of the changing degree of government intervention in the agriculture sector, there are signs that the propensity of governments to intervene in food and agriculture might be on the rise. There have been major and rapid changes in the global food system. In the mid-1990s, the new Agreement on Agriculture of the World Trade Organization (WTO) introduced measures to liberalize agricultural trade – a sector that until then had remained at the margins of multilateral trade treaties. The value of international trade in food doubled between 1999 and 2009, illustrating the rapid expansion of global trade and its growing importance in ensuring food security.[106] Trade liberalization also created new incentives for investing in farming. New agricultural superpowers such as Brazil, Argentina and Russia have emerged that produce vast agricultural surpluses for export. A growing proportion of agricultural commodities is traded between Southern countries, challenging a long-standing paradigm that involved trade on a North–South axis. But despite this rapid growth in global trade, world agriculture remains far from a free trade regime. WTO norms liberalize agricultural trade to a lesser extent than trade in non-agricultural goods, and agriculture remains a sticky issue in trade negotiations. Today, only some 15 per cent of global agricultural production is traded on world markets, and for important commodities like rice this percentage is as low as 7 per cent. The increased volatility of international agricultural commodity markets is now prompting governments to become more interventionist. Export restrictions have existed for a long time, but their use has become more frequent in recent years. During the food price hikes of 2008 and 2010, major cereal producer countries such as Ukraine, Argentina and Russia introduced export tariffs or quotas, or even outright export bans, which caused panic on global markets and sharp increases in international commodity prices. In 2008, major rice producers such as India and Vietnam also imposed restrictions. The global trade in food remains deeply embedded in politics.

In this context, it should cause no surprise that rich food-importing countries like the Gulf states are taking measures to insulate themselves from the effects of policy interventions elsewhere. And moves for governments to acquire land overseas present some parallels with shifts that are under way in parts of the corporate sector worldwide. As discussed in earlier chapters, many agribusiness companies have responded to higher and more volatile agricultural commodity prices – and to growing concerns about standards and traceability – by increasing their degree of control over agricultural value chains. As agricultural supplies become more uncertain owing to both market and policy forces, some companies previously focused on processing or trading are now pursuing vertical integration strategies that involve taking direct control of key segments of the value chain, including agricultural production. In other words, the acquisition of land to establish more direct control over farming activities has been a feature of recent policies in both government and corporate sectors.

It is too early to assess what land acquisition strategies driven by governments and corporates will mean for global agriculture in the longer term. Foreign direct investment in agriculture remains very small compared with national agricultural investment, including investment by small-scale farmers.[107] This circumstance would tend to limit the impact of transnational land deals on the global food system. But vertical integration strategies involving land acquisitions tend to compound a trend that has been ongoing for years. Today, a large share of world trade occurs within the 'close circuit' of business groups – as products or components are bought and sold between subsidiaries of the same group, rather than through transactions on open markets. This is also the case in agricultural trade, and the land rush suggests that the share of intra-corporate trade may grow in future – insofar as the acquisition of land is part of wider vertical integration strategies whereby a single business group operates in farming, processing and trading. This shift could have repercussions in multiple directions: to name a couple, greater vertical integration of value chains could squeeze local producers, and intra-firm transactions may increase opportunities for tax avoidance through transfer pricing.

Globally, there is a collective action problem, because governments in major producer countries have political incentives to defend local interests by taking measures like export restrictions, which can protect domestic food security but also increase the volatility of international food markets and inflict major costs on food-importing countries. Other measures that might be used to pursue similar domestic policy objectives (income support or targeted subsidization of food purchases, for instance) may be less disruptive of international trade but more costly, and therefore less appealing, to producer countries. Yet, in the longer term, big food producers will be major losers if the world's confidence in the reliability of their exports should decrease. The interdependence of policy choices in food-producing and -importing countries means that, to avoid the spread of national policies that promote a rush for land, responses are needed that require not unilateral government measures alone, but coordinated action to restore trust in the global trading system.

# 6 | Conclusion

This book has been a journey through the many facets of the unfolding rush for Africa's land. Along this journey, we have been challenged to rethink some widespread perceptions about what is happening, where, why, how and with what results. We have seen that, far from being a new phenomenon, today's land rush has deep historical roots. We have also found that, while the much-publicized transnational deals reflect choices made by companies and governments, deliberate agency is only part of the story. At a deeper level, the rush for Africa's land is shaped by profound social transformations at local to global levels. More than one big 'land grab', the deals reflect these multiple converging processes. In the words of two leading scholars, 'there is no one grand land grab, but a series of changing contexts, emergent processes and forces, and contestations that are producing new conditions and facilitating shifts in both *de jure* and *de facto* land control'.[1] The notion of commercial pressures on land, developed by the International Land Coalition, is a useful way to describe these multiple processes.

Rapid changes in the global economy, and policies in both investor and recipient countries, are fuelling a shift towards an increasingly large-scale, mechanized and corporate-driven African agriculture – a shift that manifests itself in the signing of large land deals. As growing global demand for food and agricultural commodities rekindles interest in Africa's 'untapped' agricultural frontier among financiers, big agribusiness, energy giants and a plethora of start-up companies, both market and policy forces create powerful incentives that favour large land deals over alternative models of agricultural investment. Shifts in the global distribution of economic power mean that, in addition to the 'traditional' capital-exporting countries of Europe and North America, new players from India, China, Brazil and South-East Asia have become increasingly involved in African agriculture. But much land acquisition in Africa is still driven by the dependence of Western societies on an expanding availability of material goods – fuel for our cars, pensions for our future, and a determination to reduce our carbon footprint without fundamentally questioning our consumption patterns. After decades of neglect, African agriculture is an increasingly crowded field, one where the interests of transnational corporations and foreign governments are directly at stake.

The land rush is also the story of profound changes in local and national societies. The growing middle classes in Africa's sprawling cities create new markets for food that fuel agricultural commercialization in areas closer to the urban centres or more suited to intensive farming. Local and national elites – from government officials and business people through to the more dynamic farmers – have been acquiring land in these areas to store value, run agricultural ventures or position themselves as intermediaries with international players. While much attention has focused on the transnational land deals, for most people in rural Africa the squeeze on the land is caused by this slower, less visible, longer-term process of accumulation and increased social differentiation in African societies – a process that started well before public attention turned to 'land grabbing'. The local-to-global processes that underpin the land rush involve different players and arenas, but they also converge and intersect – for example, where national players participate in the transnational deals as intermediaries, facilitators or partners. Studying land deals needs to be situated in these wider contexts, understanding historical trajectories and the many factors and drivers at play.

Developments outside agriculture are also important drivers of the growing pressures on Africa's land. For example, mining and petroleum operations have spread to previously marginal countries, exacerbating competition for land. The commercialization of nature through the creation of carbon markets has increased outside interest in Africa's land.[2] From the farmers in Sanso, who lost land to Mali's mining boom; to the Ghanaian cocoa growers whose land access is being renegotiated as agriculture intensifies and artisanal mining advances; to the Maasai pastoralists of northern Tanzania, squeezed by past fascinations for state farms among government officials and by today's pressures from tourism, hunting and conservation; through to the villagers under pressure from wildlife parks and biofuel projects in Mozambique's Massingir district, rural people in Africa are experiencing at first hand the results of the interplay among these multiple sources of growing commercial pressures on land. At the local level, the extent to which today's transnational land deals for plantation agriculture cause a squeeze on local landholdings is shaped not only by the widely debated yet still largely unreliable figures of the aggregate scale of these deals, but also by the way in which the deals exacerbate pressures from these multiple, longer-term processes. Where land pressures are increasing as a result of demographic growth, of extractive industry developments and of the growing commercialization of agriculture, the acquisition of even relatively small land areas can have major impacts on people's lives.

Framed in these terms, the global land rush reflects an acceleration in profound social transformations that have been evolving for a long time – namely, the growing penetration of international capital in African societies, which dates back to colonial times; Africa's integration into the global economy as a supplier of commodities and raw materials, with the prevailing modalities of agricultural production shifting over time between plantation agriculture and contractualized farming; the emergence of African upper and middle classes interested in acquiring rural land to store their wealth and seize new commercial opportunities; and the increasing commercialization of African agriculture, with the related growing differentiation among the African peasantry. While the rush for Africa's land rarely involves transfers of landowner ship, it does entail a large-scale, long-term shift in land control that penalizes small-scale growers and herders and favours divers constellations of public authorities, corporate investors and local and national elites. Indeed, land allocators – whether governments or chiefs – establish or consolidate their authority through the very process of allocating land;[3] and companies acquire largely transferable, long-term leases that are in many practical ways not that dissimilar from outright ownership.

These processes represent a growing commoditization of land relations in rural societies: land is increasingly treated as a commodity that can be traded against cash payments in the form of land rentals and taxation, or against commitments on capital contributions or jobs, for example. This commoditization of land is most visible in the discourse developed in international investor circles. In order to make land an investible asset, the investment brokers that advertise global investment funds 'render [land] abstract, show its extent, indicate its value, and allow different physical, economic and social characteristics to be visualized together for the purpose of comparison'.[4] The social and political embeddedness that characterizes land relations in the real world of local contexts, and the role of land as a basis of social identity and spiritual value, are completely lost in these narratives – land is just an 'asset class' to be invested in, alongside many other commodities. Narratives deployed by some governments also reflect this change in the way land is conceptualized. The government of Laos' strategy of 'turning land into capital' is a particularly explicit example of this. But irrespective of official narratives, the contracts that make land available to investors involve exchanges between land and varying combinations of cash payments and in-kind commitments. These contracts effectively put a price tag on the land, which prospective investors can compare across countries. The commoditization of land goes hand in hand with the monetarization of wider social relations: to make a living, farmers who lose land must now trade their labour for cash with landholding companies.

But while the land rush is premised on land being treated as a commodity, and while neoliberal reforms are widely considered to have paved the way to the deals, simplistic views of the land rush as a manifestation of the advancement of markets into rural societies are mistaken. On the one hand, land markets have existed in Africa since pre-colonial times, and land relations are increasingly monetized in many parts of the continent.[5] In Ghana's cocoa belt, local land relations outside the landholding group, and in some cases even within it, are eminently commercialized. Where land transactions are restricted by legislation, sales or rentals may be disguised as gifts or loans – as was documented in Burkina Faso, for example.[6] In other words, the commoditization of land has been ongoing for a very long time, and the land rush merely constitutes an acceleration of that process. On the other hand, today's large land deals are far from market transactions. Companies acquire land not on the open market, but through long-term leases with government or customary authorities. Land prices are often undervalued owing to government policies that aim to attract investment in pursuit of economic development goals. Some publicly available contracts include explicit commitments on the part of the host government to negotiate protectionist exemptions from regional free trade regimes – hardly the hallmark of the advancement of markets.[7] Also, companies acquiring land respond to public policies in their home countries, which are in turn driven by concerns about food or energy security, or geopolitical considerations. So the growing commoditization of land reflected in the deals is still shaped by social and political relations. And where the deals involve the compulsory taking of land that has already formed the object of transactions on informal markets, today's land rush entails the wiping out of local markets by large deals that are primarily framed as acts of public authority.

The land rush has the potential to change the face of Africa's rural societies. The shift from small- to large-scale farming involves a reconfiguration of relations between capital, labour and land. In many parts of Africa where agriculture is becoming more intensified and commercialized, the link between land and labour is already being broken: demographic growth, farm subdivision and growing land concentration can result in plots that are too small to make a living, and force many to work as labourers on their neighbours' farms. The land rush accelerates the breaking of this link, with companies taking the land, and rural people providing labour. The very fabric of society is being transformed – livelihood systems, social relations and cultural patterns. Societies usually need time to adjust to such profound changes. In the words of Karl Polanyi, who wrote about the enclosures of the commons that preceded the Industrial Revolution in England, the effect of social change partly depends on '[t]he time-rate of change compared with the time-rate of adjustment'.[8] The rapid pace of today's land rush raises concerns about the ability of local societies to adapt and avoid social dislocation, and the growing reports of local tensions and contestation should be taken seriously by those in government.

The land rush produces winners and losers. Winners include, to very different extents, complex constellations of international finance, agribusiness and energy companies, who stand to make good returns, and the corporate officials operating these companies, who stand to be rewarded for their gains; socio-political alliances and convergences of interests in the countries where the land is acquired – from politicians and government officials who may benefit from opportunities for rent-seeking and patronage, through to rural and urban elites who may act as intermediaries or land allocators; and groups that stand to consume the products of the land rush, particularly if the deals do result in more and cheaper food and fuel – from car drivers and pension holders in the West to the immigrant workforce in the Gulf, through to the growing population of Africa's sprawling cities. It is also increasingly clear who the losers are. First and foremost, the losers are people directly affected by the deals, those who lose their land and have their lives turned upside down – all without having much control of the key turning points. These adverse impacts affect not only people in the project area and its immediate vicinity. They also affect many other people in more indirect yet still dramatic ways – for instance, the farmers, herders and fishers of the Inner Niger Delta, whose resource base risks shrinking as a result of land leases and dam projects upstream. More generally, small-scale rural producers, who have thus far provided the backbone of African agriculture, risk being marginalized by the transition to larger-scale agriculture, out-competed by large farms in control over land, labour and government support. The livelihoods, ways of life and culture of millions of people in Africa are at risk.

But the land rush does not just involve a divide between global capitalists, who take the land, and undifferentiated communities, who lose it. The chasm between winners and losers cuts across those communities as well. Farmers lose land, pastoralists find their livestock corridors encroached upon and women lose access to the lands where they fetch wood or medicinal plants. Local and national elites capture the bulk of the benefits. But some benefits trickle down to poorer groups – for instance, those that get jobs as casual labourers. Local differentiation – between small-scale commercial farmers and their farm labourers, for example – translates into differentiated local outcomes. The picture is more complex than often assumed on the investor side too. Global capitalists invest money that is often not their own: asset management companies work hard to persuade rich individuals and pension fund managers to put money into their ventures. Pension fund managers handle the pension contributions of large numbers of workers. And many biofuel projects depend on high levels of bank lending, meaning that the projects are mainly financed with the savings of the broader public, which the banks are entrusted to manage. Global capitalism may be led by a relatively small group of super-rich, but ownership of capital is also a diffuse affair, at least in richer countries. Ultimately, transnational land deals involve a mediated relationship between millions of savers and consumers in richer countries, on the one hand, and people affected by the deals in Africa, on the other.

The 'land grabbing' arena is often cast as a confrontation between those who support large-scale, agribusiness farming, and those who believe in small-scale rural producers. While debates about scale in agriculture are often polarized, in practice the comparative advantage of small- and large-scale farming changes over time (with technological innovation, for instance), and there is no one-size-fits-all model that works best everywhere and at all times. Crops and contexts differ. And despite the simplistic contrasts that prevail in international debates, small-, medium- and large-scale farming work together in many places, and can mutually reinforce each other. The strong positions taken in favour of small- or large-scale farming ignore the vast body of evidence that calls for a more nuanced analysis of the pros and cons of both agricultural models.

On the one hand, the fascination among many government officials with large-scale farming neglects the fact that the bulk of private investment in Africa's agriculture comes from small-scale producers, many of whom have proved dynamic and competitive on global markets. Historically, the track record of large-scale, mechanized farming in Africa is mixed at best. The failure of many recent large land deals and the speculative nature of many land acquisitions show the risks of equating large scale with agricultural modernization. As growing numbers of agricultural investments collapse or are not implemented, they leave behind a trail of broken promises and devastated livelihoods. And even where the deals prove commercially viable, the benefits of job creation are unlikely to offset the livelihood losses caused by land dispossession, particularly in highly mechanized farms that create few jobs. The growing body of evidence on the outcomes of the land rush is to date overwhelmingly against large land deals. On current trajectory, the land rush will produce a large number of landless and unemployed people, exposing the livelihoods of many to destitution.

On the other hand, it is important not to romanticize small-scale farming, and not to ignore the inequalities that exist among small-scale producers – between men and women, youths and elders, landowners and labourers, growers and pastoralists, commercial producers and subsistence farmers. Processes of 'land grabbing from below' have exacerbated social differentiation in many rural societies. Many youths are voting with their feet and leaving rural areas for a new life in the city. For many young people, farming is too much work for too few returns, especially where farmers cannot keep up with global competitive pressures. And many farmers make major sacrifices to enable their children to get an education so that, one day, they can get out of farming. Global companies that go to great lengths to source produce from small-scale farmers may include the more dynamic growers with sufficient land and inputs to succeed, but the poorest groups may be more likely to benefit from supplying local markets, or from employment on a plantation.[9] And the demand for employment opportunities from poorer sections of rural societies cannot be simply brushed aside.

But given the widespread perception among those in government that see a transition to large-scale farming as a necessary part of agricultural modernization, there is a need to challenge accepted 'truths'; to fully recognize that small-scale farmers are the main source of investment in African agriculture, and to recognize that investing in farmers, rather than in farmland, is more likely to benefit food security at both local and global levels; to open up the full range of possible investment options for promoting agricultural development, including the many options that involve collaboration between small-, medium- and large-scale players; and to create policy spaces that ensure that it is the people whose lives are most directly at stake, not global 'land grabbers' or ideologues, who shape the future of African agriculture. In this sense, the critical fault line in the 'land grabbing' arena is not necessarily about scale, pitching small- versus large-scale farming. It is about control – who should have the authority to shape key decisions and processes. The main reason why the land rush is proving bad news for rural people has to do with a complete failure of governance – investment proposals are not properly scrutinized, investments are hijacked for capture and patronage rather than inclusive development purposes, alternative livelihood options are not considered and, most importantly, the people who are most directly affected have little control over the rapid changes that have such profound implications for their lives. This failure of governance is rooted in historical trajectories, political economies

Conclusion

181

and legal frameworks. It creates a context that is not conducive to the deals producing equitable outcomes.[10] Strategic decisions and organic transformations are happening in arenas where control is far removed from those whose lives are most at stake. Large land deals are being signed over the heads of local people.

It is true that many people affected by the deals have taken matters into their own hands – they have mobilized, challenged, resisted and in some cases succeeded. Local-to-global resistance strategies are emerging that redefine the political space for accountability and belonging. A positive, unintended consequence associated with the land rush might be greater appropriation of active citizenship and democratic space in African societies. But there is also a widespread sense of powerlessness and disenfranchisement among those affected by the deals. In most cases, the geographical dispersion of the rural population, the diversity of local interests and the 'daily precariousness of family survival' make local activism very difficult.[11] People are being dispossessed of their most important asset, land, with little or no compensation and with little opportunity to have their say – and yet they may feel too powerless to challenge the customary or government authorities that have approved the deals. A company can come, take land, make promises and then vanish under the weight of financing difficulties – and people who lost land and jobs may have no idea about what is happening, why, and how the course of events might be changed.

In a globalized world, this lack of local control is not a problem unique to land deals in Africa, though diverse contexts importantly shape specificities in the manifestations of that problem. With regard to large land deals in Africa, the lack of control has deep historical roots – not so much because the deals are themselves not new, but because the historical legacy of dispossession still influences the outcomes of today's land deals. The past still shapes the present. The legislation that regulates land relations in Africa has greatly evolved over the years. But important features remain profoundly influenced by the colonial experience, particularly with regard to the extensive role played by the state in land relations, the varying but typically limited protection of local land rights, and the legal devices that facilitate land access for commercial operators. Similarly, the customary authorities that are meant to represent local groups in the face of growing outside pressures often have contested legitimacy and are the product of much colonial manipulation aimed at controlling rural areas and opening up resources to outside interests.

In addition to the weight of history, features of the social, political, economic and legal context that shapes today's land deals undermine local control over processes of change.[12] In today's land rush, the commercial imperatives about returns and bottom lines, coupled with rapid transformations and shifting power relations in global agriculture; the legal frameworks that shape the distribution of rights and the functioning of institutions; commonly used notions of 'idle land', and of 'modernity' and 'backwardness', that legitimize or delegitimize competing forms of resource use; and deployment of the state's coercive apparatus to enforce decisions all tend to remove control from local people.[13] These multiple factors of exclusion operate in mutually reinforcing ways. For example, ill-defined legal notions of 'public purpose' are fleshed out by legitimizing discourses about agricultural modernization that identify the aspirations of the elites with the common good, and they are backed by coercive enforcement mechanisms that can ensure the surrender of the land against the will of local landholders.

The relationship between historical trajectories, political economies and legal frameworks, on the one hand, and the socio-economic outcomes of the deals, on the other, is not just one of cause and effect – with the former shaping the arena and influencing the outcomes of today's land deals. In turn, the implementation of the deals can further remove control from rural people. For example, small-scale growers that have thus far run their own farms may become casual labourers on corporate plantations, with no control over farming decisions or the business venture. Growing land concentration in recipient countries can increase the concentration of power in the hands of fewer people – in both local and national arenas. Where substantial levels of

183

investment come from a foreign country, the deals might also create the preconditions for greater interference in the domestic affairs of the recipient country. In the longer term, the deals have the potential to further entrench the forces of exclusion that are today undermining local control.[14]

Politics permeate the interplay of these multiple forces of exclusion. The fascination with large-scale farming that provides developmental legitimacy to the deals is about power relations and vested interests that mix the pursuit of private and public goods – from a genuine belief that land deals can benefit local economies to an undeclared policy of allocating long-term leases as a way to reassert sovereignty over the national territory, through to direct or covert corruption. Considerations about relations between rural and urban areas are also at play. Earlier analyses on the existence of a pro-urban bias in national policies have given way to a more nuanced understanding of the politics of urban–rural divides, and some national policies have provided significant support to rural areas. But, in many contexts, there is a deep divide between the views and aspirations of the urban elites in charge of government and the views and aspirations of rural people. To a government official in Mali or Tanzania, pastoralism is a backward and unproductive system that destroys the environment – despite much evidence that has proved the economic and ecological rationale of pastoralism in climatically unstable environments.[15] In the mind of that official, it is large-scale, mechanized farming that holds promise for the future, even though this model of farming may not respond to the aspirations of all rural people. Pastoralists see their livelihood system as a way of life, not just as an economic activity. And many farmers value having control over their land and crops, rather than becoming wage labourers on somebody else's plantation. Agricultural modernization based on large land deals may well create some jobs for farm labourers – but an important question is whether rural people want to trade their ways of life for those jobs. Either way, they should be given that choice.

So long as people have so little control over their lives and can easily be dispossessed of their land, the hopes that many have placed in a renewed interest in African agriculture are unlikely to be fulfilled. There is a need for a democratization of the processes that shape the future of agriculture. Today, much discussion about investment is developed in macro-level, top-down terms. The imperative to attract investment and current patterns of investment are largely treated as givens, and the question is how to ensure that local people benefit from those investment flows. In better-practice examples, local consultations are carried out to facilitate local participation in the benefits of individual investment projects – and also to promote local buy-in and reduce the risk of conflict. But time pressures and power imbalances tend to affect the quality and legitimacy of consultations initiated for individual projects. There is a need to depart from this approach, and place people at the centre of the investment process.

For host countries and communities, promoting investment should not be an end in itself, but a means to the ultimate goal of improving people's lives. Agricultural investment can take many different shapes, and land deals for plantation agriculture are only one possible form. There are many experiences of companies that invest in agro-processing, and source agricultural produce from local farmers. In other cases, a processing facility buys produce both from a plantation estate and from outgrowers. Some farmer associations have an equity stake in the company they supply, which would enable them to scrutinize corporate behaviour, have a voice in business decisions, and benefit from dividend payments and from share appreciation if the venture is successful. Investment models differ widely as to how they are initiated, designed, financed and implemented, or as to the segment of the agricultural value chain they focus on, for example. Different models are likely to have different implications for local economies and societies. There is no universal blueprint for more inclusive forms of agricultural investment. No single model works best in all circumstances. The starting point to determine the quality and quantity of investments that are desirable in a given context should be the needs and aspirations of those most directly concerned. Allowing people to have a say should not wait until an investment project comes in – it should be part and parcel of rural development.[16] The main question should move beyond how best to tweak prevailing investment patterns to ensure that local people participate in the benefits, and ask instead how investment can be oriented so that it responds to the needs and aspirations of those people as well as producing a financial return for the investor: what type of agriculture do rural societies aspire to develop? What are the main constraints? Where is external intervention needed to ease those constraints? What external interventions are best ensured through the involvement of commercial operators, and in what ways? And what policy measures need to be in place to promote these types of commercial investments? Tackling these questions requires inclusive deliberation at both local and national levels, and a shared vision of rural development that considers both local and national interests. This shift in perspective would not only promote models of investment that better respond to the aspirations of those concerned; it would also increase the legitimacy of investment processes among local people. Government can play a critical role in facilitating the emergence of a more bottom-up development vision and investment strategy, and so can organizations representing rural interests.

The different 'rural worlds' that coexist in any given locality – from small-scale commercial farmers integrated into global value chains through to the landless poor, men and women – are likely to have diverse needs and aspirations.[17] Therefore, depending on the context, this bottom-up approach to reframing investment may well result in a combination of different types of farming, where small-scale farmers retain their centrality in African agriculture, but also where agricultural investments are diverse in scale, production models or target markets, for example. And while no investment model can be deemed to be more 'inclusive' in every context, mounting evidence and international guidance provide important pointers. Free, prior and informed consent of local landholders; robust producer organizations that genuinely represent the interests of rural groups; supply chain relations that shift power towards local producers; fair labour relations; participation by worker or producer organizations in the ownership of the company; and proper consideration of gender dimensions are important building blocks in more inclusive models of agricultural investment.[18]

Shifting prevailing investment patterns means tackling the structural forces that undermine local control in the 'land grabbing' arena. Because politics so profoundly shape the forces underpinning exclusion, politics must be part of the answer too. A shift in approach would require a 'restructuring of the actually-existing power relations'.[19] The emergence or consolidation of active rural citizenship – 'the act of any person taking part in public affairs'[20] – will require political contestation, mediation and negotiation. The 'creation and sustenance of social and political institutions which effectively represent both the diverse and majority interests of rural people' are a critical part of this reconfiguration of the political space in favour of rural groups.[21] International NGOs have so far taken the lead in advocacy on 'land grabbing'. But local-to-global collective action through national and international federations of producer organizations is the indispensable engine for this shift in power relations.

Given the role of law in shaping today's exclusionary deals, legal processes must also be part of the solution. Wherever local rights are insecure, there is a need to reform legislation, and to provide effective mechanisms for translating law reforms into real change. Legal empowerment of local landholders – strengthening legal rights and the capacity to exercise them, and supporting collective action to give real leverage to legal rights – can help increase local control over land and resources. In addition to sustained investment in capacity support, effective legal empowerment would also require rethinking the national and international legal frameworks that regulate investment in the global South. The protection and incentives provided to investors needs to be balanced by robust safeguards for local rights and mechanisms to ensure that investment flows contribute to inclusive sustainable development in recipient countries.

Conclusion

In this context, it is critical to reverse the separation between landownership and land use, and between those who have the authority to allocate land and those who bear the consequences of land allocations. This separation characterizes, in different ways, both national and customary law, as well as the relations between the two. There is a long-standing, complex and often polarized debate about establishing private landownership in Africa. One side emphasizes the alleged economic benefits of creating individual landownership as a way in which to promote capitalistic growth and development. On the other hand, there are those who stress the specificity of land relations in rural Africa, the safety-net function of often idealized customary tenure systems and the alleged inconsistency of ownership rights with such customary systems. Yet another group defends the prerogatives of government in managing land on behalf of the nation. In practice, establishing clearly bounded private ownership rights in contexts where customary systems recognize multiple, overlapping rights over the same resource is likely to prove difficult and to create tensions among competing claimants. Clear, long-term and enforceable use rights may offer legal protection that does not significantly differ from full ownership. And even ownership rights may be lawfully expropriated if specified conditions are complied with, such as public purpose and payment of compensation.

This situation calls for rethinking the presumption of state ownership of land. Ultimately, however, the strength of legal protection depends less on abstract concepts and more on specific safeguards, including substantive protection and legal remedies against compulsory takings. And inventiveness can help devise new categories of legal right that are suited to local realities and that enjoy legal protection comparable to ownership. Recognizing to customary rights equal status to state-granted rights, and establishing the principle of free, prior and informed consent in national law would go a long way towards increasing local control – even where landownership remains vested with the government. This latter principle means that proposed investment projects can go ahead only if they secure the consent of local landholders prior to the final approval of the project. It also means that such consent must be free of coercion and based on provision of adequate information. Making free, prior and informed consent work in practice is riddled with difficulties, not least because local groups are often divided about proposed investment projects. But as practice grows, effective ways for dealing with these challenges can be developed.[22]

Experience in Ghana, where local groups own most of the land and customary chiefs have led much of the deal-making, shows that devolving control to the local level is not enough. Without the necessary checks and balances to ensure downward accountability within the group, and without the needed capacity support, devolution would only provide new routes for dispossession. This is because unaccountable local authorities can strike deals that disadvantage their constituents, and because external players can take advantage of inexperienced local negotiators. This situation raises the big challenge of developing financially sustainable approaches to strengthening local capacity and downward accountability.

In addition, local control is not just about defending rights – it is also about increasing choice, for example by expanding the legal options for landholders to use their land. In countries like Tanzania or Mozambique, villagers can use land, but they cannot rent out land that they claim but do not currently use; governments simply treat this land as 'empty' and allocate it to investors over the heads of local people. Enabling villagers to decide on the use of their land, including through leasing it to an investor if they so wish, coupled with legal safeguards and capacity support to ensure that villagers make informed decisions and get a fair deal, would increase local control in investment processes.[23]

In addition to strengthening local control, there is much that effective public policy and regulation can do to change the structural factors that currently favour exclusionary deals, and to encourage more inclusive forms of agricultural investment. The attractiveness of land as an economic asset would be reduced if governments were adequately to charge companies for it, and if they were to rethink fiscal regimes to remove biases favouring large-scale, mechanized farming. Greater transparency from the early stages of contracting processes, including disclosure of contracts, is a critical precondition for both informed local deliberation and effective public scrutiny. Wise use of public resources can improve the 'investment readiness' of small-scale producers, and increase the commercial appeal of investment models that equitably include local farmers. For example, public resources can support farmer organizations and capacity development, and public provision of roads, storage, power and communications which would offset current pressures that favour larger investments as a way to absorb private shouldering of infrastructure costs.[24] Also, policy responses to the deals are not just about promoting new, more inclusive business models. They are also about tackling old-fashioned labour issues. As a model of investment the main potential benefit of which is in the form of employment creation, land deals increase the urgency of tightening up the legislation, standards and enforcement mechanisms necessary to ensure fair labour relations, including freedom of association and collective bargaining.

The time is ripe for African countries to seek a better deal from incoming investment. Much has changed compared to just a few years ago, when the land rush story started to unfold. Many government officials I have met in different parts of Africa are more aware of the risks involved in large land acquisitions, and are eager to promote inclusive forms of investment that respect local land rights. Widely endorsed international instruments provide guidance on what good practice looks like – particularly the Voluntary Guidelines on the Responsible Governance of Tenure of Land, Fisheries and Forests and, at the regional level, the African Union Framework and Guidelines on Land Policy in Africa. The momentum, awareness, partnerships and citizen engagement catalysed by initiatives such as the Land Matrix provide fertile ground for continued scrutiny and advocacy. In addition, the growing outside interest in Africa's land and natural resources strengthens the negotiating power of African governments vis-à-vis the outside world. As pressures on land increase, governments could be more demanding of prospective investors. Collective action at the regional level can also strengthen the governments' hand.

There is also much that public policy in the investors' home countries can do to regulate agricultural investment. Governments in investor countries have a responsibility to consider the effects of policies that, directly or indirectly, increase pressures on land overseas. They also have a responsibility to properly regulate the activities of their companies operating in Africa. For example, fuller consideration is critical of social aspects in the sustainability criteria that regulate the eligibility of biofuels under the European Renewable Energy Directive. Home governments can establish more effective mechanisms to facilitate the accountability of their companies operating overseas, including both hard law (legislation regulating transnational litigation and requiring disclosure of land deals from companies listed on national stock exchanges, for example) and soft law mechanisms (for instance, complaints before the National Contact Points for the implementation of the Organisation for Economic Co-operation and Development's Guidelines on Multinational Enterprises).[25] Also, developing a more balanced international legal framework governing foreign investment is ultimately in the interest of both home and host countries – today even more so than in the past, as the divide between capital-exporting and capital-importing countries is increasingly blurred. Public opinion in Europe and North America has been much sensitized to 'land grabbing' by media reports, and can put considerable pressure on governments to act.

Diverse development agencies and civil society organizations can promote change through action on multiple levers – from supporting the voices of rural groups to scrutinizing government and private sector action, to brokering innovative partnerships that facilitate more inclusive models of agricultural investment, through to providing technical support to governments in contracting processes. And business can show leadership through innovation in the design of investment models that respond to local aspirations while generating viable returns.

Finally, research can play an important role too. The 'land

Conclusion

191

grabbing' arena is shaped by ingrained perceptions and mis-perceptions – such as the notion that much of Africa's land is empty, or that large plantations are necessary to modernize agriculture. These perceptions fuel prevailing narratives that can have a direct bearing on power relations – because some forms of resource use end up being widely perceived as being 'backward' and therefore best replaced by large land deals. There is a role for research to challenge these accepted 'truths', to provide a deeper and more fine-grained understanding of the unfolding social transformations, and to document what models of agricultural investment work for inclusive sustainable development.

African agriculture is at a crossroads. Decisions taken now will have major repercussions for the livelihoods of many, for decades to come. Some ongoing transformations are largely organic and inevitable – for instance, the growing commercialization of local land relations linked to the intensification of agriculture. For these processes, well-thought-out policy choices can affect the pace of the transformations, and mitigate their adverse impacts. But there is nothing inevitable about exclusionary transnational land deals. Powerful forces are at play, but imaginative policy and practice could push agricultural development in a different direction. Different futures are possible. It is time for the aspirations of rural people to become centre stage in the decision-making processes that shape the future of Africa's agriculture.

# Notes

## 1 Introduction

1 I visited the Massingir district in September 2008, as part of a lesson-sharing event hosted by the Centro Terra Viva, supported by the Ford Foundation and co-funded by the International Institute for Environment and Development's Legal Tools for Citizen Empowerment initiative.

2 www.limpopopn.gov.mz/.

3 Borras et al. (2011).

4 Van der Zaag et al. (2010).

5 Sugar Industry (2012).

6 Oakland Institute (2011a); Hanlon (2011).

7 Deininger et al. (2011).

8 As the book was being finalized, a military coup and armed conflict destabilized Mali, and many foreign investors have now left the country. But a discussion of Mali's experience still provides important insights on the drivers, features and early outcomes of the deals. In fact, some commentators in Mali have argued that the scale and pace of land allocations were among the factors that eroded the legitimacy of the democratic government, and which facilitated political destabilization.

9 The 'common law' legal tradition applies in Ghana and Tanzania, while the 'civil law' tradition is followed in Mali and Mozambique. Important differences in legal policy exist among the four countries. For example, in Mozambique all land is ultimately owned by the state; in Mali private landownership is allowed though much of the land is controlled by the state; in Ghana the greater part of the land is owned by customary chiefdoms, families or individuals; and in Tanzania the responsibility for managing much land is devolved to elected local government bodies.

10 Görgen et al. (2009); Polack (2012).

11 Soto Baquero and Gómez (2012).

12 See the 'Commercial pressures on land' project of the International Land Coalition (www.landcoalition.org/cpl).

13 FAO (2012a).

14 Lunstrum (2007).

15 Alden Wily (2012).

16 For an example from Mozambique's Gurué district, see Hanlon (2011).

17 Huggins (2011); Amanor (2012a); Byerlee (2012); McMichael (2012a); Alden Wily (2012).

18 Oxfam (2011).

19 Borras et al. (2011).

20 Hanlon (2011).

21 See Wightman (2011) on Scotland and Alden Wily (2012) on colonial Africa.

22 Koskenniemi (2001).

## 2 The historical roots

1 Blas (2008).

2 Koponen (1993).

3 Hobsbawm (1987).

4 Alden Wily (2012).

5 Amanor (1999); Berry (2013).

6 King (1977).

7 Plusquellec (1990).

8 Amanor (2012a); Pearce (2012).

9 Byerlee (2012).

10 Amanor (2012a).

11 Ibid.

12 Mamdani (1996).

13 See, for instance, the judgment Sobhuza II v. Miller and Others, Judicial Committee of the Privy Council, [1926] AC 518, at 525. The ruling was issued by the Privy Council, which acted as the final court of the appeal for the British Empire.

14 In French West Africa, for instance, Decree No. 55–580 of 1955 'confirmed' customary rights, reversing earlier colonial policy. See also the Portuguese Decree-Law No. 43,894 of 1961.

15 Alden Wily (2011).

16 See, for instance, Minority Rights Group International (2011). I visited Arusha in February 2011 and March 2012 as part of Legal Tools for Citizen Empowerment, an initiative implemented by the International Institute for Environment and Development together with the Tanzania Natural Resource Forum.

17 The 1911 Anglo-Maasai Agreement is available at www.masaikenya.org/MAASAI_COLONIAL_AGREEMENT_1911.pdf.

18 Askew et al. (2013).

19 Minority Rights Group International (2011); Hicks (2012).

20 Minority Rights Group International (2011).

21 TNRF (2011); Minority Rights Group International (2011); Askew et al. (2013). There is much material on this conflict, including a report, a brief and a video, at www.tnrf.org/loliondo.

22 Lyimo (2010).

23 Lane (1994); Tenga (2008).

24 Amanor (1999).

25 Hermele (1988).

26 Alden Wily (2012).

27 In contrast to Marxist-Leninist socialism, 'African socialism' tended to consider socialism not as an outcome to pursue through class struggle, but as a way of life traditional to African society (Gentili 1995).

28 *Code Domanial et Foncier*, Law No. 86–91 of 1986.

29 In Mali, Law No. 61–30 of 1961, later replaced by Ordinance No. 74–27 of 1974; in Mozambique, Law No. 6/79 of 1979.

30 Amanor (1999).

31 Tiffen and Mortimore (1990).

32 Amanor (1999).

33 UNCTAD (2009).

34 Ibid.

35 Gereffi (1999); Vorley (2002).

36 Fox and Vorley (2004).

37 Vorley (2002); De Castro et al. (2012).

38 Amanor (2012b).

39 Vorley (2002).

40 In Mali, the Land Code (*Code Domanial et Foncier*) of 2000–02; in Mozambique, the Land Act of 1997; and in Tanzania, the Land Act and the Village Land Act of 1999.

41 I visited cocoa-growing areas in Ghana's Ashanti, Western and Brong Ahafo Regions in March 2010 and January 2011, as part of a project to secure local land rights supported by the Bill & Melinda Gates Foundation and implemented by the International Institute for Environment and Development together with the Land Resource Management Centre in Kumasi.

42 Peters (2004, 2009); Woodhouse (2012).

43 Chauveau and Colin (2007).

44 I carried out fieldwork in Mali's Inner Niger Delta in February 2006, as part of a multi-country study on changes in customary law supported by the Food and Agriculture Organization of the United Nations. I would like to honour the memory of Salmana Cissé, who did the fieldwork with me and devoted much of his life to documenting the delta's complex and fascinating customary resource management systems.

45 Downs and Reyna (1988); Raynaut (1988); Amanor (1999); Peters (2004, 2009); Woodhouse (2012).

46 For example, on the ascent of Burkibabé cocoa farmers in Côte d'Ivoire in the 1990s, see Chaveau and Colin (2007) and Amanor (2012a).

47 Doka and Monimart (2004), writing about women's seclusion in Niger.

48 Toulmin et al. (2004).

49 Vorley (2002).

50 Woodhouse (2012).

51 Tiffen et al. (1994).

52 Murton (1999).

53 Woodhouse (2012).

54 Djiré (2007).

55 Alhassan and Manuh (2005).

56 Cotula and Toulmin (2004).

57 Kuba and Lentz (2006).

58 Mathieu et al. (1998); Huggins et al. (2005); Richards and Chauveau (2007).

## 3 Scale, geography and drivers

1 The conference took place on 22–24 June 2010. I attended the Farmland Opportunities Day to present on the risks involved in land acquisitions. This chapter builds on research undertaken for Cotula (2012a) and Cotula and Polack (2012).

2 Hurn (2012).

3 Oxfam (2011: 2).

4 See farmlandgrab.org/ and www.commercialpressuresonland.org/.

5 Friis and Reenberg (2010).

6 Deininger et al. (2011).

7 Polack et al. (2013).

8 Schoneveld (2011).

9 Ravanera (2011); Polack (2012); Soto Baquero and Gómez (2012).

10 landportal.info/landmatrix, data as of 19 December 2012. The ranking is based on land area acquired since 2000. Sudan, Ethiopia, Madagascar and Mozambique follow suit, and the Matrix suggests that 35 per cent of the land acquired globally is in Africa. Because the Land Matrix largely depends on public reporting of deals, it is possible that the importance of recipient countries that have attracted less media attention, for instance in Europe, North America and Oceania, are underestimated in the data set.

11 Schoneveld (2011).

12 landportal.info/landmatrix.

13 Anseeuw et al. (2012a).

14 However, it is likely that deals concluded farther back in time are under-reported, not least because media attention really took off from 2007 onwards, and that the Matrix data set underestimates the scale of mining, forestry and tourism concessions, owing to the lower level of media interest in deals in these sectors.

15 See, for example, Verhoeven and Woertz (2012) and two blogs at ruralmodernity.wordpress.com/2012/04/27/the-land-matrix-much-ado-about-nothing/ and www.chinaafricarealstory.com/2012/04/zombie-chinese-land-grabs-in-africa.html?spref=tw.

16 Cotula et al. (2009).

17 Görgen et al. (2009).

18 Deininger et al. (2011).

19 See, for instance, Oakland Institute (2011c, 2011d).

20 Deininger et al. (2011).

21 According to Friis and Reenberg (2010).

22 Deininger et al. (2011).

23 Contracts available at www.leiti.org.lr and farmlandgrab.org/home/post_special?filter=contracts.

24 Deininger et al. (2011).

25 Wisborg (2012).

26 Figures from Djiré et al. (2012).

27 Schoneveld et al. (2010).

28 Toulmin et al. (2011); Deininger et al. (2011); Anseeuw et al. (2012a).

29 Deininger et al. (2011). These issues are further discussed in Chapter 5.

30 See for instance Mujenja and Wonani (2012).

31 Djiré et al. (2012); Faye et al. (2011).

32 Kaarhus (2011).

33 Data on foreign investment flows in this paragraph come from UNCTAD (2012).

34 Land deals area from Deininger et al. (2011). Calculations on mining concessions from Cotula (2011), based on data from www.leiti.org.lr.

35 Anseeuw et al. (2012b).

36 Pensions & Investments (2010).

37 Hanlon (2011) on Mozambique; Tekleberhan (2012) on Ethiopia.

38 Kiishweko (2012).

39 Djiré et al. (2012) and Hanlon (2011), respectively.

40 The session took place on 4 October 2011.

41 Graham et al. (2010).

42 Deininger et al. (2011).

43 I calculated this percentage on the basis of data reported in Faye et al. (2011).

44 Hilhorst et al. (2011).

45 Ibid.

46 Anseeuw et al. (2012a); Zoomers (2010).

47 The contracts were accessed on 12 May 2011 from www.ethiopian-gateway.com/eaportal/node/836.

48 Cotula and Toulmin (2004).

49 Burnod et al. (2011).

50 Blas and Wallis (2009). It seems this deal is not going forward.

51 Anseeuw et al. (2012a).

52 Oakland Institute (2011a).

53 Richardson (2010); Hall (2012).

54 Anseeuw and Boche (2012).

55 Hall (2012).

56 Ibid.

57 See Cotula (2012a) for some examples.

58 Hall (2012).

59 Eleven of the twenty-three publicly available BITs signed by Mauritius are with African countries; see www.unctadxi.org/templates/docsearch_____779.aspx.

60 Woertz (2009).

61 Johnstone and Mazo (2011); De Castro et al. (2012).

62 www.mofa.gov.sa/sites/mofaen/ServicesAndInformation/news/statements/Pages/NewsArticleID88796.aspx.

63 Journal du Mali (2010).

64 www.farmland-grab.org/home/post_special?filter=contracts.

65 Deininger et al. (2011).

66 www.farmlandgrab.org/post/view/18943.

67 www.farmlandgrab.org/home/post_special?filter=contracts. This venture is owned by a dual Ethiopian and Saudi national, but given the investor profile it is best viewed as an acquisition by a member of the national elite.

68 Deininger et al. (2011).

69 Woertz (2011).

70 Görgen et al. (2009); Cotula et al. (2011).

71 Anderlini (2008); Xinhua News Agency (2008).

72 On the Going Global strategy, see www.gov.cn/node_11140/2006-03/15/content_227686.htm, accessed in Chinese, read through translation from Google Translate.

73 Smaller et al. (2012).

74 Ibid.

75 Görgen et al. (2009).

76 Stensrud Ekman (n.d.). See also Bräutigam (2009).

77 Buckley (2011).

78 www.ethiopian-gateway.com/eaportal/node/836, accessed 12 May 2011.

79 Cotula (2011).

80 Smaller et al. (2012).

81 Buckley (forthcoming).

82 One of the two deals is available at www.leiti.org.lr, the other is on file with the author.

83 www.rspo.org/sites/default/files/Summary%20Report%20of%20Planning%20and%20Management%20Olam%20NPP.pdf.

84 Campos Mello (2011).

85 Clements and Fernandes (2012).

86 Guarani (2007); Pearce (2012).

87 OECD (2010).

88 See, for example, Oakland Institute (2011d).

89 I calculated this percentage on the basis of the list of contracts accessed on 12 May 2011 from www.ethiopian-gateway.com/eaportal/node/836.

90 Deininger et al. (2011).

91 IANS (2011).

92 Ullenberg (2009).

93 Rowden (2011).

94 Schoneveld (2011).

95 Ibid.

96 Ibid.

97 Sulle and Nelson (2009).

98 Benjaminsen et al. (2011).

99 GIIN (2011).

100 Oakland Institute (2011b).

101 Anseeuw et al. (2012a).

102 Schoneveld (2011).

103 Ibid.

104 Nguiffo and Schwartz (2012); Pearce (2012).

105 Sulle and Nelson (2009).

106 Ibid.; Nhantumbo and Salomão (2010).

107 Tsikata and Yaro (2011), Wisborg (2012) and personal observation.

108 Re:Common (2012) and personal observation.

109 Nhantumbo and Salomão (2010).

110 Pearce (2012).

111 Sulle and Nelson (2009).

112 Deininger et al. (2011).

113 Cotula et al. (2011).

114 Benjaminsen et al. (2011).

115 Hanlon (2011); FIAN (2012).

116 Cotula et al. (2011).

117 Hawkins (2010); FAO (2010).

118 Buxton et al. (2012).

119 OECD (2010).

120 Ibid.; Buxton et al. (2012).

121 OECD/FAO (2010); De Castro et al. (2012).

122 Deininger et al. (2011).

123 Von Braun (2008).

124 OECD/FAO (2010) and FAO et al. (2011).

125 See www.fao.org/worldfoodsituation/wfs-home/foodpricesindex/en/.

126 OECD/FAO (2010).

127 Roxburgh et al. (2010).

128 Directive 2003/30/EC of the European Parliament and of the Council of 8 May 2003 on the Promotion of the Use of Biofuels or Other Renewable Fuels for Transport, Article 3(b)(ii).

129 Directive 2009/28/EC of the European Parliament and of the Council of 23 April 2009 on the Promotion of the Use of Energy from Renewable Sources, Article 3.

130 Borras et al. (2010).

131 Key readings on this complex debate include Lipton (1977, 2010); Berry and Cline (1979); Dyer (1998); Byres (2004); Federico (2005); Collier (2008); Deininger and Byerlee (2012).

132 Hawkins (2010).

133 Cited in Oakland Institute (2011e: 4), Holt-Gimenez (2012) and www.igc-group.co.uk/styled/styled-29/styled-33/index.html.

134 GRAIN (2012).

135 For a discussion of these issues, see Li (2012).

136 Deininger et al. (2011: 63).

137 Dolan and Humphrey (2004); Reardon et al. (2009).

138 Deininger and Byerlee (2012).

139 Amanor (2012b: 744).

140 This case is discussed as an example of how structural factors underpin the global land rush by Amanor (2012b). The analysis that follows draws on visits to Ghana I undertook in 2004 and 2005 as part of research funded by the United Kingdom's Department for International Development, and on Takane (2004), Fold and Gough (2008) and Amanor (2012b).

141 Unilever (2010).

## 4 *In the shadow of the law*

1 Campos Mello (2011). This chapter draws on research that I carried out for Cotula (2012c), Vorley et al. (2012) and Polack et al. (2013).

2 Lapucheque (2011); Clements and Fernandes (2012). This initiative was briefly discussed in Chapter 3.

3 Reuters (2009).

4 IANS (2011).

5 Campos Mello (2011), my translation.

6 Lapucheque (2011).

7 Deininger and Byerlee (2012).

8 Anseeuw et al. (2012a).

9 BBC (2010).

10 Deininger et al. (2011).

11 Wiggins et al. (2010).

12 Data from 2000 available at data.un.org/Data.aspx?d=PopDiv&f=variableID%3a14.

13 Djiré et al. (2012).

14 See, for instance, Fischer et al. (2002).

15 Chouquer (2012).

16 See Chapter 2.

17 Lund (2011).

18 Mosley (2012); Human Rights Watch (2012a).

19 Mensah Sarbah (1897: 55–6), cited by Amanor (1999: 48).

20 Mnookin and Kornhauser (1979).

21 Jul-Larsen et al. (2006). I visited Sanso in November 2008 for legal literacy trainings run as part of Legal Tools for Citizen Empowerment, an initiative led by the International Institute for Environment and Development in partnership with Malian organization Groupe d'Etude et de Recherche en Sociologie et Droit Appliqué – a group linked to what is now the University of Law and Political Science in Bamako. The mine in Sanso opened in 2001 and closed in 2009, though treatment of stockpiles was expected to continue until 2013.

22 Jul-Larsen et al. (2006); Keita et al. (2008).

23 Jul-Larsen et al. (2006), my translation.

24 Keita et al. (2008).

25 Article 3 of Mozambique's Land Act of 1997, which confirms constitutional provisions.

26 Jul-Larsen et al. (2006).

27 See, for instance, Djiré (2007), writing about a municipality

close to the capital city, Bamako.

28  Deininger (2003).

29  Article 28(b) of Mali's Land Code (*Code Domanial et Foncier*) of 2000–02.

30  Articles 12, 13 and 14 of Mozambique's Land Act of 1997, and Article 18 of Tanzania's Village Land Act of 1999. See also Knight (2011).

31  See Uganda's Land Act of 1998, Namibia's Communal Land Rights Act of 2002, and Niger's Rural Code of 1993. On Madagascar, see Teyssier (2010).

32  Article 127 of the Land Code (*Code Domanial et Foncier*) of 1986, my translation.

33  Articles 43–48 of the Land Code of 2000–02; Pastoral Charter of 2001.

34  Djiré (2007).

35  Decree No. 01-040 of 2001.

36  For instance, under Article 29 of Tanzania's Village Land Act of 1999.

37  Alden Wily (2011).

38  Articles 59–60.

39  Deininger et al. (2011).

40  Tanzania's Village Land Act of 1999, Article 4(2). See also Alden Wily (2011).

41  Norfolk and Tanner (2007); Nhantumbo and Salomão (2010).

42  Oakland Institute (2011b); Sulle and Nelson (forthcoming).

43  TNRF (2012).

44  Articles 16 and 21 of Law No. 11/022 of 2011.

45  www.tic.co.tz/TICWebSite. nsf/2e9cafac3e472ee5882572850027 f544/729d4c075f2b03fc432572d10024 bea6?OpenDocument.

46  The discussion of Tanzanian legislation summarizes provisions contained in the Land Act of 1999, the Village Land Act of 1999 and the Land (Amendment) Act of 2004. The rules are somewhat more complicated than presented here. For example, the village assembly, not the central government, has the power to authorize allocations of village land below 250 hectares. Also, investors can acquire lands in other ways too. For example, they can sublease the land or create a joint venture with Tanzanian citizens, though this route has not been used much for large agricultural investments.

47  Kasanga and Kotey (2001).

48  Articles 11 and 267 of the Constitution of 1992.

49  Article 36(8) of the Constitution of 1992.

50  See, for instance, Amanor (1999); Schoneveld et al. (2011).

51  Boamah (2012).

52  See Mali's Investment Code of 1991, as revised in 2005; Mozambique's Investment Act of 1993; and the Tanzania Investment Act of 1997.

53  UNCTAD (2012).

54  Article 2 of the Tanzania Investment Act of 1997; in Mozambique, Article 21 of the Investment Act of 1993, and Article 6 of Decree No. 14/93 of 1993, as amended by Decree No. 36/95 of 1995.

55  Data on the dominance of small-scale farmers' investment in agriculture is presented in FAO (2012a).

56 In Mali, Decree No. 08–346 of 2008, amended by Decree No. 09–318 of 2009 (Article 16); in Mozambique, Decree No. 45/2004 of 2004 (Article 14).

57 Nhantumbo and Salomão (2010), Oakland Institute (2011a) and Schoneveld et al. (2011).

58 Onoma (2010).

59 This section summarizes a detailed legal analysis of relevant investment and human rights treaties and jurisprudence (Cotula 2012b). Readers interested in greater detail, including specific references to treaties and cases, are referred to that book.

60 Guideline 12.

61 Ruggie (2011).

62 OECD (2011).

63 IFC (2012).

64 De Schutter (2009).

65 See www.rspo.org/ and rsb. epfl.ch/, respectively.

66 The principles were first proposed in early 2010 and are available at www.responsible agroinvestment.org/rai/node/256.

67 See www.fao.org/news/ story/en/item/162895/icode/.

68 UNCTAD (2012).

69 Protocol on the Establish-ment of an African Court on Human and Peoples' Rights, adopted on 10 June 1998 and entered into force on 25 January 2004 (www.achpr.org/english/_info/court_en.html).

70 See, for instance, De Schut-ter (2009).

71 Ruggie (2011).

72 See, for example, the cases *Mayagna (Sumo) Awas Tingni Com-munity* v. *Nicaragua* and *Saramaka People* v. *Suriname*, both decided by the Inter-American Court on Human Rights (on 31 August 2001, www1.umn.edu/humanrts/iachr/AwasTingnicase.html, and on 28 November 2007, www.forest peoples.org/.../suriname_iachr_saramaka_judgment_nov07_eng. pdf, respectively), and the case *Centre for Minority Rights Devel-opment and Minority Rights Group International on behalf of Endorois Welfare Council* v. *Kenya*, decided by the African Commission on Human and Peoples' Rights (Communication No. 276/2003).

73 Most-favoured-nation clauses extend to a protected investment any more favourable treatment accorded by the same state to another investment.

74 Convention concerning Indigenous and Tribal Peoples in Independent Countries, adopted on 27 June 1989 and entered into force on 5 September 1991, available at http://www2.ohchr. org/english/law/indigenous.htm. The Central African Republic is the only African country to have ratified the Convention.

75 28 U.S.C. § 1350. On the growing number of cases brought under this provision, see the web-site www.business-humanrights. org/Categories/Lawlawsuits/Lawsuitsregulatoryaction/Alien TortClaimsActUSA.

76 *Connelly* v. *Rio Tinto Corp plc*, [1997] All ER 843; and *Lubbe and Others* v. *Cape plc*, [2000] 4 All ER 268.

77 *Connelly* v. *Rio Tinto Corp plc* and *Lubbe and Others* v. *Cape plc*.

78 Hepburn (2012).

79 See, for example, Kenney-Lazar (2012).

80 Polack (2012); Ravanera (2011).

81 Görgen et al. (2009); Kenney-Lazar (2012).

82 Prime Minister Decree No. 13 of 2012.

83 The resulting report is Cotula et al. (2012).

84 Respectively at www.leiti.org.lr and www.moa.gov.et/node/150.

85 The law is the Liberia Extractive Industry Transparency Initiative Act of 2009, which applies to extractive industries but also to agriculture and forestry.

86 farmlandgrab.org/home/post_special?filter=contracts.

87 Cotula (2011).

88 Nguiffo and Schwartz (2012).

89 Tienhaara (2012).

90 Djiré et al. (2012).

91 Unless indicated otherwise, the findings discussed below are based on Cotula (2011). Some of the deals reviewed have been discontinued.

92 Deininger et al. (2011).

93 Comité Technique Foncier et Développement (2010); Cochet and Merlet (2011).

94 On the human rights and sustainable development concerns linked to stabilization clauses, see Amnesty International UK (2003, 2005); Shemberg (2009); Leader (2006); and Cotula (2008, 2010).

95 Cited in Nguiffo and Schwartz (2012).

96 Ibid.

97 Djiré et al. (2012).

98 Deininger et al. (2011).

99 Nguiffo and Schwartz (2012).

100 Oxfam (2011).

101 Sulle and Nelson (2009); Askew et al. (2013).

102 See Chapter 2.

103 Nguiffo and Schwartz (2012).

104 Askew et al. (2013).

105 For a discussion of power relations within large-scale natural resource investments in Africa, with a focus on the petroleum sector, see Cotula (2012b).

106 Mattei and Nader (2008: 107).

107 Interview with a CNOP official, August 2012.

108 Dhliwayo (forthcoming).

109 Hunt (1990).

## 5 Winners and losers

1 I briefly visited the Pru district in the Brong Ahafo Region and the Yendi district in the Northern Region of Ghana in September/October 2012. This section draws on the available literature about land deals in Africa, and in places it uses examples from these sites as illustration. The name of the farmer has been changed to protect his identity.

2 At the time of the field visit, one cedi was worth about half a dollar ($0.52).

3 Wisborg (2012).

4 See, for instance, Friends of the Earth (2010).

5 Environmental issues are a critical aspect of assessing the outcomes of the deals. To date, however, rigorous evidence of actual environmental impacts remains limited, and these aspects are not discussed here.

6 Oakland Institute (2011b); Human Rights Watch (2012a, 2012b).

7 Schoneveld et al. (2011); Tsikata and Yaro (2011); Wisborg (2012).

8 Deininger et al. (2011).

9 Oakland Institute (2011c).

10 Nhantumbo and Salomão (2010); Hanlon (2011).

11 Oxfam (2011).

12 Sulle and Nelson (2009).

13 Deininger et al. (2011).

14 Oxfam (2011).

15 Anseeuw et al. (2012b).

16 This statement refers to documentation of actual land dispossession, not to warnings about the possible future impacts of the deals. The latter warnings often involve very bold figures.

17 See Chapter 3.

18 Polack et al. (2013).

19 Oakland Institute (2011c: 28).

20 Ibid.

21 BBC (2012).

22 Human Rights Watch (2012a, 2012b).

23 See, for instance, Schoneveld et al. (2011).

24 Hertzog et al. (2012).

25 According to Sulle and Nelson (2009, forthcoming).

26 Oakland Institute (2011b).

27 Sulle and Nelson (2009, forthcoming).

28 See, for example, Article 3(1)(g) of Tanzania's Land Act of 1999.

29 Deininger et al. (2011).

30 See Chapter 4.

31 Anseeuw et al. (2012b).

32 Not his real name.

33 These considerations are based on Boamah (2012), and on thinking developed by Lund (2011).

34 Deininger et al. (2011).

35 Maertens and Swinnen (2009).

36 Anseeuw et al. (2011).

37 See, for instance, Deininger et al. (2011).

38 On gender issues in the land rush, see Daley (2011).

39 This paragraph is based on Mujenja and Wonani (2012).

40 Li (2011).

41 Data adapted from Deininger et al. (2011). This data is discussed by Li (2011).

42 Deininger et al. (2011: 63–4).

43 Ibid.

44 Carrington (2011).

45 Valentino (2011).

46 Deininger et al. (2011: 67).

47 Bugri and King (2012).

48 Tsikata and Yaro (2011).

49 See, for example, a contract available at www.leiti.org.lr.

50 Moyo (2011). Beynon et al. (1998) present different but broadly comparable figures.

51 Deininger and Byerlee (2012).

52 Ibid.

53 Bidwells (2012: 4).

54 See, for instance, Deininger et al. (2011). For a brief discussion of cases from Mozambique and Tanzania, see Chapter 4.

55 The Kolongo Declaration was issued on 20 November 2010 and is available at pubs.iied.org/G03055.html.

56 Polack et al. (2013).

57 Djiré et al. (2012).

58 CILSS (2005). I visited the Ségou and Mopti regions of Mali on several occasions between 2002 and 2011. This section benefited greatly from ongoing conversations with Jamie Skinner at the International Institute for Environment and Development.

59 Jamin and Doucet (1994); Aw and Diemer (2005).

60 Adamczewski (2011).

61 Jamin and Doucet (1994: 71).

62 Aw and Diemer (2005); Adamczewski (2011).

63 Djiré et al. (2012); Hertzog et al. (2012).

64 The appeal is reproduced in Adamczewski (2011).

65 Djiré et al. (2012). See Chapter 3 for more precise figures.

66 My translation.

67 Djiré et al. (2012).

68 See www.afdb.org/filead min/uploads/afdb/Documents/Environmental-and-Social-Assessments/mali%20fr.pdf.

69 Brondeau (2009).

70 Barry (2012).

71 Wymenga et al. (2005).

72 Brondeau (2009).

73 Wetlands International (n.d.).

74 While rainfalls present substantial fluctuations between years, they have tended to decrease over the past fifty years (CILSS 2005). Drops in rainfall of up to a third have been documented, for instance, in Mopti (for the period 1920–89; Moorehead 1997) and in Madiama, a municipality located in Djenné district (for the period 1950–2000; Moore 2005). Major droughts took place in the 1970s and 1980s. The decrease in rainfall has in turn led to a contraction of the flooded area, and to a shortening of the duration of floodings (Moorehead 1997; CILSS 2005). A dam built upstream in Sélingué, Mali, has also reduced the flooded area (Wetlands International n.d.).

75 See Cotula and Cissé (2006) for a more detailed account.

76 Article 4 of the Charte de l'Eau du Bassin du Niger, adopted on 30 April 2008, available at www.ecolex.org/ecolex/ledge/view/RecordDetails;DIDPFDSIjsession id=397CB48FB7A5D24D8C6819F0 18C917E8?id=TRE-146761&index= treaties.

77 Garuba (2011); Jägerskog et al. (2012).

78 Jägerskog et al. (2012).

79 See Chapter 1.

80 Hammar (2012). I visited Manica Province in January/February 2010 to carry out a mid-term review of the Community Land Fund, an initiative to support the delimitation of community lands financed by a consortium of donors then led by the United

Kingdom's Department for International Development.

81 Anseeuw and Boche (2012).

82 World Bank (2011). Data refer to the annual average for the period 2000–09.

83 Agencia de Informação de Moçambique (2012).

84 DNEAP/MPD (2010).

85 UNDP (2011).

86 DNEAP/MPD (2010).

87 World Bank (2011). Data refer to annual average for the period 2000–09. Because of rapid demographic growth, per capita figures of economic growth are significantly lower.

88 Cotula (2011).

89 Deininger et al. (2011); FAO (2012a).

90 Mujenja and Wonani (2012).

91 Majid Cooke et al. (2011).

92 FAO (2012b).

93 De Schutter (2011).

94 Cotula (2011).

95 Lavers (2011).

96 Evidence suggests that allocated land areas to date account for relatively small shares of national land in any given country, although as discussed the deals may target the best lands.

97 For a discussion of these issues, see Kenney-Lazar (2012).

98 *Petroleum Development (Trucial Coast) Ltd* v. *Sheikh of Abu Dhabi*, 18 ILR (1951) 144, p. 149. I travelled to Abu Dhabi in November 2012 to present at a workshop on 'Policy options for food insecure countries', organized by the Crown Prince's Court and Chatham House.

99 Woertz (2011).

100 McMichael (2012b).

101 Baker (2012).

102 See, for instance, the media reports available at www.farmlandgrab.org/.

103 On the economic, political and social risks involved in land deals, see Earth Security Initiative (2012).

104 Article 33 of the Treaty Establishing the European Community, now Article 39 of the Treaty on the Functioning of the European Union.

105 See Chapter 3.

106 Data and much analysis in this paragraph are from De Castro et al. (2012).

107 FAO (2012a).

## 6 Conclusion

1 Peluso and Lund (2011: 669).

2 Fairhead et al. (2012).

3 Lund (2011); Lund and Boone (2013).

4 Li (2012: 10).

5 Colin and Woodhouse (2010).

6 Mathieu et al. (2003).

7 Djiré et al. (2012).

8 Polanyi (1944: 40).

9 Vorley et al. (2012).

10 Anseeuw et al. (2012a).

11 Fox (1990: 3).

12 Anseeuw et al. (2012a).

13 This analysis draws on Hall et al. (2011).

14 See also Anseeuw et al. (2012a).

15 Behnke and Scoones (1992); Thébaud (2002); Hesse and MacGregor (2006).

16 Polack et al. (2013).

17  Vorley (2002).

18  For a discussion of inclusive agricultural investments, see Vermeulen and Cotula (2010); Cotula and Leonard (2010); and Vorley et al. (2012).

19  Li (2011: 292).

20  Gaventa (2002: 3).

21  Fox (1990: 2).

22  At the time of writing, the Food and Agriculture Organization of the United Nations and the Roundtable on Sustainable Biofuels were both developing practical guidance on how to implement the principle of free, prior and informed consent in relation to agricultural investments.

23  See also Sulle and Nelson (forthcoming).

24  Vorley et al. (2012). Through the African Union's Comprehensive Africa Agriculture Development Programme, African governments pledged to increase public investment in agriculture to 10 per cent of annual national budgets. See www.nepad-caadp. net/about-caadp.php.

25  See Toulmin et al. (2011).

# References

Adamczewski, A. (2011) 'Grands investisseurs privés versus "colons" de la zone Office du Niger au Mali: où on est avec la course au foncier?', Presentation made at the Journée Pôle Foncier 'Acquisitions foncières à grande echelle au sud', Montpellier, 15 September, on file with the author.

Agencia de Informação de Moçambique (2012) 'Mozambique: Guebuza praises economic growth in Manica', 27 April, allafrica.com/stories/201204300089.html.

Alden Wily, L. (2011) *The Tragedy of Public Lands: The Fate of the Commons under Global Commercial Pressure*, Rome: International Land Coalition, www.landcoalition.org/publications/accelerate-legal-recognition-commons-group-owned-private-property-limit-involuntary-lan.

— (2012) 'Looking back to see forward: the legal niceties of land theft in land rushes', *Journal of Peasant Studies*, 39(2): 751–76.

Alhassan, O. and T. Manuh (2005) *Land Registration in Eastern and Western Regions, Ghana*, London: IIED, pubs.iied.org/12522IIED.html.

Amanor, K. S. (1999) *Global Restructuring and Land Rights in Ghana*, Nordiska Afrikainstitutet, Uppsala.

— (2012a) *Land Governance in Africa: How Historical Context Has Shaped Key Contemporary Issues Relating to Policy on Land*, Rome: International Land Coalition, Framing the Debate Series no. 1.

— (2012b) 'Global resource grabs, agribusiness concentration and the smallholder: two West African case studies', *Journal of Peasant Studies*, 39(3/4): 731–49.

Amnesty International UK (2003) *Human Rights on the Line: The Baku–Tbilisi–Ceyhan Pipeline Project*, London: Amnesty International UK, www.amnesty.org.uk/uploads/documents/doc_14538.pdf.

— (2005) *Contracting out of Human Rights: The Chad–Cameroon Pipeline Project*, London: Amnesty International UK, www.amnesty.org/en/library/info/POL34/012/2005.

Anderlini, J. (2008) 'China eyes overseas land in food push', *Financial Times*, 8 May, us.ft.com/ftgateway/superpage.ft?news_id=ft00508200814383830 16&page=2/.

Anseeuw, W. and M. Boche (2012)

'Global land deals – the case of South African farmers investing in Africa', Paper presented at the international conference on 'Global land grabbing II', Ithaca, NY, 17–19 October.

Anseeuw, W., A. Ducastel and J.-J. Gabas (2011) 'The end of the African peasant? From investment funds and finance value chains to peasant related questions', Paper presented at the International Conference on Global Land Grabbing, Brighton, 6–8 April, www.future-agricultures. org/index.php?option=com_docman&task=cat_view&gid=1552&limit=10&limitstart=30 &order=hits&dir=DESC&Item id=971.

Anseeuw, W., L. Alden Wily, L. Cotula and M. Taylor (2012a) *Land Rights and the Rush for Land: Findings of the Global Commercial Pressures on Land Research Project*, Rome: International Land Coalition, www.landcoalition.org/cpl/CPL-synthesis-report.

Anseeuw, W., M. Boche, T. Breu, M. Giger, J. Lay, P. Messerli and K. Nolte (2012b) *Transnational Land Deals for Agriculture in the Global South. Analytical Report Based on the Land Matrix Database*, Bern/Montpellier/Hamburg: CDE/CIRAD/GIGA.

Askew, K., F. Maganga and R. Odgaard (2013) 'Of land and legitimacy: a tale of two lawsuits', *Africa*, forthcoming.

Aw, D. and G. Diemer (2005) *Making a Large Irrigation Scheme Work: A Case Study from Mali*, Washington, DC: World Bank, siteresources.worldbank. org/INTARD/Resources/making_a_large_scale_irrigation_system_work_DID. pdf.

Baker, A. (2012) 'Desert dreams: can the Middle Eastern country of Qatar learn to feed itself?', *Time*, 19 November, science.time.com/2012/11/19/desert-dreams-can-the-middle-eastern-country-of-qatar-learn-to-feed-itself/.

Barry, O. (2012) 'Energie – "la construction du Barrage de Fomi sur le Niger débutera en 2013", selon James Tounkara', *MediaGuinée*, 7 July, www.media guinee. net/ fichiers/blog999.php?code =calb4229&langue=fr &type =rub40&PHPSESSID=362 975 dc1be14ef71ac5afde 907661b0.

Bayart, J.-F. (1993) *The State in Africa: The Politics of the Belly*, London: Longman.

BBC (2010) 'Deadly riots in Mozambique over rising prices', 1 September, www.bbc.co.uk/news/world-africa-11150063.

— (2012) 'Why poverty? Episode 7: The great land rush', BBC4 video documentary, 4 December, www.bbc.co.uk/programmes/p010jx6v.

Behnke, R. H. and I. Scoones (1992) *Rethinking Range Ecology: Implications for Rangeland Management in Africa*, London: International Institute for Environment and Development, Issue Paper no. 33, pubs.iied. org/7282IIED.html.

Benjaminsen, T., I. Bryceson, F. Maganga and T. Refseth (2011) 'Conservation and land grabbing in Tanzania', Paper presented at the International Conference on Global Land Grabbing, Brighton, 6–8 April, www.future-agricultures. org/index.php?option=com_ docman&task=cat_view&gid=15 52&limit=10&limitstart=30&ord er=hits&dir=DESC&Itemid=971.

Berry, A. R. and W. R. Cline (1979) *Agrarian Structure and Productivity in Developing Countries*, Baltimore, MD, and London: Johns Hopkins University Press.

Berry, S. (2013) 'Questions of ownership: proprietorship and control in a changing rural terrain. A case study from Ghana', *Africa*, forthcoming.

Beynon, J. with S. Akroyd, A. Duncan and S. Jones (1998) *Financing the Future: Options for Agricultural Research and Extension in Sub-Saharan Africa*, Oxford: Oxford Policy Management, www.opml.co.uk/sites/ opml/files/o_CONTS.pdf.

Bidwells (2012) *Agriculture: Opportunities and Pitfalls. Understanding the Asset Class*, Cambridge: Bidwells, www.bidwells.co.uk/cms. php?pageid=413.

Blas, J. (2008) 'UN warns of food "neo-colonialism"', *Financial Times*, 19 August, www. ft.com/cms/s/0/3d3ede92-6e02-11dd-b5df-0000779fd18c. html#axzz20DdLBT9m.

Blas, J. and W. Wallis (2009) 'Buyer sees profit in warlord's land', *Financial Times*, 10 January.

Boamah, F. (2012) 'How and why chiefs formalize relationships with land users in recent times: illuminating the politics of land dispossessions during land transactions for biofuels investments in Ghana', Paper presented at the international conference on 'Global land grabbing II', Ithaca, NY, 17–19 October, www.cornell-land project.org/papers/.

Borras, S. and J. S. Franco (2010) 'From threat to opportunity?: problems with the idea of a "code of conduct" for land grabbing', *Yale Human Rights and Development Law Journal*, 13(1).

Borras, S., P. McMichael and I. Scoones (2010) 'The politics of biofuels, land and agrarian change: editors' introduction', *Journal of Peasant Studies*, 37(4): 575–92.

Borras, S., D. Fig and S. Molsalve Suárez (2011) 'The politics of agrofuels and mega-land and water deals: insights from the ProCana case, Mozambique', *Review of African Political Economy*, 38(128): 215–34.

Bräutigam, D. (2009) *The Dragon's Gift: The Real Story of China in Africa*, Oxford: Oxford University Press.

— (2011) *China in Africa: What*

*Can Western Donors Learn?*, Report prepared for Norfund, www.norfund.no/images/ stories/publikasjoner/andre_ publikasjoner/Norfund_China_ in_Africa.pdf.

Brondeau, F. (2009) 'Un "grenier pour l'Afrique de l'Ouest"? Enjeux economiques et perspectives de développement dans les systèmes irrigués de l'Office du Niger (Mali)', *Géocarrefour*, 84(1–2): 43–53.

Buckley, L. (2011) 'Eating bitter to taste sweet: an ethnographic sketch of a Chinese agriculture project in Senegal', Paper presented at the International Conference on Global Land Grabbing, Brighton, 6–8 April, www.future-agricultures. org/index.php?option=com_ docman&task=cat_view&gid=15 52&limit=10&limitstart=30&ord er=hits&dir=DESC&Itemid=971.

— (forthcoming) *Chinese Agriculture Goes Global: Food Security for All?*, London: International Institute for Environment and Development.

Bugri, J. and R. King (2012) *Gender Dimensions of Agricultural Investments: Case Studies from Ghana*, unpublished research report.

Burnod, P., M. Gingembre, R. Andrianirina Ratsialonana and R. Ratovoarinony (2011) 'From international land deals to local informal agreements: regulations of and local reactions to agricultural investments in Madagascar', Paper presented at the International Conference on 'Global land grabbing', Brighton, 6–8 April, www.future-agricultures. org/index.php?option=com_ docman&task=cat_view&gid=15 52&limit=10&limitstart=30&ord er=hits&dir=DESC&Itemid=971.

Buxton, A., M. Campanale and L. Cotula (2012) *Investment Funds and Agriculture*, London: International Institute for Environment and Development, pubs.iied.org/pdfs/17121IIED.

Byerlee, D. (2012) 'Foreign investment in large-scale farming: what can we learn from history?', Presentation made at the World Bank Conference on Land and Poverty, Washington, DC, 24–26 April, on file with the author.

Byres, T. J. (2004) 'Neo-classical neo-populism 25 years on: *déjà vu* and *déjà passé*. Towards a critique', *Journal of Agrarian Change*, 4(1/2): 17–44.

Campos Mello, P. (2011) 'Moçambique oferece terra à soja brasileira', *Folha de São Paulo*, 14 August, www1. folha.uol.com.br/fsp/mercado/ me1408201102.htm.

Carrington, D. (2011) 'UK firm's failed biofuel dream wrecks lives of Tanzania villagers', *Observer*, 30 October, www. guardian.co.uk/environment/ 2011/oct/30/africa-poor-west-biofuel-betrayal.

Carrington, D. and S. Valentino (2011) 'Biofuels boom in Africa as British firms lead rush on land for plantations', *Guardian*, 31 May.

Chauveau, J.-P. and J.-P. Colin (2007) 'Changes in land transfer mechanisms: evidence from West Africa', in L. Cotula (ed.), *Changes in 'Customary' Land Tenure Systems in Africa*, London: International Institute for Environment and Development, pp. 65–79, pubs. iied.org/12537IIED.html.

Chouquer, G. (2012) 'L'Afrique est-elle disponible? Ce qu'on voit quand on regarde', *Grain de Sel*, 57: 7–8.

CHR & GJ (2010) *Foreign Land Deals and Human Rights: Case Studies on Agricultural and Biofuel Investment*, New York: Center for Human Rights and Global Justice, NYU School of Law, www.chrgj.org/projects/docs/landreport.pdf.

CILSS (2005) 'Adaptation au changement climatique au niveau du delta central du fleuve Niger au Mali – rapport provisoire', Mopti: IER.

Clements, E. and B. F. Fernandes (2012) *Land Grabbing, Agribusiness and the Peasantry in Brazil and Mozambique*, Paper presented at the international conference on 'Global land grabbing II', Ithaca, NY, 17–19 October, www.cornell-landproject.org/papers/.

Cochet, H. and M. Merlet (2011) 'Land grabbing and share of the value added in agricultural processes. A new look at the distribution of land revenues', Paper presented at the International Conference on 'Global land grabbing', Brighton, 6–8 April, www.future-agricultures.org/index.php?option=com_docman&task=cat_view&gid=1552&limit=10&limitstart=30&order=hits&dir=DESC&Itemid=971.

Colin, J.-P. and P. Woodhouse (2010) 'Interpreting land markets in Africa', *Africa*, 80: 1–13.

Collier, P. (2008) 'The politics of hunger. How illusion and greed fan the food crisis', *Foreign Affairs*, 87: 67–79.

Comité Technique Foncier et Développement (2010) *Les Appropriations de Terres à Grande Echelle: Analyse du Phénomène et Propositions d'Orientations*, Paris: MAEE/AFD, www.foncier-developpement.fr/wp-content/uploads/appropriation_finale1.pdf.

Cotula, L. (2007) *Legal Empowerment for Local Resource Control: Securing Local Resource Rights within Foreign Investment Projects in Africa*, London: International Institute for Environment and Development, pubs.iied.org/12542IIED.html.

— (2008) 'Reconciling regulatory stability and evolution of environmental standards in investment contracts: towards a rethink of stabilization clauses', *Journal of World Energy Law & Business*, 1(2): 158–79.

— (2010) 'Pushing the boundaries vs striking a balance: the

scope and interpretation of stabilization clauses in light of the *Duke v. Peru* award', *Journal of World Investment and Trade*, 11(1): 25–43.

— (2011) *Land Deals in Africa – What is in the Contracts?*, London: International Institute for Environment and Development, pubs.iied.org/12568IIED.html.

— (2012a) 'The international political economy of the global land rush: a critical appraisal of trends, scale, geography and drivers', *Journal of Peasant Studies*, 39(3/4): 649–80.

— (2012b) *Human Rights, Natural Resource and Investment Law in a Globalised World: Shades of Grey in the Shadow of the Law*, London and New York: Routledge.

— (2012c) '"Land grabbing" in the shadow of the law: legal frameworks regulating the global land rush', in R. Rayfuse and N. Weisfelt (eds), *The Challenge of Food Security: International Policy and Regulatory Frameworks*, Cheltenham: Edward Elgar, pp. 206–28.

Cotula, L. and S. Cissé (2006) 'Changes in "customary" resource tenure systems in the Inner Niger Delta, Mali', *Journal of Legal Pluralism*, 52: 1–29.

Cotula, L. and R. Leonard (eds) (2010) *Alternatives to Land Acquisitions: Agricultural Investment and Collaborative Business Models*, London/Bern/Rome/Maputo: IIED/SDC/IFAD/CTV,

www.iied.org/pubs/display.php?o=12567IIED.

Cotula, L. and E. Polack (2012) 'The global land rush: what the evidence reveals about scale and geography', London: International Institute for Environment and Development, pubs.iied.org/17124IIED.

Cotula, L. and C. Toulmin (eds) (2004) *Till to Tiller: International Migration, Remittances and Land Rights in West Africa*, Drylands Issue Paper no. 132, London: International Institute for Environment and Development, pubs.iied.org/9508IIED.html.

— (2007) 'Conclusion', in L. Cotula (ed.), *Changes in 'Customary' Land Tenure Systems in Africa*, London: International Institute for Environment and Development, pubs.iied.org/12537IIED.html.

Cotula, L. and A. Shemberg, with E. Polack (2012) 'A sustainable development analysis of agricultural investment contracts in Lao PDR', Report prepared by the International Institute for Environment and Development for the UNDP-UNEP Poverty Environment Initiative, unpublished document.

Cotula, L., L. Finnegan and D. Macqueen (2011) *Biomass Energy: Another Driver of Land Acquisitions?*, London: International Institute for Environment and Development.

Cotula, L., S. Vermeulen, R. Leonard and J. Keeley (2009) *Land*

*Grab or Development Opportunity? Agricultural Investment and International Land Deals in Africa*, Rome/London: Food and Agriculture Organization of the UN (FAO)/International Fund for Agricultural Development (IFAD)/International Institute for Environment and Development, www.iied.org/pubs/display.php?o=12561IIED.

Daley, E. (2011) *Gendered Impacts of Commercial Pressures on Land*, Rome: International Land Coalition, www.landcoalition.org/publications/gendered-impacts-commercial-pressures-land.

De Castro, P., with F. Adinolfi, F. Capitanio, S. di Falco and A. di Mambro (2012) *The Politics of Land and Food Scarcity*, London and New York: Earthscan.

De Schutter, O. (2009) Report of the Special Rapporteur on the Right to Food – Addendum, 'Large-scale land acquisitions and leases: a set of minimum principles and measures to address the human rights challenge', UN Doc. A/HRC//13/33/Add.2, 28 December.

— (2011) 'How not to think of land-grabbing: three critiques of large-scale investments in farmland', *Journal of Peasant Studies*, 38(2): 249–79.

Deininger, K. (2003) *Land Policies for Growth and Poverty Reduction*, Washington, DC: World Bank.

Deininger, K. and D. Byerlee (2012) 'The rise of large farms in land abundant countries: do they have a future?', *World Development*, 40(4): 701–14.

Deininger, K. and D. Byerlee, with J. Lindsay, A. Norton, H. Selod and M. Stickler (2011) *Rising Global Interest in Farmland: Can It Yield Sustainable and Equitable Benefits?*, Washington, DC: World Bank, econ. worldbank.org/external/default/main?pagePK=64165259&theSitePK=469382&piPK=6416 5421&menuPK=64166322&entity ID=000334955_20110208033706.

Dhliwayo, M. (forthcoming) *Public Interest Litigation as an Empowerment Tool: The Case of the Chiadzwa Community Development Trust and Diamond Mining in Zimbabwe*, London: International Institute for Environment and Development.

Djiré, M. (2007) *Land Registration in Mali – No Land Ownership for Farmers? Observations from Peri-Urban Bamako*, Drylands Issue Paper no. 144, London: International Institute for Environment and Development, www.iied.org/pubs/display. php?o=12538IIED.

Djiré, M., with A. Diawara and A. Keita (2012) *Agricultural Investment in Mali: Context, Trends and Case Studies*, London: International Institute for Environment and Development.

DNEAP/MPD (2010) *Poverty and Wellbeing in Mozambique: Third National Poverty Assessment*, Maputo: National Directorate of Studies and Policy Analysis,

References

Ministry of Planning and Development.

Doka, M. and M. Monimart (2004) *Women's Access to Land: The De-feminisation of Agriculture in Southern Niger*, Drylands Issue Paper no. 128, London: International Institute for Environment and Development, www.iied.org/pubs/display. php?o=9328IIED.

Dolan, C. and H. Humphrey (2004) 'Changing governance patterns in the trade in fresh vegetables between Africa and the United Kingdom', *Environment and Planning A*, 36(3): 491–509.

Downs, R. E. and S. Reyna (eds) (1988) *Land and Society in Contemporary Africa*, Hanover, NH, and London: University Press of New England.

Dyer, G. (1998) 'Farm size and productivity. A new look at the old debate revisited', *Economic and Political Weekly, Review of Agriculture*, 33(26): A113–A116.

Earth Security Initiative (2012) *The Land Security Agenda: How Investor Risks in Farmland Create Opportunities for Sustainability*, London: Earth Security Initiative.

Fairhead, J., M. Leach and I. Scoones (2012) 'Green grabbing: a new appropriation of nature?', *Journal of Peasant Studies*, 39(2): 237–61.

FAO (2010) *Agricultural Investment Funds for Developing Countries*, Rome: FAO.

— (2012a) *The State of Food and Agriculture: Investing in Agriculture for a Better Future*, Rome: FAO.

— (2012b) *Trends and Impacts of Foreign Investment in Developing Country Agriculture: Evidence from Case Studies*, Rome: FAO.

FAO, IFAD, IMF, OECD, UNCTAD, WFP, World Bank, WTO, IFPRI and UN HLTF (2011) 'Price volatility in food and agricultural markets: policy responses', 2 June.

Faye, I. M., A. Benkahla, O. Touré, S. M. Seck and C. O. Ba (2011) *Les Acquisitions de Terres à Grande Echelle au Sénegal : Description d'un Nouveau Phénomène*, Dakar: Initiative Prospective Agricole et Rurale.

Federico, G. (2005) *Feeding the World: An Economic History of Agriculture, 1800–2000*, Princeton, NJ, and Oxford: Princeton University Press.

Feronia (2009) 'Trinorth acquires Unilever's palm oil plantations in DRC', Company press release, 3 September, farmlandgrab.org/9876.

FIAN (2012) *The Human Rights Impacts of Tree Plantations in Niassa Province, Mozambique*, Heidelberg: FIAN.

Fischer, G., H. van Velthuizen, M. Shah and F. Nachtergaele (2002) *Global Agro-Ecological Assessment for Agriculture in the 21st Century*, Rome/Laxenburg: Food and Agriculture Organization of the United Nations (FAO)/International Institute for Applied Systems Analysis (IIASA).

Fold, N. and K. V. Gough (2008) 'From smallholders to transnationals: the impact of changing consumer preferences in the EU on Ghana's pineapple sector', *Geoforum*, 39: 1687–97.

Fox, J. (1990) 'The challenge of rural democratization: perspectives from Latin America and the Philippines – editor's introduction', *Journal of Development Studies*, 26(4): 1–18.

Fox, T. and B. Vorley (2004) *Stakeholder Accountability in the UK Supermarket Sector: Final Report of the 'Race to the Top' Project*, London: International Institute for Environment and Development.

FPP (2012) 'Liberia: agri-business expansion threatens forests and local communities' livelihoods', FPP E-Newsletter, Moreton-in-Marsh: Forest Peoples Programme, April, www.forestpeoples.org/ ENEWSLETTERS/FPP-E-NEWSLETTER-APRIL-2012, pp. 2–3.

Friends of the Earth (2010) *The Scale and Impact of Land Grabbing for Agrofuels*, Brussels: Friends of the Earth Europe.

Friis, C. and A. Reenberg (2010) *Land Grab in Africa: Emerging Land System Drivers in a Teleconnected World*, GLP Report no. 1, University of Copenhagen, GLP-IPO, www.global landproject.org/Documents/ GLP_report_01.pdf.

Garuba, D. (2011) 'West Africa's many water wars', *West Africa Insight*, westafricainsight.org/ articles/PDF/102.

Gaventa, J. (2002) 'Introduction: Exploring citizenship, participation and accountability', *IDS Bulletin*, 33(2): 1–11.

Gentili, A. M. (1995) *Il Leone e il Cacciatore: Storia dell'Africa sub-Sahariana*, Rome: La Nuova Italia Scientifica.

Gereffi, G. (1999) 'A commodity chains framework for analyzing global industries', Paper available at eco.ieu.edu.tr/wp-content/Gereffi_Commodity Chains99.pdf.

German, L., G. Schoneveld and E. Mwangi (2011) *Processes of Large-Scale Land Acquisition by Investors: Case Studies from Sub-Saharan Africa*, Paper presented at the International Conference on Global Land Grabbing, Brighton, 6–8 April, http:// www.future-agricultures.org/ index.php?option=com_doc man&task=cat_view&gid=1552 &limit=10&limitstart=30&order =hits&dir=DESC&Itemid=971.

GIIN (2011) *Improving Livelihoods, Removing Barriers: Investing for Impact in Mtanga Farms*, Global Impact Investing Network, November, www.thegiin.org/ binary-data/RESOURCE/down load_file/000/000/328-1.pdf.

Görgen, M., B. Rudloff, J. Simons, A. Üllenberg, S. Väth and L. Wimmer (2009) *Foreign Direct Investment (FDI) in*

*Land in Developing Countries*, Eschborn: Deutsche Gesellschaft für Technische Zusammenarbeit (GTZ), www2.gtz.de/urbanet/library/detail1.asp?number=7529.

Graham, A., S. Aubry, R. Künnemann and S. Monsalve Suárez (2010) 'Land Grab Study, CSO Monitoring 2009–2010 "Advancing African Agriculture" (AAA): The impact of Europe's policies and practices on African agriculture and food security', fian.org/resources/documents/others/report-on-land-grabbing/pdf.

GRAIN (2012) *Squeezing Africa Dry: Behind Every Land Grab is a Water Grab*, www.grain.org/article/entries/4516-squeezing-africa-dry-behind-every-land-grab-is-a-water-grab.

Guarani (2007) 'Comunicado ao mercado', 21 December, www.tereosinternacional.com.br/tereosinternacional/web/arquivos/Guarani_Comunicado_ao_mercado_20071221_eng.pdf.

Hall, D., P. Hirsch and T. Li (2011) *Powers of Exclusion: Land Dilemmas in Southeast Asia*, Honolulu: University of Hawaii Press.

Hall, R. (2012) 'The next Great Trek? South African commercial farmers move north', *Journal of Peasant Studies*, 39(3/4): 823–43.

Hammar, A. (2012) 'The missing middle: exploring Mozambican refusals and preferences in agricultural directions', Paper presented at the international conference on 'Global land grabbing II', Ithaca, NY, 17–19 October, www.cornell-landproject.org/papers/.

Hanlon, J. (2011) 'Mozambique political process bulletin', Issue 48, Maputo: Centro de Integridade Pública and AWEPA, 22 February.

Hawkins, D. (2010) 'The world agriculture industry: a study in falling supply and rising demand', Hardman & Co., 26 May, www.hardmanandco.com/Research/Agriculture%20Funds.pdf.

Hepburn, J. (2012) 'Analysis: Interim measures granted by Inter-American Commission have featured in several recent investment controversies', *IAReporter*, 14 March, www.iareporter.com/articles/20120314_1.

Hermele, K. (1988) *Land Struggles and Social Differentiation in Southern Mozambique: A Case Study of Chokwe, Limpopo 1950–1987*, Research Report no. 82, Uppsala: Scandinavian Institute of African Studies.

Hertzog, T., A. Adamczewski, J. C. Poussin and J. Y. Jamin (2012) 'Ostrich-like behavior in Sahelian sands: land and water grabbing in the Office du Niger, Mali', *Water Alternatives*.

Hesse, C. and J. MacGregor (2006) *Pastoralism: Drylands' Invisible Asset? Developing a Framework for Assessing the Value of Pastoralism in East Africa*, Dryland

Issue Paper no. 142, London: International Institute for Environment and Development.

Hicks, W. (2012) 'Tanzania's troubling trend of land rights violations and evictions', 10 September, www.ecology.com/2012/09/10/tanzanias-land-rights-violations/.

Hilhorst, T., J. Nelen and N. Traoré (2011) 'Agrarian change below the radar screen: rising farmland acquisitions by domestic investors in West Africa – results from a survey in Benin, Burkina Faso and Niger', Paper presented at the International Conference on Global Land Grabbing, Brighton, 6–8 April, www.future-agricultures.org/index.php?option=com_docman&task=cat_view&gid=1552&limit=10&limitstart=30&order=hits&dir= DESC&Itemid=971.

Hobsbawm, E. (1987) *The Age of Empire 1875–1914*, London: Weidenfeld & Nicolson.

Holt-Gimenez, E. (2012) 'Detroit: a tale of two … farms?', *Huffington Post*, 10 July, www.huffingtonpost.com/eric-holt-gimenez/a-tale-of-two-farms_b_1660019.html.

Huggins, C. (2011) *A Historical Perspective on the 'Global Land Rush'*, Rome: International Land Coalition, www.landcoalition.org/publications/historical-perspective-global-land-rush.

Huggins, C., H. Musahara, P. Mbura Kamungi, J. S. Oketch and K. Vlassenroot (2005) *Conflict in the Great Lakes Region – How is It Linked with Land and Migration?*, Natural Resource Perspectives no. 96, London: Overseas Development Institute.

Human Rights Watch (2012a) *'Waiting Here for Death': Forced Displacement and 'Villagization' in Ethiopia's Gambella Region*, www.hrw.org/sites/default/files/reports/ethiopia0112webwcover_0.pdf.

— (2012b) *'What Will Happen If Hunger Comes?': Abuses against the Indigenous Peoples of Ethiopia's Lower Omo Valley*, www.hrw.org/sites/default/files/reports/ethiopia0612webwcover.pdf.

Hunt, A. (1990) 'Rights and social movements: counter-hegemonic strategies', *Journal of Law and Society*, 17(3): 309–28.

Hurn, L. (2012) 'Protest outside agricultural investment summit', 27 June, www.actionaid.org.uk/100621/blog.html?article=4312.

IANS (2011) 'No Indian land grab, says Ethiopian PM', 25 May, farmlandgrab.org/post/view/18669.

IFC (2012) *International Finance Corporation's Policy on Environmental and Social Sustainability*, 2012 edn, www.ifc.org/ifcext/policyreview.nsf/AttachmentsByTitle/Updated_IFC_SFCompounded_August1-2011/$FILE/Updated_IFC_Sustainability

FrameworkCompounded_
August1-2011.pdf.

Jägerskog, A., A. Cascão,
M. Hårsmar and K. Kim (2012)
*Land Acquisitions: How Will
They Impact Transboundary
Waters?*, Report no. 30,
Stockholm: SIWI, www.siwi.
org/documents/Resources/
Reports/16-406_Land_
Grabbing_report_webb.pdf.

Jamin, J. Y. and M. J. Doucet
(1994) 'La question foncière
dans les perimètres irrigués
de l'Office du Niger', *Cahiers
de la Recherche Développement*,
38: 65–82.

Johnstone, S. and J. Mazo (2011)
'Global warming and the Arab
Spring', *Survival: Global Politics
and Strategy*, 53(2): 11–17, www.
iiss.org/publications/survival/
survival-2011/year-2011-issue-2/
global-warming-and-the-arab-
spring/.

Journal du Mali (2010) 'La cité
administrative inaugurée
par ATT', 5 September, www.
journaldumali.com/article.
php?aid=2077.

Jul-Larsen, E., B. Kassibo,
S. Lange and I. Samset (2006)
*Socio-Economic Effects of
Gold Mining in Mali: A Study
of the Sadiola and Morila
Mining Operations*, Bergen:
Chr. Michelsen Institute,
www.cmi.no/publications/
publication/?2340=socio-
economic-effects-of-gold-
mining-in-mali.

Kaarhus, R. (2011) *Agricultural
Growth Corridors Equals
Land-grabbing? Models,
Roles and Accountabilities in
a Mozambican Case*, Paper
presented at the International
Conference on Global Land
Grabbing, Brighton, 6–8 April,
www.future-agricultures.
org/index.php?option=com_
docman&task=cat_view&gid=15
52&limit=10&limitstart=30&ord
er=hits&dir=DESC&Itemid=971.

Kasanga, K. and N. A. Kotey
(2001) *Land Management in
Ghana: Building on Tradition
and Modernity*, London:
International Institute for
Environment and Develop-
ment, www.iied.org/pubs/
display.php?n=4&l=5&a=N%20
Kotey&x=Y.

Keita, A., M. Djiré, K. Traoré,
D. Dembelé, A. Dembelé, M.
Samassekou and M. Doumbo
(2008) *Communautés Locales et
'Manne Aurifère': Les Oubliées
de la Législation Minière Mali-
enne*, London: International
Institute for Environment and
Development.

Kenney-Lazar, M. (2012) 'Plantation rubber, land grabbing and
social-property transformation
in southern Laos', *Journal of
Peasant Studies*, 39(3/4): 1017–37.

Kiishweko, O. (2012) 'Tanzania
takes major step towards curb-
ing land "grabs"', *Guardian*,
21 December, www.guardian.
co.uk/global-development/2012/
dec/21/tanzania-major-step-
curbing-land-grabs.

King, R. (1977) *Land Reform: A
World Survey*, London: Bell.

Knight, R. (2011) *Statutory Recognition of Customary Land Rights in Africa: An Investigation into Best Practices for Law-Making and Implementation*, Legislative Study no. 105, Rome: Food and Agriculture Organization of the UN (FAO), www.fao.org/docrep/013/i1945e/i1945e00.htm.

Koponen, J. (1993) 'The partition of Africa: a scramble for a mirage?', *Nordic Journal of African Studies*, 2(1): 117–35.

Koskenniemi, M. (2001) *The Gentle Civilizer of Nations: The Rise and Fall of International Law 1870–1960*, Cambridge: Cambridge University Press.

Kuba, R. and C. Lentz (eds) (2006) *Land and the Politics of Belonging in West Africa*, Leiden and Boston, MA: Brill.

Lane, C. (1994) 'Pastures lost: alienation of Barabaig land in the context of land policy and legislation in Tanzania', *Nomadic Peoples*, 34/35: 81–94.

Lapucheque, O. (2011) 'Governo nega ter oferecido extensas areas a brasileiros', *O Pais*, 22 August, www.opais.co.mz/index.php/component/content/article/63-politica/16050-governo-nega-ter-oferecido-extensas-areas-a-brasileiros.html.

Lavers, T. (2011) *The Role of Foreign Investment in Ethiopia's Smallholder-Focused Agricultural Development Strategy*, LPDI Working Paper no. 2, Land Deal Politics Initiative.

Leader, S. (2006) 'Human rights, risks, and new strategies for global investment', *Journal of International Economic Law*, 9: 657.

Li, T. (2011) 'Centering labour in the land grab debate', *Journal of Peasant Studies*, 38(2): 281–98.

— (2012) *What is Land? An Anthropological Pespective on the Global Land Rush*, Paper presented at the international conference on 'Global land grabbing II', Ithaca, NY, 17–19 October, www.cornell-landproject.org/papers/.

Lipton, M. (1977) *Why Poor People Stay Poor. A Study of Urban Bias in World Development*, London: Temple Smith.

— (2010) *Land Reform in Developing Countries: Property Rights and Property Wrongs*, London and New York: Routledge.

Little, P. D. and M. J. Watts (eds) (1994) *Living under Contract: Contract Farming and Agrarian Transformation in Sub-Saharan Africa*, Madison: University of Wisconsin Press.

Lund, C. (2011) 'Fragmented sovereignty: land reform and dispossession in Laos', *Journal of Peasant Studies*, 38(4): 885–905.

Lund, C. and C. Boone (2013) 'Land politics in Africa: constituting authority over territory, property, and persons', *Africa*.

Lunstrum, E. M. (2007) 'The making and unmaking of sovereign territory: from colonial extraction to postcolonial conservation in Mozambique's

Massingir region', Dissertation submitted to the Faculty of the Graduate School of the University of Minnesota, books.google.co.uk/ books?id=oHXonVEzWgYC& p g=PA62&lpg=PA62&dq= massingir+district+population &source=bl&ots=3dPG-iyBL o& sig=fNe7huPPma--uv3 MqP7KqgiqeGc&hl=en&sa= X&ei=MmjoT9beMsmf8gPywI C8Bw&ved=oCFoQ6AEwCQ# v=onepage&q=massingir%20 district%20population&f=false.

Lyimo, J. (2010) 'Tanzania: govt mulls repossessing privatised NAFCO farms', *The Citizen*, allafrica.com/ stories/201012141090.html.

Maertens, M. and J. F. M. Swinnen (2009) 'Trade, standards, and poverty: evidence from Senegal', *World Development*, 37(1): 161–78.

Majid Cooke, F., S. Toh and J. Vaz (2011) *Community-Investor Business Models: Lessons from the Oil Palm Sector in Malaysia*, London: International Institute for Environment and Development, pubs.iied. org/12570IIED.html.

Mamdani, M. (1996) *Citizen and Subject – Contemporary Africa and the Legacy of Late Colonialism*, London: James Currey.

Mathieu, P., S. Mugangu Mataboro and A. Mafikiri Tsongo (1998) 'Enjeux fonciers et violences en Afrique: la prévention des conflits en se servant du cas du Nord-Kivu

(1940–1994)', *Land Reform, Land Settlement and Cooperatives*, 1998(2): 32–43, www.fao.org/ WAICENT/FAOINFO/SUSTDEV/ LTdirect/landrf.htm.

Mathieu, P., M. Zongo and L. Paré (2003) 'Monetary land transactions in western Burkina Faso: commoditisation, papers and ambiguities', in T. Benjaminsen and C. Lund (eds), *Securing Land Rights in Africa*, London: Frank Cass and Co., pp. 109–28.

Mattei, U. and L. Nader (2008) *Plunder: When the Rule of Law is Illegal*, Malden/Oxford/Carlton: Blackwell Publishing.

McMichael, P. (2012a) 'The land grab and corporate food regime restructuring', *Journal of Peasant Studies*, 39(3/4): 681–702.

— (2012b) 'Land grabbing as security mercantilism in international relations', Paper presented at the international conference on 'Global land grabbing II', Ithaca, NY, 17–19 October.

Mensah Sarbah, J. (1897) *Fanti Customary Law: A Brief Introduction to the Principles of the Native Laws and Customs of the Fanti and Akan Districts of the Gold Coast*, London: W. Clowes and Sons Ltd, accessed in its 2nd edn (1904), www.archive. org/stream/fanticustomary laoosarbuoft/fanticustomary laoosarbuoft_djvu.txt.

Minority Rights Group International (2011) *Submission to*

the Universal Periodic Review, 12th Session of the Human Rights Council, United Republic of Tanzania, 3–14 October, lib.ohchr.org/HRBodies/UPR/Documents/session12/TZ/MRG-MinorityRightsGroup International-eng.pdf.

Mnookin, R. and L. Kornhauser (1979) 'Bargaining in the shadow of the law: the case of divorce', Yale Law Journal, 88: 950–97.

Moore, K. (ed.) (2005) Conflict, Social Capital and Managing Natural Resources – a West African Case Study, CAB International.

Moorehead, R. (1997) Structural Chaos: Community and State Management of Common Property in Mali, London: International Institute for Environment and Development.

Mosley, J. (2012) Peace, Bread and Land: Agricultural Investments in Ethiopia and the Sudans, London: Chatham House, AFP BP 2012/01, www.chathamhouse.org/publications/papers/view/181519.

Moyo, S. (2011) 'Changing agrarian relations after redistributive land reform in Zimbabwe', Journal of Peasant Studies, 38(5): 939–66.

Mujenja, F. and C. Wonani (2012) Long-term Outcomes of Agricultural Investments: Lessons from Zambia, London: International Institute for Environment and Development.

Murton, J. (1999) 'Population growth and poverty in Machakos District, Kenya', Geographical Journal, 165(1): 37–46.

Nguiffo, S. and B. Schwartz (2012) Herakles' 13th Labour? A Study of SGSOC's Land Concession in South-West Cameroon, Yaoundé: Centre pour l'Environnement et le Développement/RELUFA, www.forestpeoples.org/topics/palm-oil-rspo/publication/2012/ced-publication-herakles-13th-labour-study-sgsoc-s-land-conces.

Nhantumbo, I. and A. Salomão (2010) Biofuels, Land Access and Rural Livelihoods in Mozambique, London: International Institute for Environment and Development, pubs.iied.org/12563IIED.html.

Norfolk, S. and C. Tanner (2007) 'Improving security for the rural poor: Mozambique country case study', FAO LEP Working Paper no. 5, Rome: Food and Agriculture Organization of the UN, ftp.fao.org/sd/SDA/SDAR/sard/Mozambiquecase.pdf.

Oakland Institute (2011a) Understanding Land Investment Deals in Africa – Country Report: Mozambique, Oakland, CA: Oakland Institute, media.oaklandinstitute.org/special-investigation-understanding-land-investment-deals-africa.

— (2011b) Understanding Land Investment Deals in Africa – Country Report:

*Tanzania*, Oakland, CA: Oakland Institute, media. oaklandinstitute.org/special-investigation-understanding-land-investment-deals-africa.

— (2011c) *Understanding Land Investment Deals in Africa – Country Report: Mali*, Oakland, CA: Oakland Institute, media. oaklandinstitute.org/special-investigation-understanding-land-investment-deals-africa.

— (2011d) *Understanding Land Investment Deals in Africa – Country Report: Ethiopia*, Oakland, CA: Oakland Institute, media. oaklandinstitute.org/special-investigation-understanding-land-investment-deals-africa.

— (2011e) *Understanding Land Investment Deals in Africa – Land Deal Brief: The Myth of Economic Development*, Oakland, CA: Oakland Institute, media.oaklandinstitute.org/special-investigation-understanding-land-investment-deals-africa.

OECD (2010) *Private Financial Sector Investment in Farmland and Agricultural Infrastructure*, Paris: Working Party on Agricultural Policies and Markets, OECD, www.oecd.org/official documents/publicdisplay documentpdf/?cote=TAD/CA/APM/WP(2010)11/FINAL &docLanguage=En.

— (2011) *Guidelines on Multinational Enterprises*, www.oecd.org/dataoecd/43/29/48004323.pdf.

OECD/FAO (2010) *Agricultural Outlook 2010–2019*, Paris/Rome: OECD/FAO.

Office du Niger (2009) *Note Technique sur la Situation des Aménagements et Attributions de Terres à l'Office du Niger*, Ségou: Direction Générale de l'Office du Niger, unpublished document on file with the author.

Onoma, A. K. (2010) *The Politics of Property Rights Institutions in Africa*, Cambridge: Cambridge University Press.

Ouédraogo, M. (2003) *New Stakeholders and the Promotion of Agro-Silvo-Pastoral Activities in Southern Burkina Faso: False Start or Inexperience?*, Drylands Issue Paper no. 118, London: International Institute for Environment and Development, pubs.iied.org/9236IIED.html.

Ouédraogo, S. (2006) *New Actors and Land Acquisition around Lake Bazèga, Burkina Faso*, Drylands Issue Paper no. 138, London: International Institute for Environment and Development, pubs.iied.org/12525IIED.html.

Oxfam (2011) *Land and Power: The Growing Scandal Surrounding the New Wave of Investments in Land*, Oxford: Oxfam, www.oxfam.org/sites/www.oxfam.org/files/bp151-land-power-rights-acquisitions-220911-en.pdf.

Pearce, F. (2012) *The Land Grabbers: The New Fight over Who Owns the Earth*, Boston, MA: Beacon Press.

Peluso, N. L. and C. Lund (2011) 'New frontiers of land control: introduction', *Journal of Peasant Studies*, 38(4): 667–81.

Pensions & Investments (2010) 'Fertile ground for investment – European pension funds target farmland in emerging markets', *Pensions & Investments*, 19 April.

Peters, P. E. (2004) 'Inequality and social conflict over land in Africa', *Journal of Agrarian Change*, 4(3): 269–314.

— (2009) 'Challenges in land tenure and land reform in Africa: anthropological contributions', *World Development*, 37(8): 1317–25.

Plusquellec, H. (1990) *The Gezira Irrigation Scheme in Sudan: Objectives, Design, and Performance*, World Bank Technical Paper no. 120, Washington, DC: World Bank, www-wds. worldbank.org/servlet/WDS ContentServer/WDSP/IB/1999/1 2/02/000178830_98101904135320/ Rendered/PDF/multi_page.pdf.

Polack, E. (2012) *Agricultural Land Acquisitions: A Lens on Southeast Asia*, London: International Institute for Environment and Development, pubs. iied.org/17123IIED.html.

Polack, E., L. Cotula and M. Côte (2013) *Legal Empowerment and Pathways to Accountability in the Global Rush for Africa's Land*, London: International Institute for Environment and Development.

Polanyi, K. (1944) *The Great Transformation: The Political and Economic Origins of Our Time*, Boston, MA: Beacon Press, 2nd paperback edn (2001).

Ravanera, R. (2011) *Commercial Pressures on Land in Asia: An Overview*, Rome: International Land Coalition, www.land coalition.org/publications/ commercial-pressures-land-asia-overview.

Raynaut, C. (1988) 'Aspects of the problem of land concentration in Niger', in R. E. Downs and S. Reyna (eds), *Land and Society in Contemporary Africa*, Hanover, NH, and London: University Press of New England, pp. 221–42.

Reardon, T., C. Barrett, J. A. Berdegué and J. F. M. Swinnen (2009) 'Agrifood industry transformation and small farmers in developing countries', *World Development*, 37(11): 1717–27.

Re:Common (2012) 'Gli arraffa terre: il coinvolgimento italiano nel business del land grab', Rome: Re:Common.

Reuters (2009) 'Ethiopia sets aside land for foreign investors', 29 July, in.reuters. com/article/domesticNews/ idINLT58431220090729.

Richards, P. and J.-P. Chauveau (2007) *Land, Agricultural Change and Conflict in West Africa: Regional Issues from Sierra Leone, Liberia and Côte d'Ivoire*, Paris: Sahel and West Africa Club, www.oecd.org/ dataoecd/44/53/39495967.pdf.

Richardson, B. (2010) 'Big sugar in

southern Africa: rural development and the perverted potential of sugar/ethanol exports', *Journal of Peasant Studies*, 37(4): 917–38.

Roxburgh, C., N. Dörr, A. Leke, A. Tazi-Riffi, A. van Wamelen, S. Lund, M. Chironga, T. Alatovik, C. Atkins, N. Terfus and T. Zeino-Mahmalat (2010) *Lions on the Move: The Progress and Potential of African Economies*, McKinsey Global Institute, www.mckinsey.com/mgi/publications/progress_and_potential_of_african_economies/index.asp.

Rowden, R. (2011) 'India's role in the new global farmland grab: an examination of the role of the Indian government and Indian companies engaged in overseas agricultural land acquisitions in developing countries', Paper produced in collaboration with GRAIN and the Economics Research Foundation, www.networkideas.org/featart/aug2011/Rick_Rowden.pdf.

Ruggie, J. (2011) 'Guiding principles on business and human rights: implementing the United Nations' "Protect, Respect and Remedy" framework', Report of the Special Representative of the Secretary-General on the Issue of Human Rights and Transnational Corporations and Other Business Enterprises, John Ruggie, 21 March 2011, UN Document A/HRC/17/31, endorsed by UN Human Rights Council Resolution no. 17/4 of 6 July 2011, UN Document A/HRC/RES/17/4, www.business-humanrights.org/SpecialRepPortal/Home.

Schoneveld, G. (2011) *The Anatomy of Large-scale Farmland Acquisitions in Sub-Saharan Africa*, Working Paper 85, Bogor: CIFOR.

Schoneveld, G. C., L. A. German and E. Nutakor (2010) 'Towards sustainable biofuel development: assessing the local impacts of large-scale foreign land acquisitions in Ghana', Paper presented at the World Bank Land Governance Conference, 26/27 April.

— (2011) 'Land-based investments for rural development? A grounded analysis of the local impacts of biofuel feedstock plantations in Ghana', *Ecology and Society*, 16(4): 10.

Shemberg, A. (2009) *Stabilization Clauses and Human Rights*, Research project conducted for IFC and the United Nations Special Representative to the Secretary General on Business and Human Rights, www.ifc.org/ifcext/sustainability.nsf/AttachmentsByTitle/p_StabilizationClausesandHumanRights/$FILE/Stabilization+Paper.pdf.

Skinner, J. and L. Cotula (2011) 'Are land deals driving "water grabs"?', London: International Institute for Environment and Development, pubs.iied.org/17102IIED.html.

Smaller, C., Q. Wei and L. Yalan (2012) *Farmland and Water: China Invests Abroad*, Winnipeg: International Institute for Sustainable Development.

Soto Baquero, F. and S. Gómez (eds) (2012) *Dinámicas del Mercado de la Tierra en América Latina y el Caribe: Concentración y Extranjerización*, Rome: Food and Agriculture Organization of the United Nations.

Stensrud Ekman, S.-M. (n.d.) 'Leasing land overseas: a viable strategy for Chinese food security? Opportunities and risks of Chinese agricultural investments in Mozambique', www.scribd.com/sigrid_marianellae/d/65909633/15-China%E2%80%99s-official-stance.

Sugar Industry (2012) 'Massingir Agro-Industria plans to invest USD740mn', *Sugar Industry*, 137(2): 73.

Sulle, E. and F. Nelson (2009) *Biofuels, Land Access and Rural Livelihoods in Tanzania*, London: International Institute for Environment and Development, www.iied.org/pubs/pdfs/12560IIED.pdf.

— (forthcoming) *Biofuels Investment and Community Land Tenure in Tanzania*, Arusha: Tanzania Natural Resource Forum, unpublished manuscript on file with the author.

Takane, T. (2004) 'Smallholders and non-traditional exports under economic liberalization: the case of pineapples in Ghana', *African Study Monographs*, 25(1): 29–43.

Tekleberhan, M. (2012) 'Ethiopia suspends providing agriculture land for investment', 19 March, www.2merkato.com/201203191019/ethiopia-suspends-providing-land-for-investment.

Tenga, R. W. (2008) 'The right to food and security of pastoral resource rights in the United Republic of Tanzania', in L. Cotula (ed.), *The Right to Food and Access to Natural Resources – Using Human Rights Arguments and Mechanisms to Improve Resource Access for the Rural Poor*, Rome: Food and Agriculture Organization of the UN, www.fao.org/righttofood/publi08/NATURAL_RESOURCES.pdf, pp. 52–60.

Teyssier, A. (2010) 'Décentraliser la gestion foncière? L'expérience de Madagascar', *Perspectives*, Paris, CIRAD, www.cirad.fr/content/.../4/.../Persp04_Teyssier_foncier_madagascar_fr.pdf.

Thébaud, B. (2002) *Foncier Pastoral et Gestion de l'Espace au Sahel: Peuls du Niger Oriental et du Yagha Burkinabé*, Paris: Karthala.

Tienhaara, K. (2012) 'The potential perils of forest carbon contracts for developing countries: cases from Africa', *Journal of Peasant Studies*, 39(2): 551–72.

Tiffen, M. and M. Mortimore (1990) *Theory and Practice in*

*Plantation Agriculture: An Economic Review*, London: ODI.

Tiffen, M., M. Mortimore and F. Gichuki (1994) *More People, Less Erosion – Environmental Recovery in Kenya*, Chichester: John Wiley and Sons.

TNRF (2011) *Integrating Pastoralist Livelihoods and Wildlife Conservation? Options for Land Use and Conflict Resolution in Loliondo Division, Ngorongoro District, Arusha*, Tanzania Natural Resource Forum, www. tnrf.org/files/Integrating%20 Pastoralist%20Livelihoods %20 and%20Wildlife%20 Conservation_FINAL_FINAL. pdf.

— (2012) 'Understanding land and investments in Tanzania', Arusha: Tanzania Natural Resource Forum.

Toulmin, C., C. Hesse and L. Cotula (2004) 'Pastoral commons sense: lessons from recent developments in policy, law and practice for the management of grazing lands', *Forests, Trees and Livelihoods*, 14: 243–62.

Toulmin, C., P. Bindraban, S. Borras, E. Mwangi and S. Sauer (2011) *Land Tenure and International Investments in Agriculture*, Report prepared for the High Level Panel of Experts on Food Security and Nutrition, Committee on World Food Security.

Tsikata, D. and J. Yaro (2011) 'Land market liberalization and trans-national commercial land deals in Ghana since the 1990s', Paper presented at the International Conference on Global Land Grabbing, Brighton, 6–8 April, www. future-agricultures.org/ index.php?option=com_ docman&task=cat_view&gid=15 52&limit=10&limitstart=30&ord er=hits&dir=DESC&Itemid=971.

Ullenberg, A. (2009) *Foreign Direct Investment (FDI) in Land in Madagascar*, Eschborn: Deutsche Gesellschaft für Technische Zusammenarbeit (GTZ), www2.gtz.de/urbanet / library/detail1.asp?number =7529.

UNCTAD (2009) *World Investment Report 2009: Transnational Corporations, Agricultural Production and Development*, Geneva: United Nations Conference on Trade and Development.

— (2012) *World Investment Report 2012: Towards a New Generation of Investment Policies*, Geneva: United Nations Conference on Trade and Development.

UNDP (2011) *Human Development Report – Sustainability and Equity: A Better Future for All*, New York: United Nations Development Programme, hdr. undp.org/en/reports/global/ hdr2011/.

Unilever (2010) 'Sustainable living plan', www.unilever.com/ sustainable-living/uslp/.

Valentino, S. (2011) 'Tanzania biofuel project's barren promise', Inter-Press Service News Agency (IPS), 9 May,

www.ipsnews.net/2011/03/
tanzania-biofuel-projects-
barren-promise/.

Van der Zaag, P., D. Juizo,
A. Vilanculos, A. Bolding and
P. Uiterweer (2010) 'Does the
Limpopo River Basin have
sufficient water for massive
irrigation development in the
plains of Mozambique?', *Phys-
ics and Chemistry of the Earth*,
35(13/14): 832–7.

Verhoeven, H. and E. Woertz
(2012) 'Mirage in the desert:
the myth of Africa's land
grab', CNN, 9 July, edition.
cnn.com/2012/07/05/business/
op-ed-africa-land-grab/index.
html?iid=article_sidebar.

Vermeulen, S. and L. Cotula (2010)
*Making the Most of Agricultural
Investment: A Survey of Business
Models that Provide Opportu-
nities for Smallholders*, Rome/
London/Bern: FAO/IFAD/
IIED/SDC, www.iied.org/pubs/
display.php?o=12566IIED.

Vientiane Times (2012) 'Govt halts
new mining projects, land
concessions for tree farms',
26 June.

Von Braun, J. (2008) *Food and
Financial Crises: Implications
for Agriculture and the Poor*,
Food Policy Report no. 20,
Washington, DC: International
Food Policy Research Institute
(IFPRI).

Vorley, B. (2002) *Sustaining Agriculture: Policy, Governance, and the
Future of Family-based Farming*,
London: International In-
stitute for Environment and
Development, pubs.iied.org/
pdfs/9175IIED.pdf.

Vorley, B., L. Cotula and M. K. Chan
(2012) *Tipping the Balance: Poli-
cies to Shape Agricultural Invest-
ments and Markets in Favour of
Small-scale Farmers*, Oxford/
London: Oxfam/International
Institute for Environment and
Development.

Wetlands International (n.d.) 'Impacts of dams on the people
of Mali', www.wetlands.org/
WatchRead/Currentpublica-
tions/tabid/56/ArticleType/
ArticleView/ArticleID/1602/
PageID/629/Default.aspx.

Wiggins, S., J. Kirsten and
L. Llambí (2010) 'The future of
small farms', *World Development*, 38(10): 1341–8.

Wightman, A. (2011) *The Poor
Had No Lawyers: Who Owns
Scotland (And How They Got It)*,
Edinburgh: Birlinn.

Wilkes, H. and I. Bailey (2011)
'International farmland
markets', Savills Plc, www.
aginvestconference.com/usa/
savills.pdf.

Wisborg, P. (2012) 'Justice and
sustainability: resistance and
innovation in a transnational
land deal in Ghana', Paper
presented at the World Bank
Conference on Land and
Poverty, 23–26 April.

Woertz, E. (2009) 'Gulf food security needs delicate diplomacy',
*Financial Times*, 4 March,
www.ft.com/cms/s/0/d916f8e2-
08d8-11de-b8b0-0000779fd2ac.
html?nclick_check=1.

— (2011) 'Arab food, water, and the big landgrab that wasn't', *Brown Journal of World Affairs*, XVIII(1): 119–32.

Woodhouse, P. (2012) 'New investment, old challenges. Land deals and the water constraint in African agriculture', *Journal of Peasant Studies*, 39(3–4): 777–94.

World Bank (2011) *World Development Report 2011: Conflict, Security and Development*, Washington, DC: World Bank, web.worldbank.org/WBSITE/EXTERNAL/EXTDEC/EXTRESEARCH/EXTWDRS/0,,contentMDK:23252415~pagePK:478093~piPK:477627~theSitePK:477624,00.html.

Wymenga, E., J. van der Kamp, B. Fofana and L. Zwarts (2005) 'Ecological evaluation of dams and irrigation in the Upper Niger', in L. Zwarts, P. van Beukering, B. Kone and E. Wymenga, *The Niger, a Lifeline – Effective Water Management in the Upper Niger Basin*, Lelystad/Sévaré/Amsterdam/Veenwouden: RIZA/Wetlands International/IVM/Altenburg & Wymenga.

Xinhua News Agency (2008) 'Fagaiwei: Wu Haiwai Duntian Jihua' [NDRC: China has no plan to acquire land overseas], in Chinese, news.xinhuanet.com/fortune/2008-11/13/content_10351772.htm.

Zoomers, A. (2010) 'Globalisation and the foreignisation of space: seven processes driving the current global land grab', *Journal of Peasant Studies*, 37(2): 429–47.

# Index